My Sister
Is Missing

My Sister Is Missing

Bringing a Killer to Justice

By Sherrie Gladden-Davis with Brad Crawford

emmis books

1700 Madison Road, Cincinnati, Ohio 45206

My Sister Is Missing
Bringing a Killer to Justice

For further information, contact the publisher at

Emmis Books
1700 Madison Road
Cincinnati, OH 45206

www.emmisbooks.com

ALL RIGHTS RESERVED UNDER
International and Pan-American Copyright Conventions
Library of Congress Cataloging-in-Publication Data

Gladden-Davis, Sherrie, 1947-
  My sister is missing / by Sherrie Gladden-Davis with Brad Crawford.
      p. cm.
  ISBN 1-57860-201-7
  1. Gladden-Smith, Fran. 2. Gladden-Davis, Sherrie, 1947- 3. Missing
persons--New Jersey--Princeton--Case studies. 4. Missing
persons--Investigation--New Jersey--Princeton--Case studies. 5.
Sisters--United States--Biography. I. Crawford, Brad. II. Title.
  HV6762.U5D38 2005
  362.82'9--dc22

                                    2004028481

Cover designed by Heather Francis
Interior designed by Pamela Mitchell
Edited by Jessica Yerega

DEDICATION

Although I wrote this book in the first person, it would not have been possible without my niece Dedy's countless hours of investigation and my husband Dave's patience, support, and hard work. We have all been involved with the hours of research and pain it has taken to compile the information that follows. We have tried to gather a little understanding and bring some sense of order to a horrid situation. As a team, we dedicate this book to the memory of Dedy's mother and my sister, Betty Fran Gladden-Smith, with our love and with deep gratitude to her for her love and all our treasured memories.

ACKNOWLEDGMENTS

Our family would like to express our gratitude to the West Windsor Township Police Department in West Windsor, New Jersey, and especially to Detective Michael Dansbury (retired). Mike has lent us his strength when we were tired and weak and at times has been our sanity during this ordeal. We are forever grateful for his love and kindness. Mike has become an adopted member of our family.

We also thank Detective Brian Potts (retired) of the Wayne County Sheriff's Department in Wooster, Ohio. Brian has proved himself to be a professional and dedicated law enforcement officer who is not ashamed to be compassionate and caring. Brian and his family have become our trusted and loved friends.

We send a grateful thank-you to Special Agent Bob Hilland, assigned to the New York office of the Federal Bureau of Investigation. Special Agent Hilland has taken a beating from some of his superiors for his dedication to these cases, yet has remained constant in his belief that our case is solvable. He has worked tirelessly and has proved to be a professional and honorable agent as well as a kind and caring human being. He is a credit to the Bureau and the badge he wears. Our family feels honored to count him as our friend.

As a family, we also thank the wives and families of these officers. They have given up countless hours of family time to enable these men to pursue these cases. We are forever grateful.

I want to express my love to my family. I thank them for all the time they have unselfishly allowed me to investigate Fran's case. I know there have been times when I have not been there for them, either physically or mentally, but they have supported me and encouraged me to continue the search. I am so very grateful to my husband, Dave, for during the times I was not there for the family, he has unfailingly and consistently covered for my distraction and absence. Dave is my strength and my inspiration to do the right thing. He is my biggest supporter and fan and has believed in me and this work when I have been too discouraged to continue. Dave, I love you with everything that is in my heart, body, and soul.

A special thank-you to author Wilma Taylor, my neighbor and friend. Wilma gave me this advice: "Just write the story, Sherrie. Get up every morning and write, even if tomorrow you throw out the pages you wrote today."

I also thank Jack Heffron, editorial director at Emmis Books, for taking a chance on a first-time writer and recognizing that the written word must first begin with a good story. My editor at Emmis Books, Jessica Yerega, has been like an editorial puppet master. She took all the strings of my book-to-be and manipulated them into this finished product. My gratitude goes to her for her talent and asistance. To my helpmate, editor, and new friend, Brad Crawford, I can only express my gratitude for helping me turn my journal, notes, diary, and, finally, my manuscript into a real book with readable text.

TABLE OF CONTENTS

Part Three
The Trial

P R O L O G U E

We were a hybrid family, Mama, Daddy, Fran, and I, of disciplined military stock, a mixture of Old South and Cherokee. Daddy was a Sergeant Major in the Army (the highest enlisted rank), and when not overseas, he set up ROTC programs in colleges around the country. In later years, he was assigned to G2, or in civilian terms, Operations, which entailed managing Army posts. It fell to Mama to run the household, manage the finances, and discipline us two girls. Frequently.

She never once told me, "Just wait until your father gets home." With Daddy gone a year or more at a time, that line wouldn't exactly have snapped us into line.

I say we were Old South—not redneck. Our Old South was about dignity, pride, and respect, an intricate system built on traditional social conventions, gracious hospitality, and accepted appearances. Adults in our family referred to divorced women as widows. Rednecks don't care what other people think.

My maternal grandmother, Mary Christine Cannon, known to family and friends as Chris, was a pianist and organist for seventy-eight years, at every church we attended. I remember her best at the First Baptist Church of Niceville, in Florida. As the choir came into the church, she would quietly take her seat at the organ or piano bench, remove her shoes (so as not to scratch the foot pedals), sit up straight, nod at the choir director, and begin to play. I marveled at how beautiful and talented she was. For as long as I could remember she had a little rearview mirror rigged to her organ, which faced the congregation, to keep an eye on me, Fran, and our cousins, whom she'd seat conveniently in the first row of pews. She always kept a paint stirrer next to her sheet music. Somehow, in the midst of her rapid finger work and rhythmic foot-pumping, she could spot the slightest transgression, a chatty girl or a wiggly boy, and—it didn't matter what point in the song—would stop playing and point to the nearest exit of the church with her paint stirrer. The choir would carry on, and the congregation would continue to sing, as she marched her quarry outside the church house, away from friendly aid. Only when they had dry eyes and were ready to behave could they return to the service. Granny would return to the organ or piano and, without missing an eighth note, resume playing. Granny didn't have to stop often.

When I was about ten, I foolishly considered myself too old for the paint stirrer. As Granny took her place at the organ and before she adjusted her mirror, I slipped up and took one of her shoes. As the sermon began, Granny slid her foot into one shoe and glanced around for the other. She hobbled to her seat on the front pew and as she sat down, noticed the other shoe at my feet. She calmly pointed to the shoe, which I handed her, put it on, and marched me out to the car. I did not get a taste of the paint stirrer that day, but my lesson was worse. I realized I had embarrassed her in front of her church family. I will never forget the hurt look on her face. I promised myself and her that day that I would never intentionally embarrass anyone again, especially for a laugh at their expense.

Granny's husband, my maternal grandfather, Paul Marion Cannon, was a Cherokee and had a gentler hand. Friends called him PM. We cousins called him Pop. I could scale a Georgia pine like nobody's business, something my Mama never got the knack of, so when I was about to be punished, I'd climb a tree and wait for Pop to come home. I spent a lot of time in trees. If I could hold out for Pop, I was home free. Mama and Granny respected his authority as the elder and ultimate head of his household and would not overrule his decision. I could shimmy down from the tree, confess, and receive my punishment, usually leaf raking or some other chore. I was smart enough to pretend that raking leaves was the most onerous chore imaginable, but I liked doing it then, and I like doing it now. After the leaves were all raked, the cousins would get a big treat. Pop would bake big sweet potatoes in the ashes of the burning leaves, and later we'd smother them in butter and honey. To us, it was better than candy.

The mistake you never wanted to make with Pop was to deny what you had done or twist the facts. For him, discipline was more about emotional maturing than outside force. By coming clean, you proved to him that you had learned.

Daddy could afford to be softer on us than Mama because he wasn't around as much. We were his spoiled little girls who got gifts and hugs when he was home, and the benefit of the doubt when we weren't sugar and spice. When he did have to play the disciplinarian, it was as the disappointed parent, and that act was every bit as effective as Mama's knitting needles, which could raise a welt on bare legs better than any switch cut from a hickory tree. He was the carrot; she was the stick. (Mama, though, wasn't all brass and sass. She could also sing "Amazing Grace" and bring tears to your eyes.) While the corporal aspects of punishment fell to Mama and Granny, they were also two of the most loving and loved women I have known. They were the first to give a hug when you needed one—or just because you were close—and were always available to kiss boo-boos.

Misbehaving in front of Daddy earned you a trip to the den, where you'd sit and dread the lecture you knew he had in store. ("How could you disappoint your mother and me like this? Didn't we raise you better than that?") It might be an hour before he got around to visiting you, but you knew better than to leave that den. He usually ended the lecture with, "Now you owe me one," which meant he would wait until you had made special plans to mete out your punishment. Like when a new boy asked you out on a date, and when you went to get permission, Daddy would say, "Remember the one you owe me? I think that's the evening I'll take." Of course you had to call the boy back and explain that you "owed" your father one, which the boy would not understand, and take as code for rejection, and never call again.

That structure and those family ties kept me rooted growing up as an Army brat. A few times I went to three schools in a single academic year. But we always thought of the Florida panhandle as our home and identified with Southern values, regardless of where we were living.

Part of growing up Southern was knowing when not to ask questions. It was yes sir, no ma'am, sit up straight, make us proud, and when in doubt, keep quiet. Questions could come off as aggressive and undermine authority. We never even knew Mama had been married before until, one day, Fran and I accidentally knocked an accordion file off the top shelf of the closet. I was ten. Sifting through the records, letters, and photographs, we learned that Fran and I were actually half sisters: Daddy wasn't Fran's biological father. We knew better than to confront Mama about this while Daddy was in Korea, because we knew that this was a discussion we would all have to have together. After Daddy got home, we did discuss it. Mama and Daddy explained that when they married, Fran was only three, and because her biological father did not visit or take an active part in her life, they thought it best that Daddy adopt Fran. She had no memory of any other father except Daddy, and I can't remember our family ever making reference to Fran's biological father again. Aside from being awkward to talk about, having a half sister didn't make sense. Where was the division line? Down the middle of the nose? At the waist?

By the time I was twelve, Daddy had completed his third tour of Korea. When he was overseas, we stayed with Granny and Pop in Niceville. Mama had help, but a lot of responsibility fell to Fran to look after me. She was four and a half years older and a sort of second mother, the cool mom I could talk to about anything and try on clothes with.

Still, ours wasn't a relationship of equals. Fran was older and wiser and possessed an unerring sense for my guilt or innocence. She never tattled on me when I got into mischief. She'd just beat the stew out of me.

Fran also had another sense: an ability to discern when I was in trouble, angry, or extremely upset. It was one that I shared with her. No matter how far apart we were, or what we might be doing, each of us knew when the other had a serious problem *as it was happening.* The first time I remember it was when I was about five. I was suddenly worried about Fran but didn't have a clue as to why. I sat at the side of the road waiting for her school bus to drop her off, and when she didn't appear, I got a sick feeling in the pit of my stomach. I ran home to tell Pop that Fran wasn't on the bus. Just as I got there, Mama and Granny were pulling into the driveway, and Fran was with them. I felt relieved to see her but noticed a cast on her arm. She had fallen on the playground during afternoon recess and broken her arm. You could call it ESP, but that makes it sound as if we might have spent our summers tracking UFOs or calling the Department of Agriculture about crop circles. We weren't charging a nickel admission to the neighbor kids and exchanging winks. And we didn't *use* it. It just happened.

I took it to be a manifestation of our deep faith and unbreakable bond. I can't explain the origin of the sense, but genetics would seem to matter little. Otherwise, why wouldn't other sisters have this link?

Many years later, when my husband, Dave, and I had our own children, our approach to discipline became a blend of his family values with my mother's, father's, and grandfather's styles. We raised two beautiful daughters in small-town Indiana, where they grew up with unlimited love, all the advantages Fran and I had had, and many that we didn't. Neva and Mikel got to know one town intimately, attend the same schools year to year, and make lifelong friends. They also faced the challenge of getting away with anything in a place where everyone knows everyone else. When they were about thirteen and eight, I sat them down for a friendly lecture. "If you ever misbehave or disobey what your dad and I have told you, consider yourself caught immediately. We *will* find out. Even so, sometimes you'll be tempted to do something anyway, something so great it outweighs any possible consequences. I understand that you're going to do it, but you have to understand that I'm going to come down on you for it. And you can't be upset with me when I do, because we've had this talk. We have an understanding."

We had a friend of the family who covered a lot of ground around town. If Neva or Mikel were goofing off or doing anything unusual, he would send them on their way home or to a friend's home. Our neighbors filled in the gaps between his reports and what Dave and I were able to find out on our own. Our daughters thought nothing escaped our notice. By the time the girls were in high school, we had established an aura of omniscience. "What'd you do tonight?" I'd ask quietly, eyes narrowed, as the girls came through the door on a Friday or Saturday night. If they'd broken any rules, they spilled their guts right there. In later years I scarcely had to say a word.

This system worked more smoothly for us than Mama's knitting-needle philosophy and didn't result in any tree-climbing, so far as I can remember. I imagine too that Neva and Mikel formed a deeper sisterhood over combating Mom and Dad's all-knowing powers and looked out for each other more than they would have otherwise. Which is as it should be. There's no point in being related to people you can't relate to. Family, every family, takes hard work, empathy, a willingness to erase old scores, and a powerful, powerful love. Neva and Mikel are grown now and have far exceeded our greatest expectations. They're strong, career-minded women who still manage to make family their top priority. Both have excelled at raising their own children, whom I know have rewarding futures ahead of them. Because whether or not we like the results, our children most often become exactly who we raise them to be.

PART ONE
Fran is Missing

CHAPTER 1
"The Thing"

On October 1, 1991, my sister, Fran Gladden Smith, disappeared from her home in Princeton, New Jersey, without a trace. The rest of the Gladdens couldn't believe she would just leave without letting us know where she was going to be. We have always been a devoted family.

Fran and I were very close. We had a sixth sense about each other that we've never been able to explain: Since childhood we have known when the other was in trouble or going through an intensely stressful time. Each of us would get an all-consuming feeling that we had to communicate. We didn't necessarily know what was wrong, just that something wasn't right.

One Christmas, when we were young women, the whole Gladden clan was at my house near Indianapolis for the holidays. After everyone had left for home on December 27, my husband, Dave, had taken our baby daughter, Neva, for a nap and then fallen asleep himself. I finished getting the house in order and lay down on the couch for a nap. An hour and a half later, at three o'clock, I sat upright in a cold sweat with tears running down my face. I felt sure something had happened to Fran. I walked the floor for an hour knowing that I wouldn't be able to reach them on the road. She, her husband, Rich, and their children, Todd, Rodd, and Dedy had left together. At four o'clock the phone rang. I knew it was Fran.

I ran to answer it. "Fran, where are you? What happened?"

Fran told me that they had been in a car wreck. A car traveling in the opposite direction had crossed three lanes of interstate traffic and struck their vehicle on the front passenger side. She had hit her head and was bruised, but they had avoided a terrible accident thanks in part to Rich's expert driving. He and the kids were fine. The whole ordeal was over in less than a minute—at about three, when I woke up from my nap.

We called it "the thing." Some might dismiss it as coincidence or excessive concern, but it happened too many times in the forty-four years I knew Fran to chalk it up to circumstance. If one of us was going through an emotional time or was sick, the other one knew things were not right. Over the years, I had felt it when Fran got in heated arguments or could not meet her rent, and she had experienced it when I was in labor for three days before delivering my first daughter, Neva. We weren't just sisters. We were best friends, connected souls. We trusted each other to be there, spiritually if not physically, during our darkest and most desperate struggles. I must also tell you that "the thing" was never wrong.

On September 28, 1991, a Saturday, I felt a strong urge to talk to Fran, who was living in Princeton at the time with her husband, John. They had lived there only four months, and though Fran was quite accustomed to roaming the country as an Army brat, I don't think she felt entirely at home in New Jersey, away from the rest of her family. We talked nearly every day by phone to bridge the gap, but that afternoon I felt sure that something was wrong. I was antsy, couldn't concentrate on my sur-roundings, and could not get Fran off my mind. I tried several times to reach her. By bedtime my feeling had passed. Over the Labor Day week-end, Fran had fallen and broken her hip in the Poconos while she and John were on a belated honeymoon. She was bedridden for weeks and only now was able to get around their third-story condo using a walker and crutches. Could my desire to contact her have something to do with this? It turned out Fran's daughter and my niece, Dedy, had talked to Fran that morning, but I wouldn't find that out for three days, when I finally talked to Dedy. Fran had asked her to send patterns so she could make school clothes for Dedy's children, Nici and Jerrad. In any case, I didn't experience "the thing" at all the next day. I assumed that Fran had resolved whatever problem she'd had.

On Monday, the 30th, I called again, simply out of curiosity about what had happened on Saturday. I couldn't reach her at the condo, and I got busy at work and let it go. I tried again on Tuesday. Still no answer. Fran had talked about starting physical therapy to help her get used to the crutches on the stairs. At that point, she was still taking stairs one at a time on her rear end, and using her arms to move herself up and down. Maybe she had gone to therapy, I thought.

By Wednesday I was beginning to worry. No one answered at the condo, and they didn't have an answering machine, so I finally called John at his office. Where's Fran, I asked. John said he wasn't sure. In fact, he thought my phone call might be her checking in. Even family had trouble distinguishing our voices on the phone.

I began to consider the possibility that Fran might be in serious trouble, and sort of lost it. "John, are you telling me you don't know where the hell my sister is?"

"Basically, that's right. She's been talking about maybe doing some traveling. You know, go see Dedy and the kids, maybe your house, or even to Florida. I'm just not sure."

How did she leave, I asked. Plane, car, taxi? Most any option seemed unlikely given that even getting up and down stairs was a challenge for her. John didn't know. When he got home Tuesday night, he said, she was just gone. In the kitchen he had found a note: "Going away for a few days. Don't forget to feed the fish."

That conversation would change my life forever. After thousands of hours, and more than a hundred thousand dollars of family money, spent investigating her whereabouts, that moment would remain the gray gateway between an extended celebration of faith and family, my old life, and a single-minded mission to discover my sister's fate. Ahead lay lunch breaks spent calling county courthouses and typing letters, weekends dedicated to canvassing neighborhoods, midnight prayers, midday tears, and lots and lots of talks with the police. Through it all, I've held fast to three immutable truths: that true family owe each other allegiance at any cost; that every second, every penny of our search was worth it; and that one day, whether in this life or the next, I will find out all there is to know about Fran's disappearance and the person responsible for it. I've never felt "the thing" since.

———————

Although no one ever wants to learn that a close family member has disappeared, the timing of Fran's unusual departure was particularly unbelievable. Mama had been diagnosed with emphysema and a weak heart just months before, and her health had steadily declined. She tired easily and could manage no more than her personal needs. Granny, a robust eighty-three, had stepped in to serve as her caregiver, and Fran's older son, Todd, also helped with Mama when his work schedule permitted, but the efforts stretched them thin, to say nothing of the emotional burden. Although the demands of Mama's care took their toll, the three of them sharing a home made things easier.

In December 1989, Fran's younger son, Rodd, a U.S. Army Green Beret, was wounded during the invasion of Panama. A bullet tore through the fuselage of the jump plane and struck Rodd in the left side just as he was getting ready to parachute into battle. A Major pulled him back in before Rodd even realized what had happened. He became the first casualty of the invasion. The Army helped Fran make flight arrangements from Houston to Eglin Air Force Base, near Destin and Fort Walton Beach, Florida, where Rodd was recuperating. At some point, she decided to stay in Florida for good. After all, Dedy, the youngest of Fran's children, was grown and doing well in Houston, with two babies of her own. With Rodd on the mend, and Granny and Todd in need of extra help to look after Mama in nearby Niceville, her sticking around made sense. Now was the time to try to repay Granny for all that she and Pop had given us while we were growing up.

Fran had excellent secretarial skills and had no problem securing a job at Chromalloy Avionics in Fort Walton Beach. One of her job's perks was the option of renting an efficiency apartment on the beach in Destin at a reduced rate. She set up housekeeping there and was only about thirty minutes away, close enough to help Granny at home.

In March 1990, while working for Chromalloy, Fran met her future husband, John David Smith III. Soon after Fran took the job, John had approached her desk, welcomed her to the staff, and asked her to dinner. She was flattered but declined. Days later, he asked her to come to his office to go over some paperwork. Fran consented and followed him to an office devoid of personal touches. No photos, posters, quirky trinkets, nothing. A large teddy bear sat atop his file cabinet. She told him he ought to decorate his office properly. Shrewdly, John agreed and asked Fran to help him. Her first recommendation: Lose the bear. He suggested they have dinner and then shop for accessories and accents for his office, and she said yes.

Their courtship was brief. John traveled a lot to meet with other engineers at major airlines. He asked Fran to marry him almost as soon as they met, but having made some bad decisions in marriage before, she demurred. John was persistent. He didn't let up until she said maybe. When Fran finally acquiesced, he drove to city hall in Destin and got a justice of the peace to marry them right then, on a beach beside the Gulf of Mexico, on May 11 that year. Fran was forty-eight, and John was eight years younger.

They bought a new, unfinished house next door to Mama's and began finishing the interior. By June, it was almost complete. Her knack for decorating made the place look like a feature spread out of *House Beautiful*. When Dave and I came down from Indianapolis for vacation that year, they seemed happy and settled in their new home. It looked like the domestic ideal she had long deserved. But one aspect of their relationships struck me as odd: Fran didn't seem passionate about John. Maybe, I thought, because he traveled so much and they couldn't spend time together.

I asked her about it. Fran said she'd had the sparks and the heart-pounding before. She was older now, and besides, the breathless relationships had never worked. John was sweet, considerate, affectionate, intelligent, and a good friend. I noticed that she never once said she loved him. She just said she didn't want to end up like Mama—old, sick, and alone.

That summer, Dedy's six-year-old daughter, Nici, my grand-niece, moved in with Fran and John to enroll in an educational program offered by the state of Florida that helped provide funds for future college tuition. John was totally taken with Nici and spent many hours just talking with her. They would take walks, read books, work on math problems, watch sports, and do all the things grandpas and granddaughters are supposed to do, which surprised our family given that John had been a forty-year-old bachelor before he married Fran. He had never been around children much.

Nici loved him and the time they spent together, and John planned everything around her. While Fran and John were getting Nici's room decorated, he was a wreck because everything had to be exact, in just the right shades of pink. He had always wanted a family, and especially a little daughter, he said. John didn't want Nici to be a latchkey kid, so Fran quit her job and became a room mother and teacher's aide for Nici's class. She didn't seem to mind leaving her job; spending time with Nici and helping out her school were luxuries she hadn't had with her own children, when she had worked just to keep a roof over their heads. John made six figures, so covering the mortgage would not be a problem. He already owned a beach house in Connecticut. With Nici in the mix—despite family illness on their doorstep—they became the perfect family, in the perfect home.

CHAPTER 2
Fight or Flight

Fran and marriage had never been compatible. She was a fanatical housekeeper, a great cook, and a loving, giving person, but she was also willful, opinionated, and short on patience. When angered, Fran would rage and boil, and on occasion become physical. Then it would dissipate, the affront dismissed and forgotten. She was always surprised that someone might harbor hurt feelings as a result of her outbursts. Fran didn't hold grudges with people she loved.

And she never lost hope for living happily ever after, even through three earlier, less-than-perfect marriages had failed. Fran first married when she was just seventeen. It was probably one of the biggest mistakes Fran ever made. She wasn't ready for a lifelong commitment. Johnny, at twenty a dashing military man, tall, dark, and handsome, had some growing up to do. Family lore has it that Johnny was physically and verbally abusive, but I am positive that Fran gave as good as she got. She would never have tolerated being beaten without leaving a few scars herself. Whatever the cause, it was a stormy relationship. The one good thing that came out of the marriage was Todd. Fran and Johnny separated when she was about four months pregnant. After a particularly nasty fight, he bought her a one-way ticket to Florida, later vowing that if they hadn't separated, one of them surely would have injured or killed the other. When Todd was born, Johnny didn't acknowledge the birth.

The whole ordeal devastated Fran; Mama, Daddy, and I took over with the baby for the first few months while she recovered. For us, Todd was the most wonderful baby in the world. Though born premature, and very tiny, he was a delightful, loving, and cute baby. After a few months of feeling like a failure because of the divorce, she came to realize that with Todd depending on her, she needed to make sure he was taken care of. Fran pulled herself up by her bootstraps and continued her education by enrolling in a secretarial program.

Two and a half years after Fran and Johnny split, she married Rich Wehling, a blond-haired, blue-eyed, masculine guy who not only loved Fran but was also totally taken with Todd. Together they had two wonderful children, Rodd and Dedy, and the family really felt Fran was on the road to a happy life. Rich blended into our family well. He was fun-loving, openly affectionate with everyone, and, above all, a good man. But although Fran and Rich loved each other very much, they weren't good for each other. The pressures of raising a young family with little money to make ends meet gnawed at them. They fought often, and never kindly. After thirteen years, Fran once again found herself single. The couple did remain good friends, perhaps for the good of the children. In the past Fran had been angry with Rich for not taking fatherhood as seriously as she thought he should. I do know Fran had great respect for Rich. She wanted him to work less; she also wanted him to be a good provider. I believe Fran realized that having both was next to impossible, but she wanted it all.

The family didn't close ranks on Rich when the two split. I joked with Fran that only she divorced Rich; I didn't. The rest of the family felt the same way.

In November 1974, shortly after her divorce from Rich, Fran married Bill McClister. Fran called me and asked me to be her matron of honor, but I had just given birth to our second daughter, Mikel, in September and didn't feel we could afford to make the trip to Florida.

Consider, I told her, that I was at your other two weddings. It might just be that I'm the bad penny. And, I added, I'm not sure that you even like being married—just getting married. We shared a big laugh.

Fran and Bill were married at my parent's home in a small, private ceremony, with a reception afterward. I really felt this relationship was doomed from the start. Like Johnny, Bill had a short fuse. Combined with Fran's passionate views, I didn't hold out hope for a facile partnership. At least one partner has to remain on an even keel in any marriage. I do know that Fran loved him very much.

Once again, financial troubles created friction and led to constant arguing. After a few years, Fran felt she had had enough. She told Bill she had come into the marriage with a car and a thousand dollars and that that's what she was going to leave with. Bill provided her a car (which we later discovered he didn't have title to) and a small amount of cash. Fran contacted an attorney she had worked for in Alabama. The old boss told her to come on out to Houston: He had a job waiting for her. Fran called the family, and we scraped together enough to finance her move to Texas.

Fran and Bill continued to talk long-distance. After many phone calls and tearful, sleepless nights, they decided to try to make the marriage work. Bill moved to Houston. They bought a house. One more time, the family thought Fran might be able to have a settled life. Fran would have a man who loved her, and the home she had always dreamed of. But it wasn't to be. Fran's loyalty usually kept her from talking about private issues to other people, but my feeling is that after Fran and Rich divorced six years earlier, she just couldn't summon the vulnerability to give herself to another man. The chance of hurt and pain were too much for her to face again. Money was always an issue. Bill and Fran both worked hard and made good money, but they also loved to spend it. As the bills grew, so did the pressure on their relationship. They dated regularly for several years after the divorce, and at times thought they could put it all back together. Finally, Bill told Fran that he couldn't do it anymore. They would remain friends but build their lives with other partners. That was in 1986.

Fran dated a lot over the next several years, worked hard, and, with some emotional and financial support from the family, finished raising Todd, Rodd, and Dedy. Todd went on to junior college and settled into a career in banking. Always the macho guy of the family, Rodd went into the army and completed Special Forces training. Dedy entered college and got a job working in financial planning. All three have made us proud.

At times the boys lived with my Mama and Daddy, their grandparents, in Niceville, Florida. But Dedy was her mother's baby and wasn't happy being apart from Fran for any extended period of time. Fran continued to advance her secretarial and management skills. Her goal was to become a paralegal and court recorder. Although she held many jobs around this time, she was happiest working for the University of Houston. She got a discount on tuition and was able to audit many classes. For her, the knowledge was more important than the credit. She would have made a good professional student.

Fran had Dedy, then, and plenty of responsibilities to keep her busy. Still, I knew that during those years she was lonely. As a child, she didn't make friends easily. I was usually the one who found playmates for us as we bounced from one army post to the next. I was gregarious and assertive. But Fran would become the best friend. As Fran's confidence and beauty grew through her early teenage years, she became who Dedy refers to as Miss Popularity. Fran gravitated toward underdogs, the girl everyone else gossiped about, the new kid, the misfit. She hated for anyone to feel inferior. I've seen her take the last dollar out of her purse and give it to a homeless person. "Why?" I'd press her. She always said that she'd be okay, but that a guy living on the street might not if she didn't help him. No sacrifice was too large. She did what was right, consequences be damned. Underneath Fran's empathy and loyalty, I feel, lay a deep need to connect. An emotional philanthropist, she genuinely wanted to reach out and live through everyone.

We talked frequently at the time, as we always had. Fran never made a serious move that I wasn't aware of beforehand. Sometimes she just needed me to talk her through a problem in order to shrug off the limitations. Then she'd make up her own mind and take her lumps for any mistakes.

CHAPTER 3
Trouble at Home

In early March 1991, as we had expected, Mama's health took a nosedive. Fran called and told me to come home. I got on the first flight out of Indianapolis. Fran met my plane at Eglin Air Force Base (Eglin also serves as the civilian airport for the area), and we went directly to the hospital. Mama looked bad. Terrified, really. Her breathing was shallow. Her heart rate was 160 beats per minute—about twice what's normal. Her complexion had a blue tint. As a former emergency room tech, I recognized that the signs were grave, that she was seriously ill. I promised her I would go home to check on Granny, drop my luggage, put on a change of clothes, and return to the hospital to spend the night.

Sleep was out of the question. I spent most of the night trying to get the nurses to call her doctor. As the night progressed, Mama had gotten worse. Her vital signs were jumping all over the scale, her coloring was getting progressively worse, and her breathing became more difficult. By daybreak, I told the staff that they had a choice—either they could call the doctor or I would. They called the doctor. Upon arrival he immediately suggested moving her to the intensive care unit and putting her on a ventilator with a nasal feeding tube. With the ventilator tube down her throat, it would be impossible for her to eat normally. Mama was trying so hard to be brave and not cry.

She just kept looking at me, wanting me to make the decision for her.

"Mama," I said, "this is one I can't help you with. But I'll support you in whatever you decide to do."

She signed the consent forms. That was one of the toughest things I have ever done in my life. I had worked in a hospital for five years as an ER tech checking vital signs, taking brief medical histories, and prepping patients for the doctor or RN. I knew what patients and families go through in situations like these. The diaphragm is a lazy muscle and gets weak without regular use, so weaning the patient off a ventilator can be difficult. Doctors do this gradually by reducing the amount of assistance the ventilator provides, gambling that the diaphragm will adjust and take over the effort required for normal breathing. The day Mama entered the ICU marked the beginning of a six-week, twenty-four-hour-a-day family vigil. Fran and I decided that after my having such a hard time getting the nurses to acknowledge Mama's dire condition the night before, we wouldn't leave her there alone. Fran, John, Todd, Granny, and I agreed that some member of the family would stay at the hospital at all times. All for one, one for all.

The trip to look after Mama did have a few upsides. I could visit with my only sister, and I would get to know my new brother-in-law better. Fran and I had a hard time coordinating our trips home. Instead, we usually kept the lines at Ma Bell humming with our coffee chats. I'd make a cup of coffee in the morning, call Fran, and say, "Oh, I'm so glad I caught you at home! I just dropped by for a cup of coffee." We thought sharing a long-distance cup of coffee and the latest news were a great way to start the day. Now we could do it in person. We'd grab a few minutes together several times a month, just the two of us and a cup of coffee. We found that even being in the same location, it wasn't easy to get time alone when surrounded by a houseful of visiting family members.

I also saw a chance to know John better. Their relationship had developed so fast, the rest of us hadn't really incorporated him into the family yet. When Fran first introduced us the summer before, I was surprised by his appearance: six feet tall, thin frame, large teeth, red hair, fair complexion. He wasn't the type Fran was traditionally attracted to. Her taste had always run toward the big macho type. John reminded many in the family of John Boy from The Waltons. We even started caling him John Boy.

He had graduated from Ohio State with a degree in aeronautical engineering, but John was vague about details of his career or his family, which was foreign to us Gladdens, who delight in telling family stories.

"Mine was a very dysfunctional Mennonite family," he said. "Nothing like your family. I am so glad I truly have a family now, where the people are glad to see you when you come home."

He had grown up in rural Ohio in the '50s and '60s. His mother, Grace, married a Jewish man, Sam Malz, when John was a teenager, and the rest of the family disowned the couple. John went to live with his grandmother, whom he spoke about with love and respect.

What does your grandmother think of your being married, I asked him.

He said she told him he was a fool to marry a spoiled Southern belle. He never mentioned any other family members except a sister, Debbie, who lived in the beachfront house he owned in Connecticut. Debbie took care of his two border collies, Christopher and Amanda. Fran said she had never spoken to any of his family.

I was sorry to hear about what must have been an insecure way for John to grow up. Fran and I had grown up surrounded by family and the reassurance of knowing we were loved. He said he stayed in touch only with his grandmother and Debbie. Just as his mother had been disowned, she, too, had disowned John when he refused to go into the family business (building strip malls in Indiana) with her and his stepfather. Until he met and married Fran, he said, he was too busy building a career to even think of marriage and a family. It seemed like such a lonely life.

However difficult his past life had been, he was making up for it now. During this trip, as I visited with and prayed for Mama, I was astonished by how methodical John was. He worked in the yard constantly. The garage and driveway never missed a hosing. He and Fran would go to the grocery store together, where he paid for the food. And when he went out of town, as he did frequently for business, he'd leave a fifty-dollar bill on the counter for Fran. It didn't matter whether he'd be gone a day or a week. For growing up in such a divided, contentious family, John had stepped into the role of loving husband just fine.

The same day Mama went on the ventilator, Todd got into a bad car accident coming home. Granny and I happened to drive up on the accident about twenty minutes after it happened. Fran was ten minutes behind us. When she recognized Todd's Chevy Blazer, she raced out of the car to learn whether he had been hurt. A burly, imposing officer stepped in front of her and explained she wasn't allowed on the accident scene and would have to return to her vehicle. Fran, who's all of five foot two, looked him in the eye. "Sir," she said. "I am going up there. I can either go around you or through you. It makes no difference to me, but I am going. That's my son up there." The officer stepped aside. A doctor's examination determined that Todd had fractured his femur. Though not extraordinarily severe, it would require surgery and an orthopedic pin to repair. Thank goodness for us, he was admitted to Twin Cities Hospital, the same hospital Mama was in. I don't know how we would have covered them both if ER doctors had admitted him somewhere else.

Fran, Granny, or I stayed at Twin Cities constantly. Having Mama sent to the ICU and Todd going into surgery on the same day was almost more than we could handle. Fran and I became so exhausted and scared that we got giddy. We giggled together in the courtyard, where we escaped to smoke, for almost an hour until we got our fears under control. In our family, crying is to be done in private. For women, crying only ruins your mascara and gets you branded as hysterical and irrational. So we laughed, whatever the risk that someone Mama knew might see us and think we were callous for making light of the situation. Niceville's still a small town. I'm sure Mama would have been horrified if she had learned that someone she knew spotted us cackling in the courtyard.

I felt so much sorrow for Granny. This was one of the few times in my life I had seen her cry. Like Fran and me, she was scared that we would lose Mama. It's difficult enough when it's your mother wrapped in a matrix of tubes, but it must be doubly so when it's your daughter. She never stops being your baby, regardless of age. Granny coped in part by taking care of Nici and by cooking our favorite meals and bringing them to the hospital while we stood watch.

Todd's surgery went well, but Mama's prognosis was a roller coaster ride. One minute we'd hear she was improving and envision hot baths and real beds; the next, doctors would tell us she could go at any time. When the news was bad, we'd pray and pace. To ease the pressure, we began worrying in shifts. One of us would go home while the other stayed with Mama and Todd. Like so many other times in our lives, it was Fran and I against the world. We felt we had to protect Granny as much as possible and conserve her strength, so we waged the battle together.

John and Fran had been in their new dream home less than a year that spring when John learned that Chromalloy was downsizing and he was out of a job. While Fran and I pulled hospital duty, John spent most of his time on the road trying to land a new position. At his level, we were sure that a new job would require them to move. The market for civilian engineering jobs was limited in Niceville, an Air Force town.

When he was home, John was supportive and helpful with Mama, Todd, and Nici. He knew how rough it was trying to keep two households running smoothly, and maybe he sensed the strain Fran faced with an ailing mother and son and an unwanted move looming simultaneously. *I could see firsthand how it weighed on her.* One day as Fran and I were working in the kitchen at Mama's, a spider ran across the floor. Fran got a cup from the cabinet, trapped the spider, and went out to the yard to release it.

You're nuts, I told her. You should have killed it. It will only find its way back into the house.

Fran looked at me like I had lost my mind. "Sherrie, that is one of God's creatures. It deserved to live! With Mama and Todd in the shape they are in, we can't afford for God to be pissed at us right now."

What if the spider had been a cockroach, I asked.

She just laughed. "That sucker would have been dead. Even God hates those things."

John received at least three job offers: one each in Buffalo, New York; Borden Town, New Jersey; and New Haven, Connecticut. The family thought they were leaning toward Connecticut because the job offered better pay and benefits and was with Textron, a former employer of John's. Plus, they could move into John's beach house, though that would entail kicking out his sister, Debbie, and it would have to be remodeled and winterized. After some weeks, John decided to take the New Jersey job. I felt that if Fran and John could hold together through an uncertain period like this far from family, they could face anything together.

Todd, a youthful thirty, was on his feet within two months. We knew that his leg would never be as strong as it was before the accident, and at times he would endure some pain, but he would be able to lead a normal life. After three unsuccessful attempts to take Mama off the ventilator, the doctors managed it on the fourth. Within a few days, she was stable enough to move into a private room, and by the end of April 1991, she had returned home. Nurses would come to assist Granny with Mama's personal hygiene needs, and with physical therapy to reverse the muscle atrophy caused by prolonged bed rest. The family health crisis had passed.

Even with Fran's impending move, it was cause for great celebration. The feeding tube was gone, and Mama was hungry. Granny prepared all her favorites, and though her shrunken stomach would not hold much, she enjoyed every bite she took. Fran and I bought a case of single-serving V8 juices. Mama said she had been craving V8 for weeks— she drank four cans the first day. For Fran and me, it was wonderful to stretch out in bed and relax, to go to sleep without wondering whether the phone would ring and beckon us back to the hospital. Dave drove down from Indiana to pick me up. I had mixed feelings about returning home to work and my normal life. I wanted to go home to my two daughters, but I felt guilty leaving the rest of the family with all the responsibility of Todd and Mama's care and recuperation. And I knew I'd miss my private coffee chats with Fran, trading secrets only sisters can share. As Dave and I prepared to leave, Fran and I kept stalling for more time. We fixed a second pot of coffee and double-checked all the preparations for Mama's care. We sat in Mama's bedroom and cried. I can still see her running to the end of Mama's driveway, crying and throwing kisses, watching us drive out of sight. That's the last time I saw my sister.

CHAPTER 4
Missing Persons

John filed a missing-persons report with Detective Bob Gulden of the West Windsor Township Police Department on Friday, October 4, three days after he had found Fran's "feed the fish" note in the kitchen upon returning from work. Later in the investigation, he would meet with detectives to give a statement, an extended version of the events that he had relayed to Dedy and me when we first learned of Fran's disappearance.

John had gotten up early on Saturday, September 28, he said, to get their grandson Jerrad a birthday present. When he got home, Fran was talking to Dedy and explained the gift was on its way in overnight mail. Fran had been prepared to go out with John and buy a gift for Jerrad that day, a significant development in that she felt strong enough to go out for an entire day for the first time since she had broken her hip. It proved, we felt, that she was on the mend. They had dinner at Red Lobster and got home at about nine o'clock.

Sunday was a lazy day, according to John's statement. Fran was frisky and awakened him early to talk. Later he went out for doughnuts. It was a good day, he said, because Fran cooked dinner. They were both tired of his cooking. On Monday, they discussed their housing options; Fran had a lead on a house she had seen while driving to physical therapy, and they were debating whether to put two thousand dollars down on a house rental or use the money to finish decorating their condo. They decided that since they had already moved three times in eighteen months (first into their home next door to Mama's in Niceville, then to a temporary efficiency apartment that Fran called "the halfway house," then to their present condo), they would stay where they were.

Fran was in a good mood Tuesday. They discussed their plans for the condo and how they wanted to spend more time together. John said he felt things were good between them. Fran had an appointment that afternoon to see an attorney about suing for her broken hip—not the hotel for negligence, but the hospital for improper care. After being told she was allergic to adhesive tape, the hospital personnel had used it following her surgery. She could tolerate only paper tape. When the nurses pulled the tape off her hip, it also removed layers of skin and left scars. That night John arrived home from work around 7:30 P.M. He called out to Fran, heard nothing, and went to find her. He checked all the rooms and the balcony, then found her note in the kitchen.

A few days after Fran's disappearance, I asked John in a phone conversation what she had taken with her. He said it was like she had packed for a weekend. There were only two outfits missing: a mint green sweat suit and a pink sweat suit, each with a meadow scene screen-printed on it. I recalled that these were favorite outfits of hers. Other than her briefcase, her purse, and a yellow suitcase, everything else was there. John told us that Fran likely had only two hundred dollars or so with her when she left.

Under the right circumstances, maybe this would be perfectly reasonable for some people. I wanted to imagine that it was for Fran, too, but too much didn't add up. Fran had asked Dedy to pick out patterns and send them up to New Jersey so she could make school clothes for Jerrad and Nici. She had already sewn a dust ruffle, bedroom curtains, and bedside table covers for the condo, and was ready for new sewing projects. Even so, in the days leading up to her disappearance, she could manage to sit at her sewing machine for only a few hours a day before it became unbearable. This was not a woman getting ready to leave. I rationalized John's explanations because as long as I could persuade myself to believe them, I had hope. Nevertheless, I knew in that moment, as I listened to his emotionless voice on the phone relate this story, that events had not happened as he wanted me to believe.

Less than two months before her disappearance, on August 9, I sensed that something was wrong at Fran's. I felt it most of the next day, too, but I couldn't call her since they hadn't had a phone installed at the condo. When the phone rang on the 11th, I was relieved but not surprised. It was, of course, Fran, who was crying so hard I could hardly understand her when the operator asked if I'd accept the collect call. She had driven to her office to call me. I gave her a few minutes to compose herself.

"Fran, honey, what's wrong?"

She said she had returned home on Friday night after work to find that John was gone. He had taken all his belongings, the television, even the radio. It was like he had never been there.

"I didn't do anything wrong," she kept blubbering. "I don't understand."

He had, however, left a note: When you decide to start wearing your wedding band again, it read, I'll come home.

Fran had nicked her ring some time before, and it kept snagging her clothes. She took the ring to a jewelry store to have it repaired but felt this was so trivial she never mentioned it to John.

The situation was dire not only because John was gone but also because of how little control Fran seemed to have over household decisions. Many of their possessions were in a rented storage unit, but Fran didn't know where that was. She didn't handle money beyond what John gave her and wasn't listed on any of the credit cards. They didn't have a joint checking account.

Dave and I asked Fran if she had any money. Did she need us to wire her money to hold her over until we could decide what to do? Fran said she had about sixty dollars and was fine; she'd get paid that week. *I'll bet I know where fifty dollars of that came from*, I thought to myself.

I started asking pointed questions.

Did she think he had gone to Connecticut, to the beach house?

Fran said she didn't know. When I suggested she go there to look for John, she replied that she didn't know where it was. She wasn't even sure what town it was in.

The sheer ludicrousness of the situation infuriated me. I became angry not with Fran but with the unvarnished naiveté of a woman who should have known better. She had raised three kids, often alone, held down multiple jobs, and handled her own finances for decades. I told her (in what I hoped were sisterly tones) to get her shit together—become a partner in all phases of your marriage or get the hell out of it. And, I said, I'd damn well find out who lives in that house in Connecticut.

She started crying again. "What good would that do? When you're married to someone, you have to trust that person. Knowing about Connecticut will not change the decision I have to make. Either I stay with him, or I don't. My biggest problem right now is where to find John."

"Has he ever done anything like this before?"

He had. She said that in February, when they lived in Niceville, the Okaloosa County Sheriff's Department had served her with divorce papers. The news hit her so hard that the deputy had stayed with her for more than an hour. While the deputy was there, John called to reconcile.

"I've made a terrible mistake," he said. "May I come home?"

A few days later John withdrew the petition. I was astonished that Fran hadn't told me about something this major. There was no need to alarm anyone, she told me. Things had worked out.

Dave and I felt she was fighting an uphill battle in light of this second erratic episode. With all the mystery surrounding Connecticut, we wanted her to cut her losses and come to Indiana. We'd help her get here or wherever she wanted to go.

The Monday following John's written ultimatum, Fran reached him at his office. "Hi, cutie," he said when he recognized her voice, as if nothing unusual had transpired between them. Fran explained herself, and John seemed prepared to accept her account of the ring and the jeweler. It didn't appear she'd make it to Indiana after all. But what I really wanted to know, when Fran called me to relay the latest news, was what the dynamic would be when he returned. Would things go back to normal? And what was *normal*, anyway? Before he moves back in, she said, "I'll know where my things are, I will have an understanding about the house in Connecticut, and I will take joint control of our finances." She also intended to start saving some of her own money, just in case John ever did anything like this again. Dave let her know the offer to come to Indiana was still open, but Fran chose to stay in New Jersey and work things out.

Later that week John moved back home.

CHAPTER 5
The Investigators

Adults, the police told us, can leave anytime they want to. The fact that a person is missing is no proof that a crime has been committed. Men get fed up all the time with their lives, or wives, and disappear to start over somewhere else. Less often, and driven by need, women will take off without revealing their plans to those around them. But they're also more likely than men to later make contact with people they know or to rely on them for support.

Dedy and I had been calling the West Windsor Township Police Department every day since Detective Bob Gulden had taken the missing-persons report to follow up on developments and provide them with information we hadn't thought to give earlier. Until then, I would have walked a mile out of my way to avoid conflict with most anyone. But this was different. This was family—and a matter of life and death. Gruff dismissals and assurances of "we'll be in touch" were not going to dissuade me from finding Fran, and I knew that they wouldn't dissuade Dedy either.

Not that we had to play hardball with the West Windsor PD. Throughout our search, officers in the department displayed the utmost professionalism. Mike Dansbury, the detective permanently assigned the case, was easy to talk to and receptive to our questions and explanations.

He might actually have been too encouraging. Whether he was compensating because of the distance (he being in New Jersey, I in Indiana, and Dedy in Texas) or just trying to keep us calm and hopeful, Mike said there was a good chance of finding Fran alive and that there might not have been foul play at all. But Dedy and I knew better. If she hadn't gotten in touch with the family or turned up in a hospital some-where by now, logic told us that she wasn't going to. "She's dead," I told Mike. "There is no other possibility." Without compelling, usually physi-cal, evidence, a missing-persons case doesn't ordinarily become a crim-inal investigation, although ultimately the decision rests with the police department and its investigating officers. Feuding spouses or upset teens can take off temporarily as part of a cooling-off period, and law enforcement might decide that devoting energy and resources to a case that will resolve itself in two or three days is unwise.

With Fran we were fortunate that because of her hip injury, authori-ties declared her an endangered female and immediately entered her into the NCIC, the National Crime Information Center operated by the FBI. The NCIC is a national database that all levels of law enforcement have access to and that documents active cases and suspects ranging from missing persons to car thefts to convicted felons. (The NCIC went online in 1967 and focused mainly on traceable items, such as stolen license plates, guns, and automobiles. The Missing Persons File was developed in 1975.) Each agency is responsible for adding its own cases to the database. Getting Fran into the NCIC early gave us the theoretical advantage of announcing her plight to a large law enforcement audience in the crucial first days of a missing-persons case when a positive resolution is most likely. Yet it's far from a guaranteed anything. To give us an idea of the volume of information available on the NCIC, at one point an investigating officer searched for missing female "Smiths" in Ohio and five contiguous states and received more than 150 results.

These types of systems can be frustratingly ineffective for finding missing children; in Indiana's state database, IDACS (Indiana Data and Communication System), only 10 percent of minors listed as missing persons in the database include photos. Visual identification of kids, who aren't likely to be carrying ID, can be next to impossible using these databases alone.

Fran didn't know many people in Princeton—they had lived there only four months—so if someone else had been responsible for her disappearance, the list of known people likely to have information would be short. There was John, of course, but also Joe and Nancy Mazotas, her bosses at a Princeton title company, and Hollie Drajin, a friend whom she occasionally had lunch or dinner with. The West Windsor police started by searching John and Fran's condo, the last place anyone had seen Fran. Officers leading a team of dogs around the complex could find Fran's scent only inside the condo and the path down the stairs, ending in her and John's cars. Fran had taken neither her own car, a 1991 Dodge Shadow, nor John's, a 1991 Mazda Miata, at the time of her disappearance. Taking the Miata would have been highly unlikely given Fran's hip injury and the manual transmission, but we felt it was strange, if she had left under her own power, that she hadn't taken her car. The dogs found no other trace of her on the grounds.

Starting out, I didn't expect to influence the investigation to any great degree, but I knew that I needed to provide all the information I possibly could about Fran and her life to give the police a chance to do their job. For Dedy and me, those first weeks working with Mike Dansbury were a delicate dance. We wanted him to know we were committed to finding Fran, but we also could set aside our emotions and look at the case from an investigator's point of view. Police departments usually are reluctant to allow families to become too involved, and for good reason: Their connection to the victim can make it difficult for them to work a case effectively. Even if they can view the facts objectively, overzealous families might let slip confidential information police have shared about the case; if they were to contact a witness or informant without prior approval from the police, they could jeopardize the entire investigation. Dedy and I agreed that we'd have to prove to Mike we were level-headed, prepared to handle any eventuality, and willing to seek the truth in Fran's case at any cost. I wanted him to know that we'd never spin what we knew about Fran simply to put her in a more favorable light.

My worst fear was that Mike would write us off as hysterical victim's relatives and close ranks to protect the investigation. By this time I strongly suspected John. I didn't know him well (and, my gut told me, neither had Fran), but what I did know gave me a bad feeling. His background was sketchy, he and Fran had married quickly, and he didn't behave as I, or the investigating officers, expected a worried or grieving spouse would. The only steps he was taking to help police were prompted by Dedy and I continually issuing him stern orders. If he hadn't done something to Fran directly, I felt, then he knew who had.

But I didn't want Mike to think the family was on a witch hunt. What if he decided we had lost all reason? I covered by telling him that we knew little about John, that he was the last person to see Fran. "I do not want to cast aspersions on this man's character, but I'm telling you, I know my sister. I don't know John Smith." Mike listened attentively but didn't reveal his theories about the case.

Spouses and family members nearly always receive a lot of scrutiny from police in these situations, and John's explanations and behavior were suspicious enough to raise more than a few eyebrows. For starters, he rarely revealed more than he absolutely had to. In a signed statement he completed for police in the second week of October, one item on the multi-page form began, "We have determined that . . ." The prompt included several blank lines to describe the nature of the problem and explain what the individual knew about the case. In the space that followed, John wrote, "Fran is missing." That was classic John. The details in his more extensive answers tended to shift, making the truth a moving target. In his original statement, John said Fran might have had a couple hundred dollars when she left. By mid-October, in John's second interview, he was saying that Fran had taken the two thousand dollars they had set aside to rent a new house in order to do some traveling. Mike was amazed at how little useful information John could actually provide. "I knew more when I went in than when I came out," he said after the interview. "Getting anything out of him is like pulling teeth."

Through those crucial first weeks, Mike came to rely on Dedy and me for no-bull answers to questions about Fran and as a reality check on John's lies. Early in the investigation, Mike told us that John said he didn't have any pictures of Fran because she was camera-shy. I almost laughed out loud, and then recalled Fran's description of John's office when they first met—devoid of any pictures or personal effects, except for that teddy bear on his filing cabinet. If Fran was camera-shy, the photographers she had modeled for in Houston must have had a hell of a time getting her to pose. Our family albums were filled with pictures of her. Dedy picked out a recent photo, had missing-persons fliers made up, and sent them to John to post around town.

Everyone in the family had conspired to keep the news about Fran from Mama, but by mid-October we had to tell her what had happened. Prior to Fran's disappearance, at least one of us spoke with my sister every day. Now after two weeks without being able to reach Fran, Mama had become suspicious, and she told Todd to call his mother and put her on the phone. Todd stalled, squirmed, and finally confessed that he couldn't call Fran because no one knew where she was. He and Granny assured Mama that we were doing everything possible to find her.

That night I had a long talk with Mama. She reminded me of a conversation we had had before she became so ill. Mama had said that Dedy and I were the strong ones in the family. We should remember that, she said, because there would come a time when we would have to take over and do what had to be done, and hell be damned if anyone got in our way.

I won't say Mama had a premonition, but she certainly had a feeling there was a storm on the horizon. Mama's gut feelings were seldom wrong. I think now that in that moment she was turning the family reins over to Dedy and me.

Once we had told Mama what was going on, it freed us to pick her brain for anything she remembered about John. We asked her to go over her old phone bills for any numbers she couldn't account for, any number that John might have called from her house. I felt we had to learn more about him and find out whom else he knew. Dedy and I wanted to know where in Ohio John was from—he had never specified—and we certainly wanted to know about the house in Connecticut. Mama found three phone numbers she knew she had not called or personally received calls from. One originated in Seville, Ohio. The other two were from Milford, Connecticut. All three were collect calls. When she had paid the bills, she remembered that many times, when he was out of town, John would try to reach Fran at their home next door. If he didn't get an answer, he would then call Mama's. Mama had paid the phone bills and had forgotten about them, but she always kept her bills for at least a year, and thank God she did.

I know this job made Mama feel better; she was doing something to help. By this time she was able to leave her bed only for short periods of time. She was on oxygen and tired very easily, but the phone record searches were something she could do from bed. Mama and Granny spent hours talking, trying to remember every conversation they had had with John, anything that might provide more insight into the man.

Granny called the personnel department at Chromalloy, where John and Fran had worked while in Florida. I have no idea what she told those people, but she got a listing for John's next of kin, Mr. Chester Chaney of Seville, Ohio—John's grandfather, presumably the origin of one of John's collect calls to Mama's. This was the first we had ever heard of him.

On October 22 the local newspaper, the *Trentonian*, ran a story about

Fran's disappearance. The headline was "Depressed Wife Leaves Cryptic Note, Vanishes."

I raced through the story. Toward the end it read:

> Smith says Fran broke her hip while they were on a second honeymoon in the Poconos several months ago and she now needs crutches to walk around. . . .
>
> Police say they don't suspect foul play in the woman's disappearance, and her husband says he wasn't entirely surprised she left.
>
> "We talked about her taking a trip," he says. "When I saw the note I assumed she was heading either to Texas or to Florida."
>
> But not hearing from his wife has left him worried.
>
> "It was not unusual for her to withdraw from members of the family for awhile, but not to just take off," Smith says. "The worst thing is not knowing."

I almost went through the roof. The police and our family had decided that we needed help and had gone to the media. Someone out there must have seen a small woman, on crutches, carrying a yellow suitcase, briefcase, and purse—the picture John had painted for us. If she were really trying to manage all this, she would have had to have help. We felt the newspapers might generate interest, and someone might come forward. But I began to wonder if we had done the right thing in getting the press involved.

I called Dedy, frantic. "My God," I told her, "they are going to get her killed. The papers have told the world that she is out there, injured, disabled, and carrying two thousand dollars." Never mind that the article had also depicted Fran as "depressed" and prone to withdrawal. I called the reporter, Mark Mueller, to register a complaint. I don't know whom I spoke with, but they got an earful. (I later found out that the story itself wasn't irresponsible, since Mr. Mueller was simply quoting what John had told him. We were learning the difficulty of "using" the media to get an exact outcome. Really the best you can do is set them in motion and hope they cut your way.)

We might have anticipated this kind of twist from John. The week before, he had told Dedy over the phone that the beach house in Connecticut had been hit by a storm. He said he had spent the whole weekend there trying to get things back in order and had to haul seventeen bags of debris to the curb. He was exhausted, and the tenants hadn't even bothered to call and report the damage. Instead a neighbor had called.

The family had long felt there was something strange about the house in Connecticut. As with many other areas of John's life, the beach house was a black hole. Usually when he was out of town, John left a phone number for Fran where he could be reached. When he went to Connecticut, however, which was often, he never gave her a number. Instead he'd call Fran when he got to New York on his way home, to tell her when and where to meet his plane. Dave and I had joked that he was probably a bigamist. Fran never said whether John's Connecticut trips were business or personal. Knowing how important the house and dogs were to him, I never thought to ask. As far as we know, Fran believed that John's sister, Debbie, lived in the house.

John's relation of the storm incident was unusual because he had never before said that the house was rented. We assumed it was vacant. Debbie was supposed to have moved out that summer. That anybody would have lived there struck me as odd, because one of the reasons John originally gave for taking the job in New Jersey was that the beach house wasn't winterized. Who'd want to ride out a Connecticut winter in an uninsulated house, much less pay rent for the privilege?

John insisted that there was a young couple in the house but that the man hadn't offered to do anything to help that weekend. I was realizing by now that most any story of John's bore only a marginal relationship to the truth. "Bullshit," I said when Dedy related their conversation. "That sounds more like a wife to me. Like, 'John, you get you butt up here, I am not dealing with this alone.' Dedy, I *have* to know who is in that house." Dedy checked the local weather and could not find that there had been any storms in that area. She also confirmed that with the local police department, which gave her directions to the house and the address: 23 Point Beach Drive, Milford, Connecticut.

Dedy and I weren't comfortable calling someone we didn't know and trying to explain what we were doing, and we didn't want anything getting back to John. Using the Connecticut number Mama had provided, we decided to pretend that we were from a construction company and were looking for work. I carved a few minutes out of my workday and placed a call to Dedy, who set up a three-way call at her office with the beach house, then kept quiet while I played out our ruse.

A woman answered and I said, "Mrs. Smith?"

"Yes," she said.

I asked about the storm and a possible construction job, and again heard that there had been no storm and there was no damage to this house. I thanked her, hung up, and tried to figure out with Dedy what was going on. Who was this woman? A tenant certainly wouldn't answer to "Mrs. Smith," unless by coincidence she and her husband also happened to be Smiths. Maybe Debbie was still there and went by "Mrs." to avoid the appearance of living alone.

John's storm story broke his usual pattern of withholding any information of value. Looking back, I see that he was probably fishing for an excuse for not having handed out missing-persons fliers on Fran that weekend. Like Dedy, I was talking to John daily, and he would report where he had placed the fliers, where he had been, and whom he had talked to. John complained that he did have to maintain his job, that he couldn't devote all his time to roaming the streets. He gave me the same story about the storm as he had Dedy. I instructed him to get an agent to handle the Connecticut house. Until this case is over, I said, we need you in New Jersey to pass out fliers and talk to people. This investigation must come first. Nothing is more important. John agreed, but without conviction.

Mama had gotten one other Connecticut number from her phone records. It turned out to be a pay phone in a pizza place. We still didn't know much about the house or this Connecticut Mrs. Smith, but all the secrecy and deceit did gibe with something I remembered from Fran and John's move to New Jersey. John had turned down the position in Connecticut with Textron, the best paying of the three jobs he was offered. I was working for an automotive division of Textron, a Fortune 500 company, in Indiana, so I also knew that his benefits package would have been better there than in New Jersey. Moreover, John had worked for Textron previously and as a returning employee would have regained his former seniority and employee vesting. If he had foregone all that to avoid taking Fran to Connecticut, where he already owned a home that was clearly inhabitable, maybe there was more that he didn't want us to know. Dedy and I began making plans to go to New Jersey and Connecticut.

CHAPTER 6
Seville, Ohio

I had a powerful urge to catch the first flight to Newark and get to the bottom of the lies that were piling up around John. Each time Dedy and I quizzed him about where he had handed out fliers, we'd call Mike Dansbury. He or a patrol officer would then check it out. Not once did Mike or anyone else find a flier on Fran or talk to anyone who had spoken with John. To me, it was nothing short of criminal. It was now taking all my strength to remain civil with the man I recognized had not only played some central role in doing in my sister, but had consistently and casually lied to me about almost everything—bold, easily refuted lies that he ostensibly assumed I wasn't bright enough to discover.

In my adult life I've worked in several industries, from medicine to manufacturing, but for twenty-five years I worked as a cost accountant calculating production costs versus projected sales, assets and liabilities, and probabilities of profit. If you're setting up a ledger, the first thing you have to do is analyze what facts and figures you want to appear and make a decision on how you're going to represent the bottom line.

John wanted me to calculate based on sentiment, but I think he underestimated my ability to survey a traumatic situation with a critical, objective eye. I refused to cook the books to make his ledger balance.

Frustrated and anxious, I must have given Mike a hard time about having not come up with anything concrete on Fran. "Sherrie, what do you want me to do?" he said. "She's a little old for a milk carton." Mike wasn't trying to be cruel or sarcastic, just honest. This was one of my first reality checks.

Still, I was learning, thanks to Mike, that much lay within my own power to aid the investigation. In some respects the family of a victim has substantially more power than the police do to obtain information. We aren't subject to privacy laws for other family members, as the police are, don't have to concern ourselves with search warrants—provided we're openly invited into a home—and we present much less of a threat than an officer would, standing there on your porch with a badge and a gun. We discovered that victims' families usually elicit a sympathy that makes private citizens more likely to discuss sensitive matters with them, especially if those people feel their statements might be incriminating. With Mike to turn to for advice and support, Dedy and I saw no reason to sit on the sidelines and hope for the best.

But New Jersey and Connecticut would have to wait. Like good investigative reporters, Dave and I felt we should find out as much about John as possible without his knowledge before marching into the lion's den. Starting in Ohio made the most sense for us. John had grown up and gone to college there, and it was just a five-hour drive from home. The weekend of November 2 marked the first of many trips to Ohio. Dave, who has been a source of unwavering strength for me, agreed we needed to know for certain that John Smith was indeed who he said he was. We headed for Seville, his hometown.

Before Daddy died, I would sometimes help him locate phone numbers and addresses for his genealogical research, so I knew how valuable the library could be in people searches. Dave and I started our search at the library in Seville. Based on John's age, I estimated that he had graduated in 1969. I turned out to be right. We found photos of him in the

1969 Cloverleaf Senior High School annual, and in a few others. I marveled at how little his appearance had changed. Was the John from high school the same person we were just now getting to know? I wondered how long ago he had strayed from a virtuous path, and what had happened between 1969 and 1991 to make him abandon it. We found club pictures of John and a list of his school activities, but no senior picture, although the other annuals did have class photos of him. He ran track and cross county and participated in chess club, library, and Jet Club, a pep club. John Smith was in fact his real name. I had often felt it was too convenient, another attempt to obscure his past. Shortly after he and Fran got married, I had teased her about living a lie. "Lord, Fran, I'd never register in a hotel with him. I can just see the desk clerk now—'Oh, Mr. and Mrs. Smith, will this be by the hour or for the night?' "

From the library we set out for John's grandparents', the Chaneys', house. Finding them was easy; they were in the phone book. We drove right to their front door and Dave knocked, but no one answered. We spent the rest of the day talking to old classmates, choosing men since we knew their names wouldn't have changed, and trying to find out more about John as a kid. The most significant aspect of the trip was that, even in this town of two thousand, no one seemed to remember him. We had identified him in the yearbooks though, and felt that all in all the five-hour drive each way was worth it. On the drive home, Dave said, "You know, we probably know more about John right now than Fran did."

I agreed. "At least we know he wasn't an ax murderer or anything. People would have remembered that."

On Monday morning I called Mike Dansbury to report what we had found. I was excited and proud that we were taking matters into our own hands and helping the case. Mike's first question was, "Did you make copies of the annual?" Damn. I had not, but I had learned an important lesson in investigation: *document everything*. Mike advised Dedy and me to start a notebook and write down everything we knew about the case from the beginning. We did. Dedy bought equipment to tape her daily phone calls with John.

One should not think that during this time the police were doing nothing. They were working the case hard, too. Our Constitution guarantees us the privilege of going where we want and leaving any situation we choose, and the police were limited in their powers for a missing-persons case. Things have changed since 1991—we now have the Amber Alert for missing children and endangered adults—but at that time the police department's job was to rule on whether it should be a missing-persons investigation or a criminal case. I don't care who you are or how much you know about investigating—this is a tough call.

All Mike had to go on was Dedy and me telling him this wasn't right, that Fran didn't do this. Again I saw that with the laws as they are, Dedy and I were poised to play as crucial a part in uncovering what happened as the officers were. Mike was teaching us to be methodical, and we were learning. I sat down and wrote the questions that were really weighing on my mind:

1. Why leave a note to feed only the fish when there was also a puppy in the household? (John had bought a cocker spaniel while Fran was recovering from her hip injury to "keep her company.") Was it supposed to starve?
2. Why does a man who will not let go of the purse strings, even for groceries, suddenly turn over two thousand dollars to his wife for traveling?
3. Why did he turn down the job in Connecticut, where the salary and benefits were better, and where there was a house waiting for them?
4. Why is the house in Connecticut such a mystery? Why did John not give phone numbers or a contact name when he traveled to Connecticut on business?
5. Why would Fran ask Dedy to send patterns for the children's clothes if she didn't intend to be there to get them?

The patterns were requested on September 28 in her
conversation with Dedy.

6. If a person plans to leave, why do so with a broken left hip?
   Knowing she was at least six weeks from recovering
   enough to support herself, why would she not take the things
   she would need to take care of personal hygiene? She left
   everything, knowing she only had two thousand dollars
   to rent a place, turn on utilities, buy food, and take care of
   daily living.
7. Why would any woman continue to decorate a home she
   planned to leave?
8. Why wouldn't she at least take her jewelry, which she could
   have pawned if the need arose?

As I asked myself these questions, I fully realized that John's story did
not add up to anything resembling the truth. The last time Dedy had
talked to Fran was Saturday, September 28, when Fran had asked for
patterns to make school clothes for the grandchildren. John had returned
home from purchasing a birthday gift for Jerrad while they were on the
phone, and Dedy could overhear some of the argument that followed.
They had planned to buy Jerrad's gift together, but John said he knew
what little boys liked much better than Fran and that he had already
mailed it. Fran was seething, and Dedy had a feeling it had gotten worse
after she and Fran got off the phone. Later that afternoon was the last
time I felt "the thing." Taken together, those two points make a strong
case that Fran didn't disappear on Tuesday, as John had claimed, but met
a grimmer fate on Saturday afternoon, in a heated struggle.

Dedy continued to speak with John daily to gather insight into Fran's
case and to make sure John was ignorant of the investigative efforts we
were making. Dedy was more successful at this than I was, because nothing makes me angrier than someone treating me like an idiot. John perceived her as less of a threat. He pegged her as an innocent little girl sus-

ceptible to his superior intelligence. Dedy gamely played along but did-n't hesitate to get tough when she needed to. John would now speak to her freely about work or cars or the weather, but not Fran. He never mentioned her unless Dedy brought her up. During one such phone call, Dedy asked John for the household phone book. We felt this was important because Fran would either circle or dog-ear the pages of frequently used numbers. We thought with the phone book we'd have people, places, and ready addresses to which we could send out fliers and pleas for information. Dedy reminded him daily to get it in the mail, but he never did. He later complained to me that he'd have to purchase a replacement. "So do it," I said. He changed the subject.

When we did make him speak of Fran, he said he was still going to the shopping malls and talking to people. This is how he spent his weekends. As we well knew from Mike and the West Windsor PD, that wasn't true. Aside from Mike and the other officers, Dedy, Dave, and I were on our own.

In mid-November, six weeks after we had last heard from Fran, the three of us stood at a crossroads. We had worked the likely leads in the case, hit John's hometown of Seville, and made notes of all the events and conversations we could remember. The next logical step for us was to get to New Jersey and Connecticut and survey the situations there for ourselves, but first we had to find a time when we could all take leave to go. Dedy and I were like chained-up junkyard dogs, just waiting to be released. We hated pacing around the house not making progress toward finding Fran.

Mike tried to feel us out on our proposed Connecticut expedition, maybe to see how far we'd come in our investigative techniques in the past several weeks. One day on the phone he asked what I planned to do when we got to the beach house. Well, I'll march up to the front door and knock, I said.

"What then?"

"When they answer, I'll say, 'You're in my sister's house. Who the hell are you?'"

Mike asked if I would really do that. "In a heartbeat," I said. "If it's between being embarrassed and finding my sister, forget the embarrassment. I'm a big girl. I can handle a little discomfort."

Before I got the chance to experiment with my direct approach, Mama again became gravely ill. As careful as Granny and Todd were, somehow Mama got a cold that quickly turned into pneumonia.

I wrestled with family priorities: Connecticut or Florida? Resolving the end of Fran's life, or assisting Mama near the end of hers? I felt as if I were being pulled in four directions. My first impulse was to fly to see Mama. I called her on November 19 as the doctors were getting ready to move her into I.C.U., again on a ventilator, and told her I was coming home.

"No," she said. "You stay right where you are and find your sister." She was too weak even to hold the phone—a nurse had to help her.

I decided there was little, beyond my presence, I could give Mama if I went to Florida, and she already had family there with her. The best medicine for her would be news of Fran.

In addition to talking to Dedy and Mike every day, I now spoke with Granny and Mama's doctors on a daily basis. I kept asking the doctors if I should come home, and they kept advising me to stay where I was. The Thanksgiving and Christmas holidays were extremely hard. Dedy made the trip to Florida for Thanksgiving, but because the I.C.U. nurses would permit only short visits with Mama, she spent most of her time at the house with Granny and Todd. "Seeing Grandma Gladden was hard," Dedy said. "She is so frail. The ventilator and IV tubes look so large against her small face and along her hands. She couldn't talk, so she had an alphabet board and communicated by pointing to letters: 'F*R*A*N*?' I told her I thought Mom was just being ornery and that she'd show up soon. I lied. She knew it. The look she returned was very clear: 'Don't bullshit me.' So I told her what little I knew. She cried. It was too sad because she made no sound, just silent tears. I cried too. She knows she's dying and does not know where her child is. I cried even harder when the thought came to me that soon Grandma would know. Of course, that won't help the rest of us."

That holiday season was one of the few times I let myself give in to despair. Even though I had decided not to go to Florida, I also held off on a trip to Connecticut in case Mama had an emergency. I knew that Dave and my two girls needed me at home, and I also needed to hold on to my job at Textron. The costs of the investigation—phone calls, travel, and lots of time—were quickly adding up, and John certainly wasn't offering any financial help. On top of all of these worries, we had bought our youngest daughter, Mikel, a puppy for Christmas only to find it was ill. We took it to the veterinarian, and she told us the puppy had parvo virus and advised us to take the puppy back to the kennel where we had bought it. I felt God was now even punishing one of my children.

I was on my way home from work when the grief overcame me. I pulled the car to the edge of the road and just let it all out. For several minutes, I was too overwhelmed to drive. I kept asking myself what I had ever done to deserve this. It was the sort of question John would ask in daily conversations with me or Dedy. After dishonesty and excessive control, self-pity was probably his most notable characteristic. I despised the thought and cast around for something positive in my life to focus on. Anything. Granny used to say that God never closes a door without opening a window, but at the moment it felt like I was on the bottom floor of a house of cards. I wiped a flood of tears and tried to pull myself together and get home; my family would be worried about me. That's when I realized that they were the window. Dave, Neva, Mikel, Granny, and Fran's children and the rest of them loved me and needed me to be strong. One of Daddy's old sayings came back to me: "Pick yourself up by your boot straps and continue to march."

CHAPTER 7
Mama at Rest

If John didn't lack for self-pity, he definitely had reason to feel down. With Fran he had pursued what he considered the ideal life with a picture-perfect family. But as each day passed, he was finding it more difficult to obscure his bizarre behavior. That his façade of respectability had continued to erode was arguably more disturbing to him than anything he had done. Appearances were everything for him.

The week before Christmas, John had submitted to a polygraph. Although it was very late when he left the West Windsor Township Police Department that night, he did call Dedy to tell her about it, just as she had asked when she learned he planned to take one the week before. She wanted to evaluate whether taking the test had rattled him. "I failed it miserably," he said. A casual observer might guess that he was telling her about it to take control of the situation and put his own spin on the results before the police had a chance to tell Dedy themselves. But John had already had a number of chances to document for us what he knew about Fran's disappearance, and he invariably opted for either silence or deceit. Knowing John as I do now, I expect he was looking for sympathy and reassurance.

"John, if you were telling the truth, how could you have failed?" Dedy asked.

"I guess I'm just not good at it."

It's a shame these tests aren't admissible in court. No jury would get to hear the results of this polygraph, or even learn that he had taken one. It was strictly for police purposes, an investigative tool to gain more insight into John and the case. Until that point, I wouldn't allow myself to give up all hope of Fran returning. Underneath the professional exterior I projected for the case and the detached attitude I cultivated to cope day-to-day, I reserved a tiny bit of hope that my suspicions were incorrect. Maybe Fran had been in an accident and suffered amnesia. Now, confronted by John's polygraph results, I couldn't pretend. Fran had always loved the winter holidays. If she were at all able, she would have called. In my heart, I knew she was dead, not missing, and I also knew that John was responsible.

Mike called at the end of December and asked us to put the Connecticut trip on hold. He wanted to look into the beach house first. In light of our earlier conversation in which I had told him I intended to simply knock on the door, Mike surely felt he would handle the situation better. He didn't share it with us at the time, but he already knew from questioning John who was living in the beach house.

Delaying our trip East didn't stop us from digging into public records from every place we could find that John had been. Dedy became a champion in locating county courthouses and accessing their most useful records, all in the pre-Internet era. She was able to locate and obtain copies of John's family's birth, marriage, and divorce records. The clerks and record-keepers we both spoke to in working the case were usually incredibly friendly and genuinely interested in helping. Dedy discovered that John was the sole owner of the Connecticut beach house, which he had bought in August 1986 for $295,000. The longer Dedy and I worked together, the more impressed I became by her resourcefulness, intellect, and resolve. I don't think I had it together that well when I was her age.

Mike called Sheila Sautter at the beach house in Milford, Connecticut, the day after John's polygraph, and she agreed to meet with him. He had gotten her name from John, and he felt she was a vital link between John and Fran's disappearance. Mike went to visit her on January 3, 1992, to conduct an extended interview. Sheila revealed that she and John had shared the home for about eight years. Their relationship was unorthodox, to say the least. Prior to moving in together, Sheila had taken a job in New Hampshire and had bought a house there. John visited often and said he intended to move there with her, but that never happened. Eventually they got engaged, and Sheila agreed to sell her home and put the proceeds into the Milford house.

When John moved to Florida in January 1990 to take the job with Chromalloy, he left Sheila with the house, two dogs, and no job. His sister never lived in the beach house. John doesn't have any sisters. In March of that year, Sheila went to Florida for a long weekend and to try to make the relationship work, but she decided that she would not make the move. She told John that her life, home, family, and job were in Connecticut and that she was going home. John let her go, reluctantly. That same month, Fran met John at Chromalloy, and they began dating. It has always astounded me that he could just let Sheila go and within a few days begin to date another woman. Sheila stated that from the time she left Florida, their relationship had become platonic, although John continued to visit her at the beach house and constantly told her he wanted her back. (No doubt these were the ambiguous trips John would make while on business, when he wouldn't leave a phone number and instead called Fran when he got to New York.) Sheila said that they still held the beach house together but were no longer romantic.

She said she wasn't aware that Fran even existed until December 16, 1991, a Monday. John had gotten up and dressed about 3:00 A.M. for his three-hour trip back to New Jersey for work. Sheila was in bed, still groggy, when he said, "By the way, I'm married. My wife is missing." With that, he left.

Mike also learned that John had been at the beach house every week-end since the first of October, when Fran disappeared, and he had spent Thanksgiving weekend with Sheila and her family at her sister and broth-er in-law's home. John had a great affection for Sheila and usually tried to put on a good face for her family, but he had been withdrawn and moody on that trip.

Overall, Sheila was highly cooperative and perhaps a little embar-rassed that she was involved in a police investigation. It was a good sign for the case that someone as close to John as Sheila was would be so forthcoming about his habits and whereabouts.

The same day I heard from Mike about his phone call and visit with Sheila, Mama's doctors called to say they'd have to remove her from the ventilator. They had no choice. Her throat was deteriorating. My option was, leave her on the vent and allow her to drown in her own blood, or remove it and pray for a miracle. I had to decide how I wanted her to die. As a family, we agreed to give her what little chance she had by remov-ing her from the ventilator. The doctors said it could take days to see the outcome but that there really was no hope.

Granny and I spoke many times that night. Mama was losing ground fast. I started pulling items together for another trip home and realized that I would have to pack black this time. I had worried and prayed for Mama before, but then it was because of her physical suffering, and always with the belief that she would get better. Now I would grieve not only for her loss from our world but for my inability to bring Fran back to hers. I thought of the promise I had made to her in our last conversation: "Mama, I'll find her. You just concentrate on getting well." I had failed in my last chance to put her at ease.

The next morning I was at work trying to set things in order before leaving for Florida when Granny called. Mama had slipped in a coma.

Dave began making arrangements to get me out on the first available flight. All I could think was, *Mama, you've fought so long and hard. Please don't give up now.* Her doctors called right after that and told me to get home immediately. I hung up and just sat there, not even sure where I was. A third call came, Granny again, and I was already too late. My sweet Mama was gone.

I arrived in Florida late that afternoon. Granny was holding up as well as could be expected. Granny had Todd, her other two daughters, and a wonderful church family, and they had been with her until Dedy, Aunt Betty, and I could get there. She is a remarkably strong lady. I started to get things ready for the relatives and friends I knew would soon arrive. We still had many arrangements to make. I talked with Dave, and we finalized the plans for him to drive down with our daughters. They were to arrive the next night, Friday. I'll never forget how grateful I was for one phone call in particular. Mike Dansbury called to express his department's sympathy and to ask if there was anything they could do for us. We hadn't even met him in person yet.

Dedy called John before she left Houston to let him know that Mama had passed on. John kept saying he did not know what to do. Should he stay there and continue to search for Fran, or should he leave for Florida? He said he was concerned for Granny. Dedy told him she had to leave and for him to do whatever he felt he had to do. She also told him not to come stressed.

We decided on a visitation Saturday evening, with the funeral to take place Sunday, January 12. Many family members would be coming in from out of state, and we had to give them time to make it home. I was so relieved when Dave got there Friday night. I just felt safe and complete. We had always made good partners, but with Fran gone in the past several months, I know I was especially dependent on his strength. Without him, I might not have been able to handle the emotion of losing both Fran and Mama, much less dealing with the police investigation and interaction with John at the time and in the years to come.

At the visitation on Saturday, I remember looking down at Mama and getting an overpowering sense of aloneness. Fran and I had always faced crisis together. When we lost Daddy in April of 1985, we stood together during what we thought was the worst situation we would ever encounter. I had always counted on Fran to make things right. Then I felt a hand on my shoulder. I turned and faced Dave and again reminded myself that as long as I had him, I would be okay. The visitation was over-flowing. I couldn't believe how many people really loved my mother. I knew she was remarkable, but it was beautiful to realize so many other people thought so too. I was grateful for this show of love and respect.

When we got home that evening, John called to let us know he was coming for the funeral. I regretted that we had permitted him to come at all, but I saw no way to refuse him without raising his suspicions. He had lived next door to Mama for a year in Florida, and we needed him to believe he was in good standing with the family. Distasteful as that was, the harder part was bullying the rest of the family into playing along. Todd and Rodd were ready to wipe the floor with him. I told everyone that John must be shown the respect due my sister's husband while in my mother's home. John was the key to the whole puzzle. If we lost that key, I said, we might never know what had happened to Fran. If they were going to have a problem dealing with this, they would have to leave.

The plan was to accompany John at all times and ensure he wasn't left alone with Granny. One of us had to be with him constantly. When John said he wanted Granny to ride to the funeral with him, Dave stepped in and said she would ride with us. So John rode with Dave, me, and Granny to the church and the cemetery. My Aunt Betty ended up sitting at the back of the church during the funeral because John took the seat next to Granny on the front pew. Aunt Betty couldn't trust herself to sit anywhere near him. She wasn't sure what she might have been capable of doing to him. He was in full John Boy mode when he took Granny by

the hand and escorted her to view Mama for the last time. I took grudg-
ing satisfaction in being able to recognize the difference between who
John was and who he pretended to be. Nevertheless, I was repulsed and
thought I would become violently ill when he reached over and took my
hand as we were leaving the church. I immediately snatched my hand
away from him. I couldn't get the thought out of my head that the last
time he had touched my sister, he had killed her. I wondered how he
could have the nerve to even touch any member of my family. I just wanted him away from me and my family. His hands, to me, were filthy.

Even under the circumstances, we were glad to have seen so much of
the family again and gotten reacquainted with Mama's friends and
acquaintances. I can't deny that my memory of the funeral was tainted by
John's presence, but more than anything I marveled at the outpouring of
goodwill and love that came from such an upsetting event. Seeing John
in this setting, alone and making hollow attempts to mourn with the
family, I sensed in my gut that the unconditional love so prevalent here
was foreign to him and that he'd never really get it. It made him seem
much less formidable. Spotting his lies and inconsistencies didn't feel
like a challenge anymore.

As he got ready to return to New Jersey, Dedy walked him to his car
at Mama's house. He hadn't brought the phone book we had been nag-
ging him to send for months on the off chance that Fran had circled numbers or businesses that might offer clues in the case. But he had brought
her portable sewing machine for Nici. "Fran would have wanted Nici to
have this," he said, phrasing it as a bequeath. It was the first time any of
us had heard him speak of Fran in the past tense; he never again spoke
of her in present tense.

Nearby, Rodd, Todd, Dave, and I waited in the driveway and kept an
eye on Dedy as she and John finished their conversation.

CHAPTER 8

Clues in Connecticut, Jackpot in Jersey

itnessing John's act at Mama's funeral, the brazen manner in which he played the distraught, caring son-in-law, made Dedy and me sick with anger and impotence. The one person I had ever literally wished to destroy was untouchable. Not only could I not harm him, I could not so much as confront him about his culpability, something I desperately desired to do most any time I talked to him. The risk that we'd lose our most valuable potential evidence was too great. In his driveway conversation with Dedy after the funeral, John had revised his story about the days before Fran's disappearance. Previously he contended that there was no argument; things with Fran had been great right up until he found her note. He now told Dedy that he and Fran had argued on September 30 (the day before she supposedly left and two days after we last spoke to her), about Fran's wanting a maid. John said she only wanted a maid because Mama had a maid—which itself was not entirely true—not because she really needed one. This bucket didn't hold water. Fran was such a housekeeping fanatic that no maid would have been able to please her.

John also said that Fran was angry because she felt he wasn't concerned enough about her being alone all day while he was at work. Between his frequent travel and responsibilities at work, Fran thought he was taking her for granted. She'd retaliate by not answering the phone when he called. John was familiar with this game. She'd done it before. "Fran gave me more credit than I deserved," he told Dedy. "I didn't call."

The case was now three months old and in danger of getting pushed to the bottom of the stack as new cases with hotter leads demanded the detectives' time. Dedy and I knew that her case could only be worked hard as long as Mike was getting new leads, either internally or from us. That's the cops' dilemma: There's never enough time to investigate all the crimes and petty violations people commit. It's the same with all cases, which is why so many police departments are establishing cold case divisions. John had been of little use on that front, at least willfully, so we decided to appeal to the public.

I was wary after my initial experience with Mark Mueller and the *Trentonian* ("Depressed wife leaves cryptic note, vanishes") that going to the media could harm as much as help, but we were also running out of options. The more people who knew Fran's plight, the better our chances of stumbling across solid clues. Dedy and I used lunch breaks to call television stations and get addresses for the investigative reporting shows, tabloid magazine-style shows, and talk shows—*Unsolved Mysteries, A Current Affair, Inside Edition, Oprah, Montel, Sally Jesse Raphael,* and all the others.

We started looking for support groups for families of the missing. There's a strong network for families of missing children, but relatively little support for families of missing adults. At that time, before the Internet, there weren't as many support groups available as there are today. I belong to Hope 2 Support, which is sponsored by the Nation's Missing Children Organization and Center for Missing Adults. I did encounter a good lead by calling the Indiana State Police. A sweet lady there explained that I could write a letter to the Social Security Administration listing Fran's Social Security number; date and place of

birth; mother's and father's full names; and last known place of employment and explaining why we needed to locate her. In it we were to write
a letter to Fran and place it in an unsealed envelope with her full name
on it. The chaplain's assistant then explained that the Social Security
Administration was only a mediator. If at any time taxes were filed on
Fran's behalf, they would forward the letter to her place of employment.
Making contact would then be up to Fran. Unless we heard from her, we
would never know if the letter had actually been forwarded. This might
sound like a shot in the dark, but it was more than we had before making those phone calls.

Mike also had a bit more to go on thanks to his talks with Sheila at
the beach house in Milford, and he was applying some of that to advance
the investigation. He had gained a much broader view of John's personal life, and his new understanding only made John look worse. We knew
John had lied to us about the beach house's not being winterized and
therefore livable year-round, about a sister living there, and about the
true status of the woman who did. Sheila downplayed the seriousness of
their relationship after she left Florida, but none of us bought that John
was visiting Connecticut every weekend just to look after his Border collies. If their relationship were strictly platonic and innocent by that time,
John still felt the need to deceive Fran about the nature and object of his
frequent trips there. And there was more.

Upon arriving at Sheila's and entering the house, Mike immediately
recognized the furniture she was using as Fran's. It was the same couch,
tables, and chairs I had described to him as being in Fran and John's
Florida home. John had put most of their belongings in storage when
they moved to the condo in Jersey. After his disappearing stunt in
August—when Sheila reports that he again went to the beach house—
Fran demanded to know where their things were being stored. John rented a new storage area, this time nearer their Princeton home (it had previously been near John's Carborundum office), but it's unlikely any of
Fran's things ended up the newly rented storage unit because Sheila said

he had moved the furniture to her house in the middle of August, when John canceled the rental agreement for the larger unit and opened a new account for a smaller space.

Mike wanted to dig more into Fran's social circle in New Jersey with an eye toward tracking some of these new threads and corroborating statements he had gotten from John and Sheila. He started with Hollie Drajin, a woman Fran had mentioned to Dedy and me who had helped Fran get her secretarial job at J.A. Mazotas Title Agency. John said Hollie and Fran had had lunch on occasion and had gone to dinner a few times, when he had to work late. Mike first approached Hollie about an interview at her workplace, Schnelling & Schnelling Employment Agency. There, he sensed that she was resistant and might know more than she was willing to tell with her boss present, so he later went to her apartment. At that time Hollie told Mike that her relationship with Fran had been purely professional, and she would therefore talk to him only at the office. Then she slammed the door in his face. Mike was shocked. What was this woman's problem?

In the few months since I had entered the world of investigation, I had benefited from dozens of people who sympathized with our family's situation and went out of their way to help. So we thought I might make some headway with Hollie where Mike couldn't. I wrote to her and begged her to reply. I told her about Mama's death and how torn up our family was. On January 28, she called. Hollie insisted that she and Fran had a working relationship only. They had shared a single lunch. Hollie had been trying to find a better job for Fran. She knew Fran was overqualified for her job at Mazotas. She seemed sincere and pleasant on the phone. She said she wished she could help but did not feel she knew anything. I didn't want to risk aggravating her by bringing up her run-in with Mike, but the woman I was talking to and the woman who slammed the door on him struck me as very different people.

While I was in letter-writing mode, I also wrote to the only other people I knew to have had significant contact with Fran in New Jersey, the

Mazotases themselves. Joe and Nancy Mazotas owned J.A. Mazotas Title Agency and had been understanding with Fran's rather mixed-up life in Princeton. After Fran broke her hip during their Labor Day weekend honeymoon, she had been unable to return to work. John told Fran he had called the Mazotases to explain the situation. He said that Joe and Nancy understood and reassured Fran that her job was not in jeopardy. But weeks later, when Fran called her bosses and offered to have John pick up and drop off paperwork so she could continue her position from home, they were surprised to hear from her. They didn't know why she had stopped coming to work. Joe turned her down with regrets; they needed to hire a full-time replacement.

They got my letter and called on February 4. I always let people know that I expected them to call me collect, but the Mazotases paid for a call that lasted for more than an hour. They said they hated to let Fran go and hoped I understood their position. I told them I did, and more important, that Fran did. They said Fran had been distracted and often troubled at work, which led them to suspect a drinking problem. I quickly laid that notion to rest. Fran had a liver ailment that had caused her a lot of illness as a child. Alcohol only compounded her difficulties. We talked about Fran's reaction during the period in August when John had packed up and left. Joe had come into the office over the weekend and found Fran there. Joe wasn't surprised because Fran often came in on weekends when John was out of town or working. But Fran was a nervous wreck and, after prompting, explained what had happened. They offered to take Fran to Connecticut to see if they could find John, but were surprised to hear that she didn't know where the house might be, or even what town it was in. Joe and Nancy impressed me as having a lot of integrity and being genuinely concerned for Fran as a person, though neither seemed to know more that would be helpful in the investigation. I thanked them and hung up.

Much as Dedy and I had immersed ourselves in the case, we still felt unable to entirely bridge our physical distance from it. Anyone who has had to conduct business remotely knows the frustration of letter writing, negotiating voice mail mazes and stubborn faxes, and following up with unresponsive contacts. And we didn't yet have the advantage of e-mail. We heard back from most of the investigative shows and TV news magazines we had written to, but only with regrets. Across the board, they said Fran's story wasn't compelling enough for broadcast. We resolved to resume our New Jersey travel plans and agreed to leave from Indianapolis on February 22. We had the formal statements, the basic facts, the lay of the land. The things we wanted to know now revolved around John and Fran's life in New Jersey. We wanted to witness the sleight of hand and interpret the body language that could explain the inexplicable. We wanted to stare into hollow eyes and see if we could divine the truth. We wanted to visit the scene of the crime.

———————————

Valentine's Day, 1992: John phoned Dedy to wish her Happy Valentine's Day, but really he had called to lament the pain of his single status. "Everywhere I look, people are together, holding hands and kissing," he said. "I feel so alone. I am really going through some hard times." It was hokum . . . or was it? Did he think that if he pined for Fran to Dedy that she might interpret it as concern for his lost wife? Or was he so preoccupied with his own desires he hadn't stopped to consider that Dedy might be less than sympathetic to his lack of companionship? That was the rub with John. Head games were his favorite pastime. The more we found out about him, the more we realized how intelligent he was, which baffled us when he said things we felt disfavored him, as when he asked that we come up there to help with the investigation: Was he losing his touch, or was he masterfully manipulating us? John told Dedy he had thought of bringing home a dozen roses in case Fran showed up. He had seen a bouquet of long-stem crimson roses in a store window, except that they were not really roses but rather red panties cleverly folded to *look* like roses. John thought they were really romantic.

I got much the same phone call later. I was surprised, because John had not been calling me, but I refused to show it in my voice. I didn't want him to think he was capable of doing anything I hadn't anticipated. At least I had to hear the panty bouquet story only once. John called Dedy almost daily, so she had to endure it repeatedly, until she told him she knew her mother wouldn't have swooned over his faux flowers. We took solace in the fact that he would soon have less trivial stories to tell. Dedy informed him on February 21 that she would be leaving the next day to fly to Indianapolis and meet me, and from there we would be headed his way.

We felt it best to strike a balance with regard to timing in revealing our plan to John. We needed him to be there, but we agreed that the less time he had to prepare for our visit, the better. The beauty of our plan was that John had invited us there and would find it awkward to now refuse our help. And since we were guests, we'd be free to search and rummage through the condo while he was at work.

The 22nd, when Dedy's flight arrived, was a Saturday. Dave and I picked her up to spend Saturday night at our home, and we started our trip to New Jersey together early Sunday morning. The twelve-hour trip up gave us a chance to talk over the case, trade stories, and psych ourselves up for what lay ahead. This was the first time we were going to be alone with John, and we knew that the more we learned, the more we'd be at risk. We vowed never to be alone with him and to sleep in shifts. Also, Mike and the West Windsor PD knew where we were going to be. It was actually a thrill knowing that we were finally able to take steps to help Fran, especially because we were finally going to put John on the defensive. And facing such dire circumstances put the rest of our lives in perspective. Small hurts, gossip, financial struggles, and the undistinguished trials of everyday life now seemed both purposeful and immaterial next to the challenge before us. We had discovered many skeletons in the family closet and laughed at how stupid it was to try to hide the bones. We laughed that our family would still, in this day and age, feel that a divorce was something that almost spelled failure. Also comical was the thought that our family had had many nine-pound babies born two months premature.

John read us the riot act when we made it to Princeton. We arrived about two hours later than we had planned and hadn't called to tell him. We had stopped for breakfast to see Rich, Dedy's father, and his wife, Jan, at their home near Columbus. Dedy's paternal grandparents, Edith and Blake, were there, and we had spent more time with them than we had planned. John was in full mother-hen mode. I reminded myself that it was an act, like someone had opened a utility box on his back and flipped the switch to "John Boy." When we learned Fran was missing in October, he was so unconcerned we had to threaten to fly to New Jersey to get him to file a police report, but now our late arrival warranted furious hand-wringing.

Walking in, Dedy and I were struck by the décor of the condo. Fran had a way with a room, and knowing her as I did, it wasn't difficult for me to differentiate her touches from the rest. It's hard to explain, but we knew things had been moved from the places Fran would have put them. In the kitchen, she always had her coffeemaker on the counter to the right of the sink as you walked in, but here the microwave was on the right, and the coffeemaker was on the left. I couldn't imagine why the appliances would have been rearranged since Fran had left the condo. It would have taken more effort than it was worth.

After we settled in, Dedy and I asked John to again relate everything he remembered about the weekend prior to Fran's disappearance. He gave pretty much the same story as he had given the police and us in the beginning, but with an additional comment about Fran's irritation with their level of intimacy: "Fran was often annoyed that I didn't act like a normal husband," he said. "I didn't check on her as often as I should have when I returned to work after her accident. I'd tell her, 'Fran, I don't know how a husband should act. I've never been married before. I have no experience to draw from.' We decided that I would call more, be more conscious of her needs." Dedy asked specifically if there had been a real blow-up or argument; he said there had not. John had obviously forgotten what he had told Deby at Mama's funeral, when he said they had argued about Fran's wanting a maid. We let it pass.

John then presented us with one page of what he said was a nine-page letter he had found the evening he came home and found Fran missing. He said there had been no "feed the fish" note, just this letter. He had invented the note because he felt what she had actually written was too personal. (It also was apparently too personal to share with the rest of us.) On the one page John showed us, Fran mentions suicide over the possibility of suffering one more failed marriage. I took the note and saw that the writing was indeed Fran's, and ached for what she must have felt being so far from her family, nearly immobile and dependent upon a man who perverted the meaning of love and whom she couldn't love in return. She probably *had* had those thoughts. In the pantheon of John's greatest head games, this could have been his best. Yet I never took the letter seriously. Fran was afraid of death. She felt suicide was a one-way ticket to hell: Do not pass go, do not collect two hundred dollars. It was a study trick she had taught me years before: Write down all the known facts, and then appraise their value. This was something she meant to throw away after she had written down all that bothered her. It could have been written any time.

And there was this: John had conveniently left the other eight pages at his office, presumably because they would have contradicted what was on the page he had, or reflected poorly on him. Dedy read the page and said, "No way." A comment later made by the Mercer County prosecutor in New Jersey deftly refutes the possibility: "Normally suicide victims don't hide their own bodies."

If John was convinced Fran had done herself in, he still continued to canvass the community looking for her. Again we heard about all the places he had been trying to get information about Fran. John told an elaborate story about how he had even traced where Fran bought her makeup and had stopped by the store several times to talk to any clerk that might have waited on Fran. He called these his "walk-and-talk trips." By 1:30 A.M. we had heard enough of his good intentions and rolled into bed. It was a one-bedroom condo, and John hadn't picked up much Southern hospitality during his stint in Florida, so Dedy and I took the couch and love seat that sat on opposite sides of the living room coffee table. We tossed and turned the rest of the night. We had decided to sleep in shifts, but neither of us slept for more than thirty minutes at a time, both us aware that the other was awake but too scared that John would hear us to talk.

The next morning, John left for work early, maybe 6:45. I heard him making noise and pretended to still be asleep; I didn't want to have to talk to him again just then. A figure hovered over the couch, but when I looked up, I saw it was Dedy. She had started taking the place apart soon after John left. It's a good thing he's so habitual and kept a highly regimented work schedule, because we took that place apart. As we ticked off what was there, our strangest discovery was not what was missing but how much was there. Fran's good jewelry was in a small satin bag in the dresser, her reading glasses in a dresser in the sewing room/office. Fran couldn't read so much as a bus schedule or menu without them. Her watch sat on the phone table in a small glass. In the bathroom, her deodorant, razor, shampoo, makeup, manicure set, and various other toiletries were all there. They were easily replaceable, but if we were to believe John's first story about a spur-of-the-moment trip, why wouldn't she take those items with her? She had taken her suitcase, so no doubt everything would have fit.

We found the shoebox for her Keds sneakers she had supposedly taken with her, without the shoes. That didn't mean that John's account of those held up, however—Mike had already told us they had found the shoes in the kitchen trash can when they originally visited the condo for an informal interview with John, but couldn't remove them without a warrant. The clothes in her closet, near as we could tell, were all there save for the pink and green sweat suits John had told us earlier she'd taken with her. But one dresser drawer raised a red flag. Dedy had found a pair of panty hose and a pair of underpants twisted together. "Mom would never leave her things like this," she said, "and she would never put dirty underwear back in her dresser."

While Fran's side of the bedroom closet was loaded to the gills with outfits, we got the sense that John had moved back in for our visit. A couple suits and a few changes of casual clothes hung on his racks. I recalled that in Florida he had filled two oversized closets with his wardrobe alone.

As with other rooms in the apartment, the bedroom was not as Fran would have arranged it. It was not balanced. The carpet had marks where furniture had been moved, with little vacuuming done since. The present arrangement didn't even make sense. Fran spent most of her time in bed in her last month here, yet the phone was on a table across the room. Fran answered too quickly when I called to have had that setup. The TV screen wasn't visible from the bed. A matching bedroom table was missing. During her recuperation Fran had described an elaborate strategy to deal with the pain when she had to go the bathroom (take a pain pill and wait twenty minutes for it to kick in before hauling herself out of bed), but here, the bed was as far away from the bathroom as was possible. Dedy and I took the bed apart but couldn't find anything that pointed to a fight or struggle.

A mirrored double closet just inside the entryway held some of Fran's evening-wear makeup and the missing-person fliers Dedy had sent to him. They were all there, still wrapped as Dedy had mailed them. I looked out the balcony doors to the deck and spotted a storage area, which proved to be unlocked. If John put all of the missing-person fliers in the closet by the front entrance, what did he keep in out-of-the-way storage areas? It was small, like a generous closet, with old boxes, a few files, and the usual stuff in limbo between valued possession and trash. Under some of the junk, I dug out two yellow suitcases. John had told us and the police that Fran had taken one of these with her.

All the gifts Fran had received over the years, the little treasures that a mother and grandmother keeps, were there. Our net impression from searching the condo was that John had moved on with his life, while Fran's was very much there. Only she wasn't. Dedy described it as a "paper vacuum." No bills, no birth certificates, photo albums, marriage licenses, nothing. About the only paper, aside from the missing-person fliers, was a note from Fran to John to pick up her medicine at the pharmacy.

Fran hadn't taken those papers, because John had called Dedy after her disappearance and asked about them. Who were these other men, he wanted to know—Sveda, Wehling, McClister? Dedy, perhaps revising her appraisal of John's intellect, reminded him that Fran's children, including Dedy, were all named Wehling, and Fran's surname had been McClister when they married. Sveda should have been the only unfamiliar name. During this phone call, Dedy asked him if he and Fran had ever discussed anything about their lives before their marriage. John just said that was the past, and at the time they were only interested in their future. Clearly John and I had opposing agendas.

Monday, 10:30 A.M.: For the first time, we met Mike Dansbury and the other detectives who were working Fran's case face-to-face. Dedy and I had discussed many times what we thought Mike would look like: forty-ish, dark hair, and physically fit with a mustache. It turns out the picture we had painted in our minds was quite accurate. We were delighted. Mike is actually thinner and more handsome than we had imagined, the kind of man that women turn around to look at twice. Bob Gulden was the surprise. We had him pegged as the older, fatherly officer. In fact, he was more late-twenties to mid-thirties and also very handsome.

The one thing I will never forget about our first visit is the picture of Fran on the bulletin board to the left of Mike's desk. Finding Fran had

always been my ultimate goal, but day to day I kept myself going by finding enough new information to keep her case from getting buried in an
archive somewhere. Seeing that photo in his office reassured me that he
wasn't going to give up this fight until we had all the answers. We knew
we had very little time to convince this man that Fran didn't leave on her
own. We spent several hours reviewing the case with Mike and going over
John's statements, which we picked apart. There were so many lies in
them that it was hard to believe he hadn't been arrested just on the cir-
cumstantial evidence. Dedy and I told him about our search of the
condo: the missing-person fliers; the yellow suitcases, and the personal
items still there, as if Fran had never left. We also gave him the one page
we had of the nine-page letter, which he made a copy of, and told Mike
that John had lied about the note he first said Fran had left. Mike directed us to analyze everything that seemed amiss in the condo, ask ourselves why it's wrong, and take pictures of and notes on all of it. I asked
Mike what he thought the chances were of finding Fran alive and well. I
could tell that he was reluctant to answer, but he had also learned that
we were pretty strong women and wouldn't ask a question we weren't
prepared to hear the answer to. Maybe 20 percent, he said, based on
what I know about your family and Fran's personality, and that figure
goes down with each passing day. It still wasn't easy to hear.

We left the police department and spent the afternoon photograph-
ing and noting our morning discoveries and making sure we hadn't
missed anything. I made a quick sketch of the floor plan of the condo.
Both of us had a strong feeling that Fran should be here, or like she had
been there recently, and it wasn't due to sleep deprivation. "I was totally
overcome with the smell of Mom," Dedy would write of the experience.
"It had been four months since her disappearance, and it smelled like
she had just walked out. I grabbed some of the sleeves [in her closet] and
wrapped my face in them. She could have been right there. I drifted off,
remembering how she looked in them, what she was doing, where she
was going. I dropped to my knees and began to cry very quietly. I did not

want to upset Aunt Sherrie." I found Dedy in the closet reeling with emotion just then. This was probably the closest she had felt to her mother since Fran's disappearance. I saw the tears trickling down her cheeks, and my heart ached. Fran and I had been close, yes, but I had gotten to spend more than forty years with her. Dedy had been robbed of potential decades of love and memories with her favorite person and had to deal with the loss at a much younger, more vulnerable age than I did. I took her in my arms and resolved to make it up to her as best I could. But I knew there can be no replacing a mother.

Monday, 3:00 P.M.: We left the condo to meet John at his office at Carborundum. The night before, we had asked him if the people at work were supportive. John said, "Somewhat. They just look at me kind of strange." I suggested that Dedy and I visit him at work to show family unity. John felt it might help. Dedy and I couldn't have cared less about how he was being treated at work but thought a visit there might shed some light on his work life and the atmosphere there. We also had a plan. Dedy would ask John to show her to the ladies' room, and I'd use the time to sift through his office for any evidence, and the other eight pages of the letter John had shown us the night before. I prayed the bathroom wouldn't be too near his office, and that John wouldn't just give her directions. If they were anything like the directions he had given us to the office, she'd definitely need an escort. We encountered many of the same landmarks on the way there but weren't sure how we had ended up driving by them again. After about thirty minutes of driving in circles, we stopped at a guard shack of a factory and called John to get better directions. After the trip, Dedy and I went back over John's original directions, and we're sure that they weren't intended to get us to his office. We've never been able to figure out why he would do something like that. Maybe this was just one more head game played on stupid females.

John was in his element when we got to Carborundum and friendly enough after our hassle in getting there. I thought it strange at the time that he came to the parking lot and escorted us to his upstairs office via the back stairway. He explained the office area was being renovated. Stranger still, he never introduced us to anyone. We passed a number of people on the way. I had expected him to make sure we met everyone there. His office was a Spartan hodgepodge that included the missing bedroom table and table cover from the condo. It looked ridiculous next to the file cabinets and bare surfaces in the rest of his office, though it would have looked ridiculous anyway. No man should have a lavender flower-covered table like that in his office. We commented, polite as you please, on how he had decorated, and John said Fran had done it for him. I spotted a picture of Fran in a black dress propped prominently on the credenza behind his desk. She was bending slightly backward and wore a lighthearted expression.

After a bit of small talk, I did manage a few minutes in John's office while he showed Dedy to the bathroom, but our grand plan was useless. All I found were some specs for jobs and other work-related papers. His desk and file cabinets were locked. With no chance of digging up anything on him at work, Dedy and I made our excuses and prepared to head out. John never did really show us around. In hindsight I should have pushed him to introduce us to the people in his department or, failing that, walked around and introduced myself. His reasons for encouraging our work visit became clear to us several weeks later when I talked to Mike about his investigative follow-ups and learned that after we left that day, John had asked the receptionist what she thought of his wife and daughter. Once I get past the shameless flattery, I see a lie that perfectly exemplifies John's methods. Often he'd rely on a grand deception; not something irrefutable or clever, but so basic and accepted that, without evidence to the contrary, the average person wouldn't dream anyone might lie about it. Normal people try to redeem expired coupons or shade recollections to put themselves in a better light. They don't manufacture an alternate reality to cover their tracks. The Achilles' heel of John's strategy was that, pressed by skepticism and real scrutiny, the fabrications disintegrated. I should say for the record that Fran and I have similar facial features, but I'm untold pounds heavier than she was, and not even the casual observer would confuse us. Our biggest similarities were our eyes and our voices. No wonder John didn't like to call me.

Once again, following John's directions, Dedy and I got lost on the way to find a grocery store, gave up, and waited in a sour mood for John to get home. We had been pushing full-bore since we left Indianapolis and were beginning to run out of steam. Sleeping in shifts meant getting maybe three hours' rest, and our day of detective work was taking its toll on our reserves. We realized that we hadn't eaten anything since 7:30 the night before. After finding those yellow suitcases in the storage area, I wasn't counting on a fitful slumber that night either. John got home, and we ordered pizza.

You'd think based on the condo's haphazard arrangement that John wasn't an especially detail-oriented guy, but he hadn't been home five minutes when he asked me why the microwave's digital clock was blinking. We froze. That morning, Dedy and I wanted to take a look in the attic—aren't the darkest secrets always in the attic?—but we didn't have a chair high enough to get us up there. I unplugged the microwave and set it on top of a barstool to create a makeshift ladder. Dedy climbed up and scanned the attic floor. Nothing there. But when we got done, we couldn't figure out how to reset the clock. How to cover now? "Oh, we needed an extra outlet for a curling iron," I told him. "Sorry about that." You couldn't go wrong playing the ditzy damsel with John. To this day I haven't developed a moral balance sheet for John and me, but I know what my column looks like. I've never repented for the lies I've told him, because every one was part of an attempt to get him to tell the truth. I haven't heard it yet.

We ate pizza and talked into the wee hours of the morning. This trip was the first time we had really gotten a chance to explore John's personality, see how he responded to direct, in-person questioning, and analyze his different tones of voice, facial expressions, and body language. We were learning that how you asked John something greatly affected what kind of answer you'd get. Mike Dansbury had told us that morning about the day in late December when they did a consensual search of the condo and took John back to the station for questioning. No lawyer present, no interrogation, just a formal interview, though he was read and signed off on his Miranda rights. Detectives talked to him for hours and showed him pictures of Fran. He had no reaction; he'd just look away, like he was withdrawing into a safe place. That's when they asked to administer a polygraph.

As innocently as possible, we asked John where Fran's personal papers were. John said, "The papers are one thing that makes me think she's been back home. The papers were here, and on October 1 they were gone." John again said it was as if Fran had packed for a weekend, not to go away for good. That was one reason he was not overly concerned when he came home to find her gone.

It was no good. We hadn't figured out how to get past the pre-recorded John, and it seemed anything we asked him now was going to yield the same lines we had heard a dozen times over.

Dedy and I were bushed and again resigned ourselves to a restless half-night's sleep. Dedy, bless her heart, volunteered for the first shift and insisted on taking the love seat again. Exhaustion, unfortunately, wasn't going to be enough to knock us out. Curled up on the cramped couch and love seat, we mentally replayed the events of the day, our minds racing. Morning would come early. John planned to work a half-day, and we had little time as it was for all the things we wanted to do.

Tuesday, 6:00 A.M.: I heard John and looked over to the love seat where Dedy was sleeping. He was sitting next to her, watching as she slept, like he wanted to touch her.

The thought nauseated me. We had had numerous uncomfortable

conversations since arriving. Most everything we had to discuss was unpleasant in one way or another. The worst, though, were John's impromptu chronicles of his and Fran's sex life, which he related with zest to both of us. Throughout our visit, he talked freely of where all they had done it, or maneuvers Fran had "taught" him. According to John, Fran enjoyed the romantic possibilities of their balcony, which he said was embarrassing because Fran could be so loud. Actually, I was the one who was embarrassed, for me and Dedy both. "John," I said, "if you feel the need to discuss these things, I am here to help. I'll listen, but cool it in front of Dedy. After all, Fran is her mother. . . . She does not need to hear this."

He had brought up sex again the previous night before bed, and now I watched him shadow Dedy, looking for all the world as if he might massage her or start stroking her hair. She *does* look a lot like Fran. I wondered if John felt any pangs of guilt as he sat and gazed at her. If he had tried to touch her, I think I'd have finished him right there. I groaned and pretended to be just waking up, hoping to put Dedy on her guard. When John realized I was awake, he slid a short distance away to the foot of the love seat. Dedy seemed roused by the sound and movement and quickly got up as well. She'd tell me later that she hadn't been asleep either, just lying still with her eyes shut, and had been equally creeped out by John's hovering.

We saw John off to work and again discussed what we had and hadn't found. The biggest piece left to cover with John was the beach house. We knew far more than John could have suspected and now hoped to squeeze more out of him by confronting him with the facts and asking for explanations. The trick, I thought, was to do it gingerly, without revealing how tirelessly we were really hunting him. If we made him overly insecure about his perceived advantage, he might cut off contact with us or panic and get a lawyer. So far he hadn't, I suspect because he needed to convince himself that he wasn't in any trouble. If he were to secure legal counsel, he'd become the one with all the civil rights. Once we had more to go on from John, we planned to go to the beach house ourselves and see what else we could uncover. We checked in with Mike by phone and let him know our plans. He said that while we were in the area, we should do whatever we felt would make the trip worthwhile.

In the early afternoon when John came home, we were still debating the best way to approach him about Sheila and the beach house. John knew we had met with Mike but didn't know how much we had been told. We decided to try to make him as comfortable as possible but plunge right in. "John, it's okay. We know everything," Dedy said, although she didn't elaborate. She was sitting on the love seat with him. I was on the couch directly across from the two of them, and neither of us was looking at John, so I can't be sure what his reaction to this statement was. We went on to explain that family is family, and nothing else ought to take precedence over Fran's case. We told him we knew that Sheila was living in the house. John sighed. "I guess I should start at the beginning."

I told him I felt this would be a good idea.

He said the job with Chromalloy in Florida came open unexpectedly and he had to be down there ready to start work the next Monday. He knew he'd have to find someone to take care of the dogs. Sheila had recently moved back to Connecticut, and he approached her about temporarily moving into the house. She told him that this was workable because she had an alcoholic brother ready to leave rehab, and he could move into her condo. John reported that this worked fine until he met Fran in Florida and got serious. He could never make Fran understand that Sheila was an old friend, not an old lover, and he flatly denied that he and Sheila were ever engaged.

"Then Fran knew about Sheila?" I asked.

"Sure," he said, "from the second date. Fran and I were at my condo, and the phone rang. I asked her to answer it. It was apparently Sheila. I heard Fran ask, 'Do you love him?' I don't know what the rest of the conversation was about. They hung up." John told us Fran had been to the beach house once, but not inside—and I didn't have to think too hard to answer why. Fran told John it was "a piece of shit" and that she couldn't believe he had spent so much on it. The house seemed to be a major point of contention in the relationship. Before John had taken off in August 1991, Fran didn't quibble about his control of the overall finances or the household, but she did see that house as a drain on their finances and a major reason why they weren't living in a better place in New Jersey. She wanted to get it fixed up and move Sheila out of the house so they could rent it out at the market rate. It was true they were losing money on the house; John claimed he was paid a token amount in rent, though Sheila had already stated that she never paid anything. No doubt he had been just as steadfast in his position as Fran had been in hers. "Forget I had the house long before we were married—IT'S MY HOUSE!" he exclaimed to us, and it was apparent we were getting a glimpse of the temper he had when someone crossed his path at the wrong time.

He admitted to taking all of Fran's furniture to Connecticut but said Fran knew about it and that the furniture was going to be repossessed. Fran had told us before they paid cash for the furniture. Dedy said, "John, you're trying to tell me my Mom knew about Sheila and still let her furniture be sent for another woman to use? Bullshit. That did not happen." John shut down, as if he couldn't believe we would doubt his words. We knew that Fran would never agree to have her things sent to the home of another woman. Mike later confirmed the furniture was free of debt, and had been paid for in cash. As he ran out of excuses, John seemed to withdraw into himself. He'd look down, cross his arms across his chest, and push back into the couch. Far from just changing positions or contentedly sinking into the cushions, he looked like he wanted to disappear into them and come out the other side. I asked John if Sheila and the beach house had had any influence on this investigation. He looked me in the eye and said, "No. No, it has not." This is probably the only true eye contact I have ever had with John during a conversation.

Dedy and I divulged that we wanted to go to Milford to talk to Sheila. We asked what Sheila had said when he told her Fran was missing. We really were trying to get an idea of the type of personality we would face if we went there. John answered: "She said, 'My God, you mean this woman could show up on my doorstep?' I told her it was possible." He said the drive to Milford would take hours and that we had better plan on leaving as soon as possible. To tell you the truth, I think he was a little relieved that we were so focused on the house. Questions about Sheila and a possible visit to the house shifted the pressure ever so slightly off John, and he welcomed it. With a little bit of his showman's confidence back, he piled it on deeper still: He said he thought Fran had been back to the condo many times and that when he gave up the storage unit on October 29, the unit had been entered two times that he knew he had not been there. He gave an elaborate description of accessing the unit and preparing to lift a heavy box only to practically throw it over his head before he had time to react to the unexpected change in weight of an almost empty box.

It was hard to buy any of this, but there was a chance we could verify John's storage unit claim. If we could find out from the management when the unit had been accessed, and it corresponded to a weekend when John would have been in Connecticut, maybe we'd have something. Still, his stories didn't gibe with Sheila's, and we were inclined to believe her versions if for no other reason than she had less to cover for. That afternoon talk did bring about one important discovery: I might not be able to prevent John from telling lies, but I could back him into a corner and shut him down, something my husband, a formidable man who at six-foot-three could look down on John, hadn't been able to do. I could literally put him up against a wall and turn him into a frightened child. I hadn't realized before how fearful he could be of a strong-headed woman, and I didn't recognize it soon enough to take full advantage on this trip, but with that newfound knowledge, I was becoming more powerful all the time.

CHAPTER 9
Eternal Bachelor

iguring out John better was both a blessing and a curse, in the same way that improving as a bull rider is a blessing and a curse. We could better control an unpredictable beast, but knowing how he worked also meant getting inside his head, and that's a dark place. Many a night I'd lay awake, on edge, John's tortured thoughts my own. His advantage, as I've said before, is that he could out-crazy you with his erratic intellect. Was he making a tactical blunder in betraying his true feelings, or was it a red herring to distract you from the right path? Dedy and I opted to stay in New Jersey and investigate the storage unit lead, which might prove definitively whether Fran had resurfaced, rather than drive to Connecticut and cover ground Mike and his crew had already trod. I've since felt, but don't know for sure, that Mike thought we should have made the trip to the beach house.

John, Dedy, and I made our way to the Publix storage unit, a fifteen-minute drive from John's condo. As with most modern storage areas, every tenant is given an access code that allows them to use the facility at any time. Since this was Publix's system, and since the contract with John was closed, the manager there said it would be no problem to study the computer tapes and tell us of which dates and times the unit was visited. With John's consent, we asked that this information be sent directly to Mike Dansbury. Mike later verified that the unit had been accessed a few times since October 1, but only for a few minutes each time, and that no one at the storage facility remembered seeing a small blond lady on crutches or a walker. No one at Publix had seen a missing-persons flier, so we left one for them.

It was now 2:30 P.M., and we still wanted to drop by Joe and Nancy Mazotas's office. We had never met in person, and I really wanted to pay them for the phone call and thank them for befriending Fran. Joe Mazotas, a middle-aged professional-looking gentleman, introduced himself and led us back to his office and called in Nancy and a coworker, Pete. Fran had told me about him before. He was in his early thirties, with a baby face and a welcoming smile. He and Fran had gotten along well and enjoyed working together. They had become close coworkers because of Fran's computer skills and Pete's dry sense of humor. She said his personality reminded her of Todd's.

John had chosen to wait in the car because he said the Mazotases didn't like him, and we soon found he was correct in his assessment. Perhaps Joe, Nancy, and Pete were unhappy that John had not called them to report Fran's hip fracture and therefore put them in the position of denying her future work, or because they saw what Fran's home life did to her at the office. The three were aware through the police that Fran had not been found. Joe and Pete had been in law enforcement in earlier careers, and they both thought we should take a good look at John. They couldn't cite a specific reason, just a gut feeling. Joe reiterated his belief that Fran's occasional distractions at work were the result of troubles at home.

The three of them again went over what they remembered of the time in August when John took off, but they could think of nothing they hadn't told me before. Nancy felt that Fran talked to her more about personal things than she did Joe and Pete. But she said that Hollie had been closer to Fran than she was, that Hollie called all the time and that Nancy often took her messages for Fran. Everyone in the office had seen Fran and Hollie having lunch across the street at the pizza parlor many times, and Nancy recalled that Hollie had told Fran where to make reservations for her and John's Pocanos trip. We explained that Hollie had been less than cooperative with the police, which led Nancy to remember that on one occasion, she was sure Hollie had called, but when she tried to take a message, the caller said to have Fran call her Aunt Carol. We don't have an Aunt Carol. Nancy later told Fran that Hollie did not have to leave fake names and that receiving personal phone calls at work wasn't a problem. Good thing, too. For a few months after they moved into the condo, Fran and John didn't have a home phone, so I could reach her only at work.

The most puzzling comment we heard from the Mazolases wasn't about Hollie leaving messages with fake names. It was about John. As Nancy was empathizing with Fran's relationship difficulties, she acknowledged that Fran had been married before and also mentioned that this was John's second marriage. I corrected her. Nancy insisted that she was sure Fran had said this was his second marriage. Perhaps, she cautioned, she had misunderstood. We thanked them for their time and said our goodbyes. Joe and Nancy were upset that I would even try to pay them for their long-distance phone call. As we were leaving, they told us to try to talk to Hollie at her office, which was just across the street. That should be interesting, we thought. What little Hollie had told me so far had been entirely false. By the time Dedy and I returned to the car, John had been waiting for more than an hour.

John drove us across the street in Fran's Dodge Shadow. Obviously, using John's directions, we had been having trouble finding our way around in new surroundings, so we thought it best that John drive. We also wanted to keep an eye one him and observe his reactions to the people we were talking to and the places we wanted to visit. Since his primary car was the Miata, a two-seat roadster, that meant taking Fran's car, the one John said he had been driving the day Fran disappeared. Early on in the case he said he didn't know why he had taken her car that day; it was just there. At Mama's funeral, he told Dedy that he thought Fran had been trying to do too much and that if he drove the Shadow, Fran would be forced to stay at home and rest. A third possibility is that his first two answers were nonsense and John had actually taken her somewhere in his car but wanted us all to concentrate on the Shadow.

Dedy and I went into the office of Schnelling & Schnelling to speak with Hollie while John once again chose to wait in the car. It was as if by driving he hoped to avoid participating in our efforts to find Fran. One would think a concerned husband would not miss an opportunity to gather even the smallest bit of information about his missing, disabled wife. From the name you'd think Schnelling & Schnelling would be a class place, but the office was hardly decorated to impress clients or customers. Everything looked old and misused. As we introduced ourselves to Hollie, she ran, literally ran, to her boss's desk. Carol Izen was in the middle of a phone call. When Hollie told her who we were, Carol didn't even say "Goodbye." She just hung up the phone. Everyone in the office herded out of their cubicles and stood staring at us. From the moment we walked in, the vibe was that we were unwelcome and should leave. Hollie had been so friendly on the phone; we expected to be treated more cordially. No one asked us to sit down or invited us to her office. Hollie stated again that she and Fran had gotten together for one lunch, not several, and that what she and Fran had had was a professional relationship. Dedy and I assumed that she was holding back because of her boss's presence. What were these people holding back? Going back to the car, we were shaken. These two people were the only ones during our New Jersey trip who had treated us unkindly. We wanted to know why.

In two days we had accomplished more in Fran's case than John had in five months. Since we were in the neighborhood, we opted to stop by a bakery, a beauty salon, and the pizza parlor where Joe and Nancy Mazotas had seen Hollie and Fran have lunch. These would have been on the top of my list of places to ask about Fran's whereabouts, but John said he hadn't been to any of them. "Just malls and places like that," he said of his standard weekend rounds. The lady behind the counter at the bakery remembered Fran, because she had noticed her pinkie ring. It's a unique, cat's-eye-shaped ring set with many small diamonds. The woman's husband questioned her memory, but she felt that, because of the ring, she had seen Fran recently. Dedy became a little emotional that Fran might really be out there. Back at the car, John saw that Dedy was upset and put his arm around her. "We'll find her," he said. Then he took the opportunity to say how self-centered Fran could be—undoubtedly, I thought, the reason she hadn't bothered to contact us in five months, as she was too busy entering their storage unit and buying macadamia nut cookies from the bakery across from her old employer. I rolled my eyes and asked for strength, or at least patience to keep from wrapping my fingers around his neck.

Tuesday, 4:00 P.M.: There had to be more than we were getting from Hollie. I was determined to hear something resembling the truth from her after the blow-off we had gotten at Schnelling & Schnelling. Our plan was to follow her home. The problem was, we were in Fran's car and assumed she would recognize it too easily, common though they were. We returned to the condo to trade cars. We knew the Miata might also be identified, and at any rate it was too small for the three of us. So we returned to Hollie's office in my OSHA-yellow GEO Tracker. It's only slightly less visible than a taxi and much more conspicuous, but we were new to playing detective, and yes, we were spotted. Hollie pulled off to the side of the road. Traffic was so heavy we had no choice but to continue on, and by the time we found a place to turn around, she had vanished. We came off the trail and tried to think fast. I remembered that I had written to Hollie at her home address. I dug into my briefcase, found the letter, and within a few minutes we had located her address on a map. She lived in the same complex as Fran and John.

We arrived at Hollie's condo before she did. John took Fran's picture and approached several residents as they left their cars, asking them if they had seen Fran. They all replied that they had not. When Hollie arrived, she brushed past John. Hollie did not appear to recognize him. We had to assume the two were strangers. John signaled for Dedy, who got out of the car and hustled to the security doors to head her off: "Please, Hollie, talk to me. This is my Mom!" Hollie once again said it was an office matter and went inside. Dedy looked utterly forsaken by the world out there, bewildered and alone, and I felt a hot flash of indignation when Dedy related how Hollie had again denied any knowledge. I made John pull directly behind Hollie's car and block it to get the license number. Mike's investigation into the Pocanos trip had uncovered only one Drajin, a Mr. and Mrs. Jeffrey Drajin. I wanted to know whether her husband's name was Jeffrey, and if this was the same Drajin couple, I knew Mike could verify it using the license plate number. Hollie denied the idea that she had given Fran the name of a place to stay on their visit to the mountains. I was more inclined to believe Nancy Mazotas because so much of what Hollie told Mike and me turned out to be untrue. As we drove away, Hollie was standing in the second-story window of her condo, right above us, watching us. For the first time in my life, I gave someone the middle finger.

The arrangement of the parking lot, though, made it impossible to leave the area without going deeper into the complex and turning around. As we neared the back of Hollie's condo, we saw her and a man, who turned out to be her husband, standing in the road. He looked ready for a fight. John cracked the window and I did a lot of fast talking to keep her husband from opening the door and dragging John out of the car. I told him about Fran's disappearance, what the Mazotases had said, and also asserted that we felt Hollie was not comfortable talking in front of her boss. I told her husband that she had been uncooperative with the police and had slammed the door in Mike Dansbury's face. If looks could kill, Hollie would have dropped dead right there. It was obvious that her husband did not know any of this. I also explained that we had come to their home because Fran might have tried to contact Hollie and even if she was not at home, someone else in their building might have seen Fran. With this information, Hollie's husband became much more agreeable and sympathetic. He even offered to help John pass out fliers within the complex. He said to let them know if there was anything else they could do. "At the office only," Hollie quickly intoned.

We got back to the condo at about 7:30 P.M., after I had purchased groceries to prepare dinner. We were ready to drop. Dedy went straight to the bathroom for a bath while John and I prepared dinner—or rather I fixed dinner while John sat on the counter and talked. (This is a pet peeve of mine. I don't like anyone to put their butt where I am preparing food. Counters are for glasses, not asses.) With Dedy in the tub, he couldn't resist recounting some of his and Fran's more adventurous sexual exploits, and while I had developed a powerful appetite over the course of the day, I felt confident this would kill it. "That doesn't sound like Fran to me," I said. She had never fully recovered from the abuse of her first marriage. She did love romance, however, and would spend hours planning the perfect outfit, hairdo, and dinner when John was returning from a business trip. Nothing I knew about Fran indicated she was the lustful type. John's response to me cut: Obviously, you didn't know Fran very well.

Equally damning were his stories about being an inadequate husband that invariably culminated in his pleading ignorance, as a terminal bachelor, about the intricacies of a successful marriage. Before we talked to Nancy, those yarns sounded like John's usual whining and refusal to accept responsibility for the hardships in his life. Now it was like he was needling me. Dedy had the same thoughts, but we wouldn't be able to discuss it until the next morning when John left for the office.

After her bath, Dedy discreetly called the West Windsor Township Police Department as they had instructed us. Bob Gulden answered.

"Where have you been? We had you in the Shadow, then the next thing we knew, the Shadow was in front of the condo and Sherrie's car was gone. Don't ever do that again, and remember to call in frequently." Dedy called me to the sewing room and told me about the conversation. We giggled that John didn't have a clue about what was really happening, but we were also pleased that Mike and Bob were watching out for us. We had no idea they had been tailing us, which I suppose is the way it works when a professional does it. At supper, we asked John about the weekend in August that he had disappeared, making Fran frantic. He said he and Fran had had an argument about his lack of concern. Fran had taken off her wedding band and placed it on the coffee table and said, "I might as well be single." John left the next day for the Jersey Shore, where he slept in the car and thought about their marriage. When Fran reached him Monday at work, he knew he wanted to come home and patch things up. That night, Fran hit him with what he calls "the List": all the things that had to change before she would allow him to return home. He told us he agreed to all the terms she had listed. Later that week they made up, and he returned home. John told us that Fran had taken his AT&T phone card, or at least he thought she had, because it was missing. His Visa was also missing, but neither had been used since Fran had left. He wanted us to know what a good guy he was because he hadn't canceled the cards. Even if things hadn't happened exactly the way John explained them, it did seem their relationship was far from perfect in the months leading to her disappearance and that Fran had taken bold measures to turn it around. My heart cheered for her take-charge attitude, but my head told me that no amount of chutzpah could keep the beast at bay when it was finally cut loose.

Wednesday: 7:30 A.M.: John left a little later for work that morning. We spent some time with goodbyes. John kept telling us he wished we had come sooner, and about how lonely and depressed he had been. We sympathized outwardly, but inside we kicked ourselves for not making him take us to Connecticut. We could have parsed his and Sheila's stories simultaneously and maybe blown the whole case wide open. Instead we had allowed ourselves to be manipulated once again. Water under the bridge, I guess.

Our last stop before Indianapolis was the West Windsor police station. We had a lot to report to Mike and wanted to make sure we had time for a good talk before the long trip home. At the station Mike came out to meet us and took us into his office. It was comforting to have some expert guidance and advice on all the troubling things we had learned: John's revelation that the "feed the fish" note was a fabrication and that Fran had instead written of suicide; the discovery of so many of Fran's possessions, even the suitcases, still in the condo, while John appeared to have moved out; the notion that Fran had known about Sheila in Connecticut and approved the move of her home furniture to the house in Milford; and Hollie's maddening refusal to share anything she might know to help out a supposed friend in dire need. In discussing the case at length with Mike, it occurred to us that John had not talked to a single person we had interviewed in our three days there, nor had he spoken with anyone when he accompanied us on our excursions. He had talked to the police, but only when they initiated the call. Then there were the fliers we found in the closet, which ended our belief in his "walk-and-talk" stories.

We started to tell Mike about our encounters with Hollie and Carol, but he knew all about them. They had filed a formal complaint against us (just short of a restraining order) that morning, and Mike instructed us to stay away from them, their office, and Hollie's apartment. This was a complete overreaction, we thought, and anyway we had gleaned what little information we were likely to get from Hollie and Carol. We found it comical—but believe me, Mike Dansbury was not smiling.

I told Mike that women in our family are more prone to ask for forgiveness than permission, but I did apologize—not for what we had done but for any problem we might have caused Mike. We moved on, bringing up Nancy Mazotas's comment about this being John's second marriage. Mike looked at me as if I were crazy and said, "Yes, I thought you knew." John had married on June 30, 1970, at age nineteen in Detroit, and it had ended in a no-fault divorce four years later. John said he had last seen his first wife heading to a commune in Florida. I found that strange because growing up there, I had never heard of communes in the state. Back then, it was still the Bible-Belt South. Her name was Janice E. Hartman, and she had two brothers: Ross, who was in the military, and Gary, whose occupation was unknown. Everything seemed to check out, and Mike said that no one from the department had spoken to her or her family. This just didn't feel right to me. I knew there had to be a reason other than the pleas for sympathy why John would consistently present himself to us as previously unmarried. In four years of marriage, Janice must have suffered a few of the same indignities at John's hand that Fran had. In just the few minutes that Mike had described her, I began to think of Janice as family. "I will find this woman," I told Mike. "I have to find these people, and I have to know that she is okay."

PART TWO

A Second Investigation

CHAPTER 10
No Secrets

Mike would say many times that our trip to New Jersey was the turning point in the case. Everyone, from Mike to Hollie, now understood how serious we were about finding Fran and that we wouldn't rest until we learned what had happened. The most crucial piece of the puzzle was something "we" already knew—that John had been married before. Fran seemed to have known this, so John's stories to the contrary felt bold: He was gambling on the odds that Fran had never told us about his first marriage. Surprisingly, she hadn't, and I don't know why. John's behavior, however, made sense. After Fran disappeared, I have to believe he knew we would spare no cost or effort to locate a first wife if we were aware that he had been married before. He was right. With the police, it wasn't that simple. They would have his records and already know his marital history. If he didn't come clean right up front, detectives would have a strong incentive to find out why. John had to hope that we would never bother to share information, and we resolved never to let him take advantage of that oversight again.

We formed what we now call "the team." Mike adopted the phrase "no secrets" as our motto. He explained that there would be elements of the case he couldn't share with us, but that he wouldn't keep us in the dark unnecessarily, simply out of desire to maintain the police/citizen divide. We became used to hearing, "I can't talk about that right now, but someday, you will know all." And Mike has always been true to his word. He is one of the most honorable men I have ever had the privilege of knowing. We told him if that occurred to just tell us, and we would back off. If he told us he was handling something, we would know this was an area we didn't have to cover, and that to get in the middle of it could harm the investigation.

Returning to our respective homes, Dedy and I could finally let our guard down, emotionally and physically. My first night home, February 26, was one of the few times I can say I got some fitful sleep for many years after Fran disappeared. Despite being rested, we continued to be hard on ourselves for letting John steer our agenda on the trip. It took us awhile to realize that by not going to Connecticut we found out so much that would have gone undiscovered, one victory being the rental space we visited with John on Tuesday. It was a no-brainer: Once Mike saw the size of the unit John had rented, he knew there was no way it could have held a household's belongings. It was far too small. Like so many aspects of John's life, the storage unit seemed to be strictly for appearance' sake.

Our progress in New Jersey notwithstanding, we had a long way to go to conclusively prove any wrongdoing on John's part. We had much that went to cause, such as John's shifting stories and total disinterest in Fran's disappearance, but a defense attorney would have laughed the case out of court. We had no victim, no murder weapon, no crime scene, no witnesses, and only a speculative motive. The failed polygraph would get us nowhere. Most important for us at the moment, we had nothing to further interest the media. No television producers were anxious to publicize an undefined case or shove cameras in the face of a man who wasn't even close to being charged with a crime.

Despair was an attractive option. Five months of frantic work and nothing tangible to show for it. Instead, the cost accountant in me took over. I decided if I couldn't balance out the figures in Column A, I'd move on to Column B. Janice Hartman became an obsession for me. I spent every spare minute on the phone with directory assistance. Since John and Janice had married in Detroit, I started there. I wanted every R. Hartman, Ross Hartman, G. Hartman, and Gary Hartman in the 313 area code. I dialed directory assistance so many times that I kept getting the same gentleman. (They could give me only two numbers in any one call.) Finally the man said, "Excuse me, lady. What are you trying to accomplish?" He kindly put me on hold and got a list from that area code for me. Gary Hartman might not sound like a common name, but you'd be surprised by how many there really are. It was a long list, so Dedy and I split the list and began calling numbers. No dice. We had long since given up trying to locate Janice directly given the likelihood of a woman's name changing with marriage. We also knew locating Ross was possible through military records, but with no military serial number or Social Security number, it would be difficult. In the Internet age, the entire process would have been so easy. We could have jumped on one of the people-search databases, searched with specifications for the approximate age and town of residence, and within a day or two had a handful of likely candidates along with their marital status, credit history, and any criminal record. If only.

No, we were still in the phone age, and Dave was painfully aware of that every month when the phone bill arrived. My calls on the case frequently pushed it above five hundred dollars. That March it was only three hundred, the first time in months it had been that low. Dave mischievously suggested we go out to dinner—we had two hundred dollars to spend. It was around that same time that we were on our way out to dinner when Dave said, "Babe, you know, given their ages, so young, they could have been high school sweethearts." I agreed and tried going back to the 216 area code, the Cleveland area code that at the time also included Medina County, north of Wooster, to see if I could dig up a Gary or Ross Hartman. This time I was smarter. I told the operator straight out what I needed and got a supervisor, who was an angel. Once again, thank you God, Ma Bell, and all of your employees! I started dialing and left a lot of messages saying something like, "My name is Sherrie Gladden-Davis, and my phone number is (317) 555-6942. Please call me collect at your earliest convenience." The phone didn't ring all day. I was low the next day when I spoke with Mike about my progress. "Sherrie, just what are you saying on these machines?" he asked. When I related my standard message, he said, "You sound like an aluminum siding salesperson. You've gotta give them more. Peak their interest." I started over that day leaving a new message: "I am Sherrie Gladden-Davis. I am looking for anyone related to or having knowledge of Janice E. Hartman-Smith." I encouraged people to call me collect, and that evening, at about 7:30 P.M., my phone finally rang. It was Gary Hartman, Janice's brother. I told him I very much needed to talk to Janice.

"That's not possible," Gary said. "Please explain what this is all about."

I told him that my sister and his sister had one thing in common—they had both been married to John David Smith III—and that my sister had been missing since October 1, 1991, while married to John.

Gary says now that the hair on the back of his neck stood up. "My God, lady. You have a problem. My sister has been missing since November 1974. She disappeared, never to be seen again."

"Oh my God." I repeated the phrase over and over to talk myself through the shock. I remember that when I recovered, I said, "I guess our sisters had two things in common." Gary went on to say that John and Janice had separated and that their divorce had been final for about a week when she disappeared. Gary and Janice had talked about a week before Thanksgiving to make holiday plans with the family. When Thanksgiving came and went with no word from Janice, they knew something terrible must have happened.

I couldn't believe what I was hearing. I told him I needed to contact the police in New Jersey and asked him to stay by the phone. The West

Windsor police would be in touch with him within thirty minutes. Gary agreed to wait. "By the way," he said before we hung up, "the "E." stands for Elaine."

Gary and I agreed to talk the next night. With a lump in my throat and my heart pounding, I fought the tears and dialed the West Windsor Township Police Department. Mike had left for the day, but I talked to Bob Gulden and, later, to Mike when he called after hearing the news. "Mike, did I find enough?" I asked.

"Sherrie, we still have a lot of work to do, but yes, you found enough. Now we have to contact the authorities in Ohio and see if we can get enough to build a case." With two wives unaccounted for, we were approaching something like hard evidence. Fran's investigation was being moved from a missing adult to a possible homicide investigation.

Dedy and I now found we were working with two police agencies. We were grateful for the development and at the same time overwhelmed by the new demands and possibilities. If Janice had been the victim of foul play, it had happened seventeen years before. The cops working at the Wayne County Sheriff's Department in Wooster, Ohio, which had jurisdiction in the investigation, had either retired or were in leadership positions on the force. Our contact in Wooster, Sergeant Brian Potts, mitigated any additional stresses we shouldered with the new case. Brian, like Mike, is a cop's cop, a highly professional, thoughtful, and considerate law enforcement officer. Dedy and I soon had great respect for him. Unlike Mike's case, however, Brian's came with baggage. He was embarrassed by the department's lack of follow-up in Janice's case. There might have been a better paper trail of the investigation, but after so many years it is hard to know exactly what took place almost two decades ago. In 1974, it wasn't unusual for young people to just decide to take off. This was the end of the era of free love and self-expression. Further complicating matters, the officers working Janice's case originally were now Brian's superiors. No one wanted to come out looking foolish, and Brian had to watch where he stepped.

Whatever went awry in those early years, the sheriffs in Wooster County made up for it now. Brian and Dedy found they had much in common on a personal level. Both were divorced and the custodial parents of children. They could relate to one another in matters of family and children and quickly became phone friends. Mike's and Brian's trust in us made coping with the situation and aiding in the investigation so much easier. They came to know that there was nothing they could tell us that we hadn't imagined as worse. I've often told people that while I knew these men were not saints, I was sure they could walk on water and not cause ripples.

Finding out about Janice provided the insight into the young John that we had never gotten out of yearbooks or in talking to old neighbors. Garry (as I soon found his name was spelled) said the family had never been happy with Janice's choice of husbands, and John's family didn't appear any more pleased than the Hartmans were. It's been said that when John's mother, Grace Malz, learned about the marriage after they returned from Detroit, she threw all of his clothes outside and set them afire. John, for his part, was nasty-mouthed and opinionated. The "F" word was every other word out of his mouth. He was the bad boy, the biker with the leather jacket. Janice herself was a little wild, and her family thinks she got a thrill from dating John.

They had met at a school dance, although they weren't classmates and didn't start dating until sometime later. Janice was an attractive girl with blond hair, sprightly eyes, and apple cheeks. She had a wide, beautiful smile. As in his and Fran's marriage, John controlled all the money in the household, and Garry recalls him as being both verbally and physically abusive to Janice. One visit in particular stands out: He and a friend had gone to Columbus, where the couple lived, to visit Janice and maybe go out to eat. He suggested many places, but Janice vetoed every one. Finally she admitted she had no money. Just as Garry was ready to tell her not to worry and that dinner would be his treat, John came home. He was furious that visitors had come unannounced and made such a scene that Garry and his friend decided to leave and not make things harder for Janice.

After John and Janice married, the isolation got worse. John attended classes at Ohio State, and Janice found work as a night manager for an all-night gas station. Garry and the rest of his family visited infrequently because of John's temperament. The only member of Janice's family who John welcomed was her little sister Dee, who was eleven or so at the time. Dee spent weekends with the couple on occasion. In an interview with Brian Potts, she told of one weekend she stayed with Janice and John. The couple was on the bed watching television, and John tried to get Dee to come over to the bed and touch his privates. Janice got up and yelled at John to leave her alone and told him that he had better never do anything like that again. That settled it, according to Dee, and nothing ever happened afterward.

John dropped out of Ohio State after two years and got a job working with computers. I was *shocked* to learn that he did not have a degree in aeronautical engineering and only passed himself off as an engineer. He had not even studied aeronautics at Ohio State, but rather industrial engineering. Old resumes state that he planned to complete his degree in engineering at a university in Connecticut. John's saving grace, if you can call it that, was that he was a quick study. His step-father, Sam Malz, was an engineer by training, and John had picked up enough principles and terminology from reading Sam's books to play the part. From examining old resumes and doing some legwork at former employers, we found a friend who he had followed from job to job. The man had found John working as a database specialist for an outside firm early in his career, and vouched for his skills and credentials from that point on. John did complete a course in computer science through LaSalle.

This professional front was absolutely essential to how he would operate in the coming decades. Working as an engineer brought him instant credibility, and more or less all of his relationships, romantic or otherwise, were based on his ability to provide. Dangerous psychopaths, the conventional wisdom goes, just don't pull down six figures and drive expensive sports cars. But by 1974, Janice had seen more than enough to know what John really was. She told a friend who had witnessed John slapping her that she was tired of being knocked around. The Hartman family called her four years of marriage to him "hell on earth."

The divorce settlement was simple: Janice would keep her Mustang, and John would keep his GMC van. Janice loved her Mustang, her first new car, and she refused to let even family drive it. The rest of her life, even with distance from John, was less rosy. She stayed mostly with her father but sometimes with friends, and worked as a go-go dancer at a place called the Sun Valley Inn. I need to emphasize that she was not a stripper. Although the dancing was physical and perhaps erotic, she was not removing clothing for tips. There was never any physical contact with customers. Her family wanted her to find more conventional work, but she enjoyed it. She had told family members she worked at the bar as a narc helping agents put drug dealers away, conceivably to make her job look more respectable to those who disapproved. We have found no evidence that would prove Janice was an informant for any police department or drug-enforcement agency. To be sure, rumors of drug involvement did surround the couple. In police interviews many people talked of John staying wired on uppers, and Janice might have smoked pot from time to time.

Seven days before the missing-persons report was filed on Janice, she got off work at the Sun Valley Inn and went to a party with her friend Leonard Bennett. In keeping with the times and their crowd, the party was fairly wild, and she wouldn't have known many of the people there. A couple in the bedroom was having sex. Bennett said when the couple came out, one man there asked Janice to dance for them. She still had her work costume on under her street clothes, so she took those off and offered up a quick dance. The man asked for another dance, and when she refused, he became angry, grabbed her, and forced her into the bedroom. She couldn't get away; four others joined in. The man who had asked for the dance was verbally abusing her and calling her a tease. There were no other women around. He ordered Leonard Bennett to have intercourse with her. Bennett got on top of Janice but couldn't perform for them.

At some point Janice got her hands free, so the man who had dragged her to the bedroom trained a shotgun at her. Janice saw a knife on the nightstand, and when he leaned the shotgun against the wall in the corner, she grabbed the knife and slashed the waterbed many times. She ran out and filed a police report that night, citing assault and attempted rape. Some of this account comes from her report, and some comes from principals the police interviewed. One anonymous individual police interviewed was asked why he had gone to the party that night. He responded that the host was the only one who knew where the drop was. Again, we hear innuendoes of drug involvement.

Police who investigated the incident at the time didn't connect it to Janice's disappearance, but it doesn't appear they connected much of anything. Sloppy police work could be to blame, but left unsaid is that Janice's work and personal life at the time, and her family's round disapproval of her lifestyle, may have led police to investigate her case less vigorously than they otherwise would have.

Even after years of work on Janice's case, we're still unable to piece together a cohesive account of what happened the night of her disappearance. We understand that on the night of November 16, 1974, Janice and John met to celebrate their divorce over a few drinks with a friend of Janice's, Kathy Paridon. Kathy told police that John had dropped by the bar to talk to Janice. We aren't sure which is correct, but the fact remains they were together that night, and they did have an argument. John slapped Janice. Janice and Kathy left together, and Janice took Kathy home. In some statements and conversations, Kathy says that John was with them when they left. In others, she says there was another man with her and Janice, but she has never supplied his name. No one has seen Janice since the early morning of November 17, just three days after her divorce from John was final.

Janice was scheduled to appear in court the next morning, the 18th, to file formal charges in the assault case. When she didn't show, there was no follow-up on her. The assault and attempted rape investigation were dropped. Her family wasn't especially alarmed since she frequently stayed with friends and other family. But when she didn't come for their Thanksgiving get-together, they grew concerned and contacted John. As in our case, John said he did not know anything and was of no help. He did file a missing-persons report on November 19 in which he identified himself as Janice's husband, not her ex-husband. For some reason, he filed the missing-persons report from Kathy Paridon's home and listed the contact person as Kathy's mother, not John or Janice's family. It's only a guess, but most people feel John was trying to distance his report from any member of Janice's family in case the police investigated the matter. If one were to lay the reports of Janice and Fran side by side, their similarities would be striking. All of Janice's personal things were there, but no Janice. While Fran was supposed to have taken a yellow suitcase, John reported that Janice had left with a red suitcase. Her prized Mustang was parked *at John's mobile home.* At first John said he did not know how it got there. Later he changed his story, saying it had been towed there by the Ohio Highway Patrol. This did not check out; the Highway Patrol never towed the car to his home. Janice, like Fran, had an important meeting that she never reached. And most important, they were hard-pressed to prove foul play without a body as evidence.

At the time of Janice's disappearance, the Hartmans were going through a difficult time and lots of domestic changes. Janice's parents had been divorced, Garry and Isabel had recently married, parents were being re-married, and John and Janice had divorced. Family communication was strained. The burden of the investigation fell to Janice's mother, Betty Lippencott, and to the police. Right after the Christmas holidays of

1974, I believe, Janice's mother hired a private detective. He billed the family for about two thousand dollars but turned up nothing except a belief that John was involved. Some detective. Even back then, that shouldn't have been a surprise. Several people had heard John say that if he couldn't have Janice, no one would.

The discovery of Janice and her disappearance changed my entire outlook on the case. For the first time since we lost Fran, I felt like we had been blessed with divine intervention. We needed Janice to help prove Fran's case, and without Fran, no one would have looked twice at Janice. In my mind, this was no coincidence. I felt God was giving us a chance to help both these women. Some with a firm traditional faith, as our family has, are reluctant to acknowledge the spirit world and see it as a distraction, a sort of New Age hocus pocus. I never viewed it that way. To me, they are all part of the same world. If you believe in heaven and hell and that people's souls live on after they have left our realm—and I do—you have to acknowledge that it's possible to communicate with those souls just as we can communicate with God. Strangely, I never felt "the thing" with Fran after she passed, and I haven't been able to connect with her in any meaningful way since. But I still held out hope that someone else, someone with a spiritual sensitivity that exceeded my own, might be able to. And by that point, I was ready to try anything.

Mike was receptive in March 1992 when I told him I wanted a psychic opinion. He located and contacted a lady I will call "Dorothy." She had worked with many police agencies before, and with some success. With only superficial information about the case, Dorothy said we were looking for Silver Lake, or Silver Creek, an old white house that might now be a restaurant, water, caves, and a tunnel. These are all vague clues, but the connection to the spiritual realm is fuzzy, and psychics often see things in flashes, almost in a blur, and without context. It's up to the police or investigators to make sense of the clues. Mike found an area that might match Dorothy's clues, secured a helicopter with infrared capabilities, and lined up air-scent body-recovery dogs in case they found anything promising. The searched areas were within a twenty-mile radius of the condo and Carborundum. Regrettably, the search didn't turn up anything, and Mike took a lot of harassment and good-natured kidding from his department. They called him "Psychic Mike."

Dedy and I busied ourselves that month working with Brian on Janice's case, and we remained confident that something else would turn up. Plus, Brian and Mike spent endless hours briefing each other on their respective cases and coordinating efforts. We all kept the phone lines humming. Dedy and I found working together with Brian easy and pleasurable, and he quickly became an indispensable member of "the team." Not just anyone tied to the investigation earned that status. After Mike sent Dorothy a map of the West Windsor area at her request, we never heard from her again. We're uncertain whether she didn't want to continue on the case or whether she thought she had given us all she knew. I was disappointed and angry, therefore, when I turned on a television show some years later and saw that she was using one of Fran's missing-persons fliers to make it appear as if she had been instrumental in solving the case. The most upsetting thing about this was that her interview made it appear as though Fran's case had been solved, so anyone with information on the case would think they didn't need to come forward. Not everyone, I've learned, has scruples or that team spirit—not even psychics.

CHAPTER 11
The Hartmans

The grief we shared with the Hartmans, seventeen years apart, gave us an immediate connection. Both of our families had lost so much because our sisters had chosen to marry the wrong man. I spent many hours on the phone with Garry and his wife, Isabel. We held long conversations familiarizing the other family with our sisters. We wanted each other to realize that these weren't grainy images from an irrelevant past but real women with likes, dislikes, ambitions, families, friends— and flaws. Acknowledging imperfections is a real but complicated part of the grieving process. These women weren't saints because they had died. But neither did their flaws in any way justify the cruel misfortune they suffered. Loving the whole person is important to preserving their memories and allowing them to live on. I believe that retaining and treasuring those memories brings us closer to those who have left us. It's all we have, although it's not all they were.

The year after her disappearance, Janice's family erected a marker for her at their family burial plot in Millersburg, thirty-five miles south of Seville. "I just wanted something that said she had passed through this world," Janice's mother, Betty Lippencott, said. I tried to grasp what it must be like to have your daughter go missing for nearly twenty years with no resolution. For too many years, that marker at the family plot was their only source of peace with Janice.

Ever the loyal soldier, Dedy remained in contact with John to gather information and neutralize his threat. Finding Janice changed our outlook in so many ways, among them the realization that John wasn't just loathsome to us but an ongoing danger to all the women around him. And the greater the risk he seemed to present, the more I reveled in dominating him. No mistake: Our dynamic had changed since New Jersey, and we both knew I had the upper hand. I sensed his fear. He could never be sure what I was thinking or what I might do. So Dedy was his main point of contact, but he did call me on April 2 to wish me happy birthday. Really it was his birthday; mine would be in two days. He said he was going to Illinois on business and would be out of town for a few days, and that he didn't want to leave without telling us where he would be. Now it was second nature for me to analyze John's statements, find the holes, and then either call him out or tuck the discrepancy away in my mind— and case notes—for future reference. In this case the red flags were that he wasn't leaving any hotel information or phone number for his Illinois trip, even though he had called to keep in touch, and that today was Thursday. That meant his business trip would begin on Friday. John always seemed to be going out of town on business on Fridays.

I called Isabel to see if she or Garry could drive by John's grandparents' or mother's house and see if he was there, and not in Illinois. The Hartmans had just purchased a jewelry store in Wadsworth, five miles east of Seville, and that coming weekend would be their grand opening, so Dave and I decided we would go there ourselves on Saturday to check things out. That day, I turned forty-five, and Dedy has said she wished I could have spent it celebrating and relaxing, but we tended not to think about personal pursuits while working on the investigation. The key to my sanity was compartmentalization: Keep the case in one box, work in another, motherhood in a third, marriage in a fourth. Personal time was unthinkable for long stretches (and usually resulted in my thinking about the case). Dedy and I had a rule: For us the case came first, but we wouldn't sacrifice family members' special occasions to pursue this investigation. We helped each other out on that front by picking up the ball and running with it on days when the other couldn't do it.

So it was that we headed to Seville on my birthday to keep tabs on John. We had wanted to see the area again anyway, now that we had an entirely different perspective on the youthful "John Boy" we had known before Garry's account. After driving by John's grandparents' home in Seville, in his mother's neighborhood in Hudson, and around town for many hours without seeing either of John's cars, we decided to try to locate Garry and Isabel's store to meet them in person.

We found the store, Stonier's Jewelry, and parked the car. Stonier's was located on what appeared to be the main drag in Wadsworth, in a well-established business district. I knew that Garry and Isabel had purchased a long-existing business and wasn't surprised to see that they were redoing the display cases and putting their own face on the store. I approached an attractive, small-framed lady and asked for Isabel. She was very businesslike and said, "I am Isabel. How may I help you?" When I introduced myself, Isabel came from behind the display case and quietly embraced me as I introduced Dave. She was very excited that we were finally meeting after so many phone calls. She said that she and Garry talked so often about how it was a comfort, after all these years, to finally have someone who completely understood what they had been going through—the worry and frustration of not knowing. Garry express-es it this way: "It's like there is a hole in your heart that never heals." Isabel explained that Garry was with their daughters but would be back soon. She then invited us to their home to wait for Garry and rushed around making arrangements with an employee so she could leave. We followed her home. Garry was still out.

Isabel led us to their living room and shared family pictures. At last I could put a face to Janice. Isabel was right about her beauty. She had sparkling eyes, a cute, rounded nose, and a strong, oval jaw. I showed Isabel pictures of Fran, and we both agreed that John had excellent taste in women. It was coming up on four o'clock by that time, and Dave and I started glancing at our watches. We had a five-hour trip home. Isabel really wanted us to wait until Garry got home so we could all meet. She suggested a tour around town to kill time until Garry and the girls returned. We agreed and climbed into her van.

As we cruised down the streets of Wadsworth and Doylestown, Isabel pointed out the house where Janice, Garry, Ross, and Dee had been raised. She showed us where their father had lived when Janice disappeared, and we drove past the Sun Valley Inn, the bar where Janice had danced. It was a worse-for-the-wear local bar in need of exterior repair. But all and all, it looked very much like most of the watering holes you find in small towns. Isabel explained that it had been much nicer when Janice had worked there. We continued our little tour of the area. About ten minutes after seeing the Sun Valley Inn, we came upon an area that especially captured my interest. Isabel was now driving down a country road through a park-like area. To the right the land was swampy and over-grown, but to the left appeared a beautiful man-made lake. Isabel said biking and hiking trails criss-crossed much of the land. Garry and their daughters came here frequently. She pointed to an overgrown area at the back of the lake and said, "Garry and I have always thought John might have put Janice here, maybe because they've found other bodies dumped in this area."

I asked Isabel the name of the lake.

"Silver Lake or Silver Creek," she said. Silver Lake apparently had been created to help control flooding along Silver Creek.

My heart went into my throat. Isabel said she looked into the rearview mirror and that Dave was white as a sheet. I composed myself enough to relate the psychic reading that Dorothy had given Mike, and we looped down toward the lake and drove back to the Hartmans'.

When we got back, Garry and their three daughters had arrived. The little girls were very pretty and strongly resembled Isabel. Garry looked just as I had pictured him during our phone chats: light-brown hair flecked with gray, glasses, and an ever so slightly awkward demeanor. His face carried the weight of many unanswered questions over long years. We met, talked, and compared notes for about an hour. Because it was early spring, we had the advantage of longer days, so Dave then suggested we return to Silver Lake and take pictures to send to Mike. Isabel volunteered to drive me back out there. I took many pictures and lamented that I wasn't dressed to walk the entire area that evening. It was after midnight when Dave and I pulled into our driveway. We had talked all the way home about being able to meet and talk to Garry and Isabel. We also decided to return as soon as possible to walk Silver Lake. Mike has often said I'm not satisfied until I've wrapped my eyes around a place and have a gut feeling for it.

Monday morning, Mike was amazed to hear about our Silver Lake experience, and nearly as pleased that I had photographs to send him. We weren't professionals, but we were getting the hang of the investigative techniques he was always trying to teach us. And now that his contact with Dorothy had yielded something other than dead ends, he could hold his head a little higher at the station when someone called him "Psychic Mike."

CHAPTER 12
The Siege

Our knowledge of Janice's missing-persons report resulted in Mike's obtaining a search warrant from the Mercer County Prosecutor's office for the condo, John's office, both cars, the storage units, and the beach house. He called John and asked him to meet with the authorities at 6:30 A.M., before work, on April 9 to go over the case. That was true. What John didn't know is that they'd read him his rights and question him at the station for fourteen hours until the searches had been completed. This was definitely going to interfere with his work schedule.

All the places to be searched were hit at the same time. The condo search proved fruitful. They found several of Fran's personal belongings in the trash. The police immediately noticed that much of Fran's clothing had disappeared since Dedy and I had visited and taken pictures of the closets. They felt John was systematically ridding the condo of Fran's things.

The office yielded mostly financial records, checking account records, and credit card transactions. Officers held and documented these items for further investigation. They found and documented the portfolio pictures of the camera-shy Fran and also noted the receptionist's comment about John asking what she thought of his wife and daughter. To other people at work, he said that Fran had been found living in Texas working as a dancer and that we had come to get her things. I've often wondered whether he was confusing his wives.

The cars turned up very little. The police vacuumed both the carpets and then took the carpets from both trunks into evidence. They found blood on the Miata's trunk carpet, but no more than someone might leave if he had cut himself. The new, much smaller storage unit (5 x 9 x 7) that John rented on August 15, 1991, had been closed out and was now empty, but police hoped to determine whether any remains might have been stored there. They applied luminal, which reveals blood under fluorescent light, and got a negative result in the interior.

Throughout these searches, Buffy, an air-scent, body-recovery dog, had been used, again with negative results. These are remarkable, highly trained canine officers that are used in rescue missions and in the recovery of bodies. People picture bloodhounds and German shepherds when they think of police dogs, but body-recovery dogs are trained to smell only for decomposing flesh and can be of most any breed. They don't distinguish between individual human scents. After scent detection, the most important consideration is temperament. These dogs can work a search for hours on end and have to be highly motivated to continue their efforts to the exclusion of all else. Training starts early using surplus tissue samples from morgues and research facilities. For the dogs, it's a game: Find the object, bring it back, and get a reward. Later they progress to barking and bowing, known as "sound and down," over a found scent rather than retrieval of actual tissue. If a search ends unsuccesfully, handlers throw out a small encased sample that has the target scent to reward the dog's efforts, so there's never a reason for it to lie.

They can also locate bodies that have been submerged in water because of the gases the body begins emitting during decomposition that are lighter than water and rise to the surface. While this is not a pleasant thought, and though it must be emotional for the human officers that work with these wonderful animals, these animals are very valuable officers for any case in which foul play is suspected. (One of the best cadaver dogs of all time, a Doberman/German short-hair mix named Eagle, died only recently. He was so accurate his testimony was allowed in courts of law. Handlers once did an unscientific experiment with him in a nursing home where he sounded and went down in front of certain patients in which he detected the early shutdown of vital organs. Out of sixty patients, he sounded and went down in nine. All but two of them were dead within two weeks.)

In Connecticut, John and Sheila's beach house neighbors told authorities that John and Sheila were good neighbors and were presumed a married couple. They were quiet, spent a lot of time working in the yard on weekends, and walked a lot along the beach property.

John appeared unmoved during his stint at the police station. For the first nine hours, he sat somberly in a hard wooden chair with his overcoat on. It was like a silent protest, or a refusal to concede that this was anything out of the ordinary. Finally someone told him this could take awhile, and didn't he want to at least remove his coat? He continued to sit. As before, John averted his eyes when officers put pictures of Fran and Janice in front of him. Dedy and I spent the day at our jobs, praying for a phone call that would end our search for Fran. I resisted calling the department at all that day, knowing how tense and hectic things would be for Mike running the whole operation (and that he'd call when he had the chance). A communication officer, a liaison for all the investigative teams, did call once to ask about Fran's pinkie ring. They had found some of Sheila's jewelry in Milford and wanted to find out whether some of it might have belonged to Fran. Fran always wore the pinkie ring, and we were unable to locate it. For the rest of the search, Dedy and I stewed in our juices, traded a few phone calls, and speculated about what they might find.

Mike and two officers from the Connecticut State Police interviewed Sheila at the beach house and built on the background she had given Mike in his January visit. Sheila repeated that John had been in Milford almost every weekend since the beginning of the previous October and added a key detail: Her mother's birthday was the weekend of October 7, the weekend after Fran disappeared, and they threw a party in her honor at the beach house. Sheila recalled that John was supposed to come out the previous weekend and rent a carpet shampooer to get the house ready for the party, but he had arrived around 4 P.M. on Sunday, too late to get it done. She rented the shampooer and took care of the carpets herself. John spent most of the party weekend upstairs pacing the floor. The family could hear his footsteps above them for hours at a time. He appeared downstairs to socialize, but only briefly. Sheila also volunteered the information that her family did not like John.

She knew that he was divorced, but not because he had told her. She had been helping him prepare a resume using an old version that listed his true marital status. She asked him about it. John just told her that it was a mistake make by a secretary. "Secretaries don't make those kinds of mistakes," she replied. John confessed that he and Janice had divorced. She did not, however, have any idea that his first wife was also missing.

The weekend of August 10, 1991, she took a short vacation with her family and returned home to find furniture and many boxes inside. When she asked John about all the stuff, he explained the new storage unit he was renting in New Jersey was too small to accommodate all the furniture and other things. Sheila did not yet know about Fran and didn't think too much about the arrival of the furniture. John had his quirks. Because the furniture was better than what she had, she used it instead. I don't buy for a second that Fran knew her furniture was being moved, and we knew from Fran and Mike that it wasn't being repossessed. One could argue that John was moving the furniture out to Milford in anticipation of their leaving the condo and transitioning Sheila into other housing. If so, John never communicated that intention to Fran or Sheila, and neither knew about the other. The furniture factor taken together with John's continuing affections toward Sheila and his neglect of Fran suggests to me that he was consciously planning to push Fran out of his life, one way or the other.

The only weekend John hadn't come out to Milford since the first week of October was in late February, which would correspond to the trip Dedy and I made to New Jersey. John told Sheila that Fran had been located in Texas and did not want to see him ever again. He told her Dedy and I were coming to get Fran's things. But this does not ring true. What did she think Dedy and I were coming to New Jersey to pick up? A woman's mentality would make her open the boxes as soon as John left for New Jersey, and she would see what all of Fran's belongings were already there. I assume John told her this story to cover for not being able to visit her that particular weekend.

The new storage unit could have been the catalyst for John and Fran's final showdown. We already knew the unit was much too small to store even a roomful of furniture and felt sure John had rented it to pacify Fran as to the whereabouts of her things when she confronted him. Management records showed that the first access to the unit was on September 25, three days before we think she was killed. Most people involved with the investigation, especially Mike, Dedy and I, feel that this entry might have been Fran. We do know that it had to have been either Fran or John, because no one else had the access code to enter the unit. If it was Fran, she would have known on sight that this was a ruse, but she didn't say anything to me about it in the few days afterward.

Sheila also told of an annual visit she and John made to Ohio at Christmas to visit John's grandparents, mother, stepfather, and other family members. In 1990, they had taken a vacation to Disney World with her family between Christmas and New Year's. That was Fran and John's first Christmas together. I remembered that on that Christmas Day, she was a little blue when I called her. She said that John would have to leave that week on business but that at least he was home for Christmas Day. I knew Fran had made lavish plans for the perfect holiday. She had such high hopes for their life together. Whenever John came home from a business trip, Fran always was dressed to the nines and had a special dinner waiting for him. She usually had a little gift sitting next to his plate at the dinner table, or on his pillow at bed time. She loved making little surprises for the people she cared about. She would even make little gifts to celebrate their couple's monthly anniversaries.

Mike sounded exhausted the next morning. He said when they released John that he had walked out of the station like nothing happened. Nevertheless, he hired an attorney immediately after that, and it became impossible for the police to call him about the case. The attorney put it this way: "If you are not ready to charge my client with a crime, leave him alone." The gauntlet had been thrown down. It was go time. The authorities' powers were more limited now that John had legal counsel, but the only thing they could do to little old me was sue. And we were putting a good bit of our money, at least $1,500 a month, into the case. Let them sue. I prayed for them to sue. I knew it would be apparent to any judge that they were dealing with a person who didn't know the meaning of truth. John would come off as a laughing stock. I took a deep satisfaction in having come far enough that he now needed a lawyer. Now we just needed to get him and his lawyer into the courtroom—at the defense table.

CHAPTER 13
Grace Malz

Miraculously, even with our observing his every move in West Windsor and shattering his invincibility by discovering Janice, John continued to talk to us—which is more than we could say for Hollie Drajin. Dedy spoke with him every day. Two days after the searches, she got an earful about how the police had left everything at his office, the condo, and his cars a mess. John complained that the police had confiscated his personal financial papers and that he wouldn't even be able to file his taxes. (That's going to be the least of your problems, I wanted to tell him.) He said the police were looking in from the outside and targeting him unfairly simply because he was the last person to see Fran.

Through months of whining, lying, and crass innuendo, Dedy had been mostly patient with John. The stronger and more restrained she was, the bigger the patsy John took her for. Until the day of the searches, he had no idea we were aware of Janice or anything about his true life in Connecticut. Dedy was tiring of her role.

"John," she said, "you give me just one reason why I should believe anything you have to say. Now that we've heard about Janice and Sheila, don't you think it would have been better coming from you? Especially when we gave you every opportunity to tell us everything when we were up there!"

John said he didn't blame her for not believing him or his story. He declared the police knew more about Janice's disappearance than he did. Even after she had laid it on the line, John never told her he had filed the missing-person report on Janice. He asked Dedy to remember that he and Janice were divorced and out of each other's lives. Why would he have any knowledge of her being missing?

Dedy asked John why he continued to lie to us. "I just don't have an answer for that," he said.

Mike and the other officers started going through the evidence they had confiscated during the searches. They found evidence confirming John had indeed been in Connecticut the weekend of September 28. There was a credit card receipt showing he had done at least one thing to prepare for Sheila's mother's party: He had purchased a pair of balloon curtains. Though a small fact, this disproved John's claim that he and Fran had spent a nice weekend at home. One of the sweetest things that Mike did with the evidence was to make copies of the portfolio pictures and send them to Dedy and me. This is just one example of many that explains why this man has become an adopted member of our family, and why we love him.

The sense of urgency had grown since police had declared the case a possible murder investigation, and the leads required more time to pursue and promised more progress. The last week of April was crazy for Mike, Brian, and another officer with the West Windsor Township Police Department, Dave Mansue. The three were planning to meet in Seville to interview John's family and other people connected with John's early years.

Dave and I decided to take advantage of the time off to make final arrangements for a cruise to the Bahamas for our twenty-fifth anniversary. We had settled on the trip not long after we were married, when money was tight and a cruise to the Bahamas was the most exotic getaway imaginable. But I had a hard time overcoming my guilt in abandoning the case to party on a ship. I remembered a conversation Fran and I once had about marriage during one of our morning coffee chats on the phone. I had just given birth to my first daughter, had been feeling the stress of being a new mother, and was feeling guilty about snapping at Dave just before he had left for work that morning. Fran told me, "You must now and always put your relationship, marriage, and love for Dave before everything. If the waters there are calm, the two of you will be able to handle anything outside the relationship." This was good advice from a woman who had never been able to find happiness in marriage. Some people say that one should never put anything or anyone ahead of their children. Fran disagreed. If the couple is strong, they automatically put their children first.

Compartmentalizing my different lives to make time for the case worked well for keeping my head together, but I knew that not every compartment—the case, my job at Textron, the girls, and Dave—was getting equal treatment. If I were to drop marbles into different jars that represented my efforts in each of these categories, my husband's jar would have had by far the least. You could say that Dave was losing my marbles. I knew I loved him totally before we married, but I couldn't possibly have appreciated what I would one day feel. I love him so much more today than I did on our wedding day, and I vowed to prove that to him.

We departed Cape Canaveral the last day of April for the Bahamas and enjoyed a wonderful cruise. Dave made sure I kept busy with only fun things, though I wasn't able to let go of the investigation altogether. It affected me too intensely to push it entirely out of my mind. Dave and I did get time to get to know each other again, and I'd like to think I haven't taken his love and support for granted since. I hope not.

Mike, Brian, and Dave Mansue met in Seville the week we were at sea. John's family treated them less than cordially, though I wasn't sure whether that was just the way their family was or whether they were suspicious of out-of-state cops questioning them about the potential murder of someone they'd never met. But they did know Janice, I told myself.

By coincidence, Garry Hartman worked for the same company as John's mother, Grace Malz: Westfield Insurance. Westfield's complex there is a town in itself. It even has its own Zip Code. Garry and Grace had little, if any, contact. Garry said the two of them weren't exactly in the same coffee-break league. She was much higher on the corporate ladder, though she had moved around to a lot of different departments. Few employees cared to spend much time around her. Garry described her as short, stocky, red-headed, and bossy. Mike and Dave Mansue thought having a female officer in the interview who could go head to head with Grace was a sound idea. West Windsor's department doesn't have a female detective, so they brought in Eileen Gillece from the Connecticut State Police. Eileen proved to be ideal for the job. She can be an imposing presence herself when the work demands it.

Grace came as advertised when Mike, Brain, Dave, and Eileen arrived. She lectured them about approaching her during the workday and insisted she would speak with them only after hours, at 7:00 P.M. They agreed but met grief again when signing in at the front desk that night. Grace didn't want their names on the registry. A Westfield security officer stated bluntly, "They are required to sign in." Grace grumbled and herded them back to her office. She immediately handed Eileen a paper stipulating that if anything were released to the press, etc., she would sue, and made it clear she wouldn't talk until they had signed the paper. Eileen promptly wadded the paper up and told her in so many words that it was pure crap. They did not intend to sign anything, and the interview would proceed. Grace remained hostile and expressed concern about her position at Westfield and what press coverage could do to her husband's business. She never asked why they suspected her son or why they were doing this to her son.

When the authorities tried to interview John's grandparents, Mrs.

Chaney informed them she had a doctor's appointment and couldn't talk to them. Mr. Chaney just said, "John should have married Sheila." Later, when Mike and Brian tried again to interview him, he would not answer the door. He held up a sign that said, "Flu." I have wished many times that Mike had simply gone on through the door and told Mr. Chaney that it was okay, he had had his flu shots that year.

They still had John's brothers to interview, and they turned out to be more helpful, relatively speaking. Michael was a few years younger than John and had been close to him growing up. He said he didn't know of any violent threads in John's fiber. When they were young, John had quit trapping because he didn't like having to kill animals. Michael did tell them that John had always had trouble telling the truth. Mrs. Chaney arrived while Brian and Mike were talking to Michael, and they thought her intention was to warn him, but the interview continued and went well. Michael said he and John weren't close anymore and that he didn't really know him.

Steve, the youngest in the family, told Mike and Brian that he had never really liked John and they had never been close. Sam Malz was the principal parent in Steve's upbringing, and neither spent much time around John. He said John was very good with computers and that their relationship was based on using John's computer knowledge, nothing more. He had little else to add.

Sam took the cake among the Smith/Chaney/Malz clan. He declined to do a face-to-face interview with police but did say he would speak with them on the phone. He had only one reply for every question: "I don't care." They tried to explain that John could be in a lot of trouble, and Sam repeated, "You don't understand. I DO NOT CARE." John was right about one thing. He grew up in a dysfunctional family. He took Grace's heartless, controlling, deceitful personality and expanded it into a cottage industry. From early on, John was considered the black sheep of the family and has at times been disowned for bucking Grace's demands. He refused to help with the family business when Sam was seriously ill and was consequently shunned. That might have been the only wise decision he ever made. His two brothers were totally dependent on the goodwill of Grace and Sam. Grace owned their homes, their vehicles, and, because they worked in the family business, their very livelihoods.

Periodically, John would redeem himself with some gesture that brought him back into the family's good graces. It's the measure of his misdeeds, then, that none of those gestures was enough to persuade Sam Malz to care about him during the police interview. Michael tells the story of when they were teenagers swimming with the family at a local park. Sam got into trouble in the water and was floundering, scarcely able to breathe. John swam out and pulled him out of the water just in time. He saved his life.

CHAPTER 14
A New Dimension

The case grew ever more complex and delicate now that so many players on both sides were involved and John had an attorney. Time on the investigation became more focused but protracted. Searches, like Mike's uneventful effort in New Jersey with the dogs and infrared-equipped helicopters, required extensive coordination between officers and agencies and depended upon cooperative weather. Since our trip to Seville and the Hartmans' jewelry store in early April, Dave and I had been waiting for an opportune time to return and walk Silver Lake. Though vague, Dorothy's articulation of that name without prompting gave us what was so far our only real lead on finding an actual body, the biggest barrier to proving John's guilt. The first good conditions for us to cover the wooded marshland around Silver Lake came over Memorial Day weekend 1992.

Our first order of business on reaching Seville was to photograph the Chaneys' home on Pleasant Street for Mike. He wanted them as a tool to help Mike and the authorities in New Jersey. John did seem to have feelings for his grandmother, Mrs. Chaney. Mike felt that using the photos for what is called, in police speak, a throwdown, just might be useful for his next interview with John. (A throwdown is when photos of important things or people in a suspect's life are placed directly in front of them during questioning.) Mike and the other officers hoped to get some—correction, any—emotional reaction from John. We all felt the grandparents were the only emotional connection between John and his family. Brian Potts was in nearby Wayne County, south of Seville, but the fact that it was such an old case and that his supervisors had handled—and botched—the initial investigation meant he received little support for his efforts. He wasn't really permitted the time. Dave and I had asked Garry and Isabel weeks ago to take the pictures—they did, after all, live in the same area—but they generally were too busy or too plain scared to take the photos. The John they had known was brash and threatening and wouldn't hesitate to exact revenge for any plot against him. They feared he would come after their three young daughters. Their reluctance to take the photos delayed Mike's next interview with John for two weeks, until we could go do it ourselves. As I came to know the family through our common pain and challenge, and to care for them greatly, I also began to see why Janice's case had never received the serious attention it deserved. The Hartmans loved Janice's memory, but they had moved on with their lives.

That made the investigation more difficult to an extent, but I tried not to let it interfere with our budding relationship. Isabel and I talked frequently and exchanged news not only of the investigation but also of family. In one of our conversations at the time, Isabel related a story that qualified as both. A gentleman had approached Garry at Westfield. The man said that he knew the police had come to interview Grace Malz and that he and John had been childhood friends. As adults, they had drifted apart. A few years prior, he had run into John's grandparents, the Chaneys, at a street fair in Seville and went over to say hello. The Chaneys told him John was at home and in the garage working. He paid his respects and went to visit John but was surprised by the welcome he received. Or, more accurately, the lack of welcome. John had changed. His expression said it clearly enough: Get out of my face. The man left hurt, having thought John would be glad to see him after so many years.

I got his name and phone number from Isabel and called him as soon as we hung up. To date we had learned of John's childhood only through his brothers. His parents and other family members were of no help. I was curious to see what a less partial witness would have to say about his youth. Because this man also worked at Westfield, I asked him whether he would be uncomfortable talking to me. He replied that it was no problem. He related the same story he had told Garry but added, "Something has happened to John. He was never like that before." I asked him what he could remember about the years he and John had been friends. "John was older. I was really more Michael's age," he said. They had all played together, but John was the leader. He taught the two younger boys to hunt, fish, and camp. He said John and his brother were close and united in their hatred of their mother, who was domineering and controlling. Although he spent many years with the brothers, he couldn't recall a single show of affection between them and their mother. If they were out playing and Grace called the boys in, they didn't finish what they were in the middle of and come in good time, like most kids. They bolted home. I asked if he thought this might be because Grace had been a single mother and felt she had to be strong to remain in control of a difficult situation. "Perhaps," he answered. "Looking at it as an adult this might be true, but I believe it went deeper. They were afraid." He felt Grace did only what society demanded of a mother, nothing more and nothing less.

Dave and I took many pictures of the grandparents' home from different angles. I stood in a gazebo across the street and used a Polaroid camera. Being a five-hour trip away, we didn't want to get home and find that we had nothing to send Mike. We left Seville to walk the lake area. I don't know if I really thought I would find Fran or if I just knew I had to look. The best way to explain it is, I was afraid of what I might find but more afraid of what I would not. Dave and I split up but stayed within sight of each other. It's a large area, and as the afternoon rolled on, we knew we had very little daylight left for the search. We concentrated on areas in which the dead grass and underbrush appeared to be disturbed. Spring was late that year, so there wasn't a lot of new growth. At dark, we left the lake having found nothing and paid a visit to Garry and Isabel. We got home late, weary, and somewhat let down. I had prayed we would find something.

The first week of May, Mike let Dedy and me know Sheila was willing to talk to us. After the search of the beach house, Dedy and I had asked him whether Sheila would. This was emotionally important to Dedy and me because we wanted to hear for ourselves the voice of the woman who, because of John's not wanting to give her up, had cost Fran her life. We really wanted more insight into her personality and a feeling for her relationship with John. We decided it would be best if Dedy contacted her first, and she called Sheila that evening. We didn't want to risk her changing her mind. Sheila and Dedy spoke about many things, but most of all the location of the small gifts the children had given Fran. We now knew exactly what John had done with Fran's things. It was more of a shock for Sheila. As they were on the phone, Dedy described a set of three crystal birds, and Sheila then identified two of them in her china cabinet. "I'm looking right at them," she said. There was an unusual coffee table with a ginger-jar base and large unattached glass top. Dedy heard the sound of glass hit glass. Sheila said, "I'm sitting on your mother's couch. Everything you have described is here." She told Dedy that she would be glad to box up the smaller things that they had discussed and send them to her. The news of two missing wives and the ongoing investigation of John shook her. After the searches, Sheila resolved to get out of the beach house. She had John served with a restraining order and started looking for a place to move.

About two weeks after she and Dedy had spoken, I called Sheila. I needed to get my own impression of her, and we talked for more than an hour. She confirmed that John had moved the furniture to Connecticut in

August 1991 and spent his weekends there since the beginning of October. She told me John had tried to rekindle their romance and told her frequently that he wanted her back. John also told her Fran had been found. Sheila told him it was over. They never fought, according to Sheila. If they got into an argument, John would just throw a cheap shot at her and leave. He wasn't violent. But she had trusted John, and she was scared. One of her anecdotes resonated with me. She talked of her trip to Florida in March 1990, when she and John broke off their engagement and she returned to live in Connecticut. As she prepared to leave, she placed her engagement ring on the coffee table, just as Fran had supposedly done when she challenged him to think about their marriage.

———————

The first week of June, during our morning check-in, Dedy told me about a story she had read in the June 2, 1992, issue of *Woman's Day*. The story, written by young-adult author Lois Duncan, was titled, "Who Killed My Daughter?" Duncan tells the story of how she located and used the help of a psychic to investigate her daughter's murder. Dedy faxed me the article. Duncan had gone in search of a credible and proven psychic. By happenstance, she located Dr. Marcello Truzzi, who is involved in researching paranormal happenings. It turned out that Duncan and Dr. Truzzi were one-time college classmates.

Both of us were well aware that the psychic world, especially the world of psychic criminal investigation, where families are often desperate to try anything that might locate their loved one, is rife with schemers and charlatans. Yet based on our faith, belief that it's possible to communicate with the spirit world, and, yes, a sense of desperate urgency, we had decided months before that we wanted to involve a psychic in Fran's case. We had also given up any illusions of finding Fran alive and well. After reading the *Woman's Day* story, I sat down and composed a letter to Dr. Truzzi begging for his help. He replied the last day of June. Dr. Truzzi wrote that he could not recommend a psychic, but he did send three names of psychics that he knew to be honest in their dealings with police and families. He also supplied addresses and phone numbers. Each possessed the ability to work over the phone, an important quality in the geographically scattered cases we were involved in.

The "team," Dedy, Mike, Brian, and I, took part in a conference call to develop a consensus on using a psychic. Mike—Psychic Mike—is of course a believer; Brian is more skeptical about the use of paranormals. We agreed, however, that we had nothing to lose in contacting the three psychics. After placing some calls, Dedy and I selected Noreen Renier as our first choice. We liked her sense of humor. The outgoing message on her answering machine said, in a low, raspy voice, what Daddy used to call a whiskey sour voice, "I knew you were going to call. . . . That's why I left the machine on."

That evening, Noreen's associate, Margaret, returned our call. I explained that Dr. Truzzi had referred me and that we were begging for Noreen's help. Margaret told us Noreen would help only if she were given an invitation by the investigators on the case and that she works with police departments only when foul play is suspected. I hastily explained that Fran was one of two wives missing and that foul play was definitely suspected. I asked if they would reconsider if Mike Dansbury contacted them. Margaret assented but made no promises.

When they connected, Margaret told Mike that they didn't want to know anything about the case, just that the police were in agreement that Noreen should be used as an investigative tool. She said that most credible psychics claim only to be tools, never case-solvers. Her services, if we could get them, would come at a steep price for us: $525. Margaret said they usually did two sessions, a preliminary reading and a follow-up. The fee covered both sessions. After a client had had time to digest what Noreen told them in the first reading, she could contact Margaret, never Noreen, to let her know when they wanted to schedule the second reading. With assurances of the department's support and agreement to the fee, Mike scheduled a session with Noreen for August 12, 1992, two months away. Noreen is a busy woman. Fortunately, that gave us time to pass the family hat yet again to come up with $525. Love doesn't come cheap.

Now in Gainesville, Noreen lived on the west coast of Florida at the time and had worked with the FBI and police agencies around the country since the early 1980s. She worked on the Laci Peterson case and has had a convincing number of successes, although it can sometimes be difficult for victims' families and officers to prove conclusively that one, she's using psychic powers; and two, the information she's providing is what made the difference in solving their case. Skeptics tend to explain the appearance of psychic phenomena by citing analytical interpretation of existing case information, exploitation of seemingly specific generalities that could apply to many cases ("I see the victim . . . she's near water, and trees . . . in a shallow grave . . ."), and a variety of careful hedging. Clues can indeed be vague, and sometimes Noreen is unsure how much she has aided an investigation. The bottom line, though, is that many of these cases do get solved and that families put up large amounts of money betting that they will.

In many cases Noreen works, she employs psychometry, the reading of energy fields emitted by objects owned by the victim or suspect. Holding those objects helps her tap into feelings and images their owner has had. Metal objects, such as jewelry, seem to work best. Because the sessions are so expensive, Margaret sent us a list of Noreen's credentials, teaching credits, and a list of books that mention her to give us as much insight as possible into how she works and to enable us to make the most of our time with her. Margaret also coached us on how to phrase questions to enhance Noreen's psychic flow. We must never interrupt her with another question, but were to let her know when she was hitting on known information with comments like, "That's right," or "That makes sense." Considering the way her psychic energy works, handling the session properly would appear to be crucial to getting good results. In one interview she gave in May 1992, she said, "I get lost going to the grocery store, but I found a plane, once. I gave them two numbers; it turned out to be the longitude and latitude for it."

Now we needed some good items to send to Noreen for the reading. Dedy and I had asked John for Fran's things when we were in New Jersey, and he had told us that everything not at the condo was in Connecticut. He said he would pack them up and send them to Dedy. We left New Jersey with very little. I had driven my Tracker, and with our luggage, there wasn't much room for anything else. Mike had given us the things he had collected from Joe and Nancy Mazotas: computer disks, another pair of glasses, a bottle of Tylenol, and her dictionary. As we left the condo in February, I went back to the kitchen cabinet and took a small demitasse cup and saucer. Fran had loved these cups and displayed them in her kitchen in Florida. The cups were special to me because while I was home during the time Mama was ill, Fran and I sometimes used them to throw adult tea parties. Dedy picked up a few of the small gifts that she and her brothers had given Fran. This was all we had. We spent hours on the phone trying to get John to send the rest. Dedy's cedar chest in particular was dear to her. She had lent her mother the chest when she had no room for it at home. We offered to pay the shipping cost to return it and heard plenty of excuses, but had no luck getting it back. Janice's family had similar trouble getting any of her belongings returned in 1974. When Janice's mother insisted, Mrs. Chaney met with her and Janice's aunt to give them a shoebox of things and a hope chest. John never made an effort to return anything of Janice's. We took an inventory of what little we had and with some disillusion realized we did not have the things Noreen would need to help us.

We opted to give it one more shot. John had told Dedy he planned to go to Seville for the Fourth of July weekend and that he would pack Fran's things and meet Dave and me in Hudson, Ohio, where his mother and stepfather lived. We could then transfer the things to our car and return home. Dedy revealed that we were trying to locate a credible psychic to help us and that if we could find someone, we would not want to have to wait for personal items for the psychic to use. We did not tell him we had already found Noreen.

On July 2 Dedy called me at work crying. John had called to tell her he would not meet us. I was so angry I saw red. If he didn't want to lift a finger or spend a dime on finding Fran, I could deal with that. We would take care of it. But to insolently deny us the tools we needed . . . I just wasn't going to have it. I sat at my desk and fumed, then decided to call John myself. When he answered I said, "John, what's the problem? I just got off the phone with Dedy, and I'm pissed." John repeated the excuse he had given Dedy. He had just given up the condo and was living in Connecticut. Through the work week, he rented a place at Fresh Ponds, the temporary housing that he and Fran had used after their move to New Jersey and before they leased the condo. John said it would take about three hours one way to commute between New Jersey and Connecticut through holiday traffic, and he was trying to help his new tenant, Dave, move into the beach house. Sheila had left things a total mess when she had moved out and had even taken the appliances and furniture.

"I talked to Mother, and she is very concerned for Fran," John said. "When I told her about Sheila taking the things, Mother said I should file charges against Sheila for grand theft. Mother said, 'Who does Sheila think she is, Fran?'"

I ignored his sob story and reminded him that Fran had to come first. Even now, before his tenant, his job, the beach house, or anything else. Getting these items was an investigative matter as well as a personal matter. "John, you have constantly put everything above and in front of finding Fran. That ends *right now*." I reiterated that the children had asked for very little and never anything that had come out of the marriage, just things with sentimental value.

He said he was vague on exactly what they wanted.

"For now, I need the following: something of Fran's in metal, something in glass, a few items of her clothing, and paper." I wanted to be sure

I had covered all the elements that my research told me a psychic might use. For metal, I suggested Fran's watch.

John said he had moved so haphazardly from the condo that he had no idea where to locate the watch. I told him where it had been at the condo, beside the bedroom chair, in a glass, on the table that held the phone. "Find it," I said.

We planned to meet him as previously arranged at the McDonald's in Hudson, about twelve miles north of Akron, at 1:00 P.M. I told him he had best be there or it was my intention to go to his mother's home and ask her why her son would not help locate his missing wife. I pushed and asked if it would be better if we met at Grace's house. At that time, I didn't know the exact address for his mother's house in Hudson. When Dave and I had previously driven around the area to check his Illinois trip story, I just had an idea of the neighborhood. I had been more interested in seeing whether I could identify one of his cars, but I was confident John didn't know that.

John started to complain again and did manage to wheedle a 4:30 meeting time out of me. He went on about how hard it would be to find the other things. "I haven't even had time to go through things or to be able to organize a garage sale."

He would have been in physical danger if we had been face to face. "John, don't you dare put a fucking thing of my sister's belongings in a garage sale," I said. "Don't you even, for one moment, entertain the thought. I'll come up there and break your damned neck, you son of a bitch." I don't know if I've ever been so angry.

John began to talk about how he wished Fran would come home.

"Bullshit," I said. "I have had forty-five years with Fran's personality, and Dedy has had twenty-seven. We all know Fran is not coming back. John, you and I both know she is not coming home."

He became very quiet.

I told him we should end this conversation before anything else hurtful was said. "John, I'll see you in Hudson at 4:30 P.M. tomorrow afternoon. And John, you had better be there."

CHAPTER 15
The First Session

The next day, a Friday, we arrived in Hudson before noon, found a nice place to eat lunch, and took our time before rolling into the McDonald's parking lot at 3:45. John had sold both the Shadow and the Miata, so we didn't know what kind of car he would be in. I was eager to see what he'd be driving and whether he'd be with his family. John showed up at 4:10 but didn't appear to have driven himself. The first words out of his mouth were, "I'm so glad you guys are here." His eyes were wide and the words tumbled out of his mouth. "I got here about three and looked in the lot for you. You weren't here so I went to Mom's. She said she was so glad I had come early because the annual family outing to the Indians game was moved up to tonight—you know fireworks and stuff. They're going to pick me up here." He looked everywhere but at us.

John said he didn't know how he got everything done. The traffic was awful, and he'd been forced to pull to the side of the road for a few hours' sleep. He had also hit dense fog. I told him that not getting this done would have caused problems.

I wanted him to know I was still angry. I told him it would be in his best interest if he never made Dedy cry again. John just hung his head. I wanted to see what his reaction would be if I continued to bully him. I told him that if I had been able to get my hands on him the day before, I would have killed him. He changed the subject. As in New Jersey, seeing him fold up like a lawn chair felt really good.

John trotted over to his car, a late-model Honda, and produced what he had brought along: a sweater dress, a red sweater that Dedy had given Fran, a red blouse, a yellow-and-white crop top, a coffee cup, and Fran's watch. Just things I had asked him for, nothing more and nothing less. John told of finding the clothing in the garage and the remainder of her things in the second bedroom. He complained that he could have just mailed the stuff.

"Not good enough." I shook my head. "We waited from October until months after Mama's funeral for a phone book."

Dave interjected: "Then it was useless. It was old and not even the phone book we needed. The phone book was from the area that you worked in."

Change of subject again. We were back to what an awful trip it had been. He did show interest in the psychic. I told him I'd keep him posted. I had already decided that he would be told nothing about our sessions with Noreen. I wanted him relaxed. I didn't understand enough yet to know whether his being nervous or upset would have an effect on the reading we got from Noreen. I explained that using a psychic would be expensive, but he never offered to assist with that. I started getting the urge to tear into him again and didn't want to go too far, so I said it was getting late and that we should be getting on the road. Then I caught a look from Dave and, in that second, picked up that he was determined to wait John out and see who was going to pick him up.

We began making small talk to keep him interested. Cars and dogs were choice topics. He showed more emotion over his Border collies than he ever had over the disappearance of his wife. His voice cracked with emotion, and he said, "They're hiding them from me because of all

I've put them through. It's just not fair." I assume he was talking about Sheila taking the dogs and the embarrassment caused by her family knowing about the police search at the beach house. Just then a dark Mercedes pulled into the lot. John ran just like a little boy over to the car. He didn't even say goodbye. But it wasn't his ride. Even this was significant to us. We now also knew that John's mother and stepfather had a dark-colored Mercedes. When John returned to where Dave and I were standing, he seemed nervous that our meeting wasn't over. A few minutes later a navy Lexus pulled into the lot and parked behind our car. Again he raced over to the car, calling out over his shoulder, "That's them. See ya."

John and company were directly in front of us as we left the McDonald's. I took advantage of our position to get the plate number of the Lexus. The plate was from Summit County, which is where Hudson is located. Mike later ran it and traced it to his stepfather, Sam Malz. It was a lease. We were headed in the same direction on State Route 303 as we pulled into traffic, and we'd discussed with John what route we'd be taking home, so what happened next surprised us. At the next intersection, without warning, the driver swerved into the left-turn lane and made a rabbit-fast U-turn, then waited a few seconds like they thought we might follow them. When we continued to go straight, they sped off the other way on 303 with John in the back seat and the person who I assumed was his mother, Grace, in the front seat. The occupants turned around to watch us until we lost sight of them.

On July 6, a Monday, Mike, Dedy, and I had a three-way conversation about what we'd send Noreen for our first session. Since John was a suspect, Mike supplied a date book and a metal pen for Noreen to use. He would also include a date book of Fran's, her glasses, and a blue comb that Dedy and I had found in the trunk of her Shadow while in New Jersey. One year Granny had bought all the women in our family combs, all alike except in color. Fran treasured hers. She would have gone out to her car in her pajamas to get this comb. I planned to mail Noreen what John called Fran's favorite coffee cup. I told John I didn't know how he could be so sure that this was her favorite cup since it was part of an eight place setting of their everyday dishes. "Believe it or not, Fran could tell the difference," he said. I did not believe this for a single second. I also mailed the watch that John had brought to Hudson for us. I didn't bother to send the red blouse. I don't know where John found it, but it was several sizes too large. The crop top he brought was so tacky I knew Fran would never have worn it.

I mailed Fran's assorted items and a cashier's check for $525 to Noreen. Family members had kicked in enough to cover that cost before we had even contacted everyone. If Dedy and I had been forced to come up with all the money, we would still have been waiting to make an appointment. Dave went that day to purchase recording equipment to tape the phone sessions. Margaret had told us taping the sessions would free us to concentrate on phrasing questions and getting answers instead of trying to document her every comment. We wanted to get every scrap we possibly could, but we had some angst about betting the family's money on such an uncertain technique. There are no guarantees.

We were ready to go, but Noreen wasn't. We still had six weeks before the first session, which Margaret had moved from August 12 to August 19. We anticipated the date the way kids anticipate the holidays. Every day that passed meant one less moment between us and our prize. At long last, August 19 arrived full of promise. It was a little before 1:00 P.M. when the session get under way. I checked to see that the tape recorder was working. Mike, Dedy, and I were all on, and in Florida were Noreen and her assistant, Jo Cantrell. Mike would direct the questioning. We had read everything we could get our hands on about psychic detection and prayed we'd manage the fragile psychic atmosphere well enough to expand the meat of the case. We didn't want Noreen getting lost on the way to the grocery store, so to speak. There was little likelihood the police would file charges without a body or bodies to prove a crime had been committed.

The 1989 photo of my only sister, Fran Gladden-Smith, that we used for our missing-persons flier.

Master Sergeant Thornley Thomas ("Dick") Gladden in Korea, 1950, holding a photo of our Mama, Margaret Marion ("Mickey"). This went in a double frame with a photo of Mama, Fran, and me. Daddy's duties overseas meant this was as close as we got to a family portrait. The two photos were taken at the same time but, because of the International Date Line, not on the same day.

Fran's son, Todd Wehling, age 10

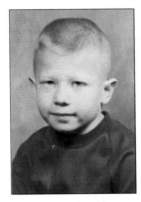

Fran's son, Rodd Wehling, age 8

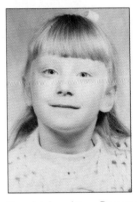

Fran's daughter, Deanna ("Dedy") Wehling, age 6

Todd, age 18

Rodd, age 16

Dedy, age 14

Mama holds Fran (age 7) and me (age 3) close in our near-family portrait at home in Niceville, Florida.

Granny and Pop, my maternal grandparents (Paul M. Cannon and Mary Christine Cannon), who always put family first.

John David Smith III, Fran's
fourth husband, in 1992, taken
at the West Windsor Township
Police Department.

Fran and John in May 1991, shortly before they moved from Florida
to Princeton, New Jersey, where John got an engineering job with
Carborundum.

Fran and John's Princeton condo, from which Fran disappeared October 1, 1991. Their unit was on the third floor, left side.

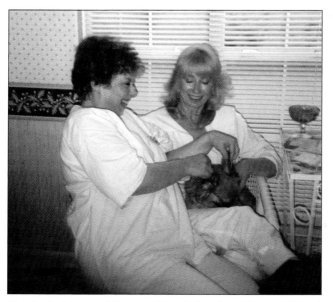

The last picture of Fran and me taken together, at Mama's house in Niceville, Florida, March 1991.

Detective Mike
Dansbury of the West
Windsor Township Police
Department.

Detective Bob Gulden of the
West Windsor Township Police
Department.

Lieutenant Dave Mansue of
the West Windsor Township
Police Department.

(left to right) Captain Greg Eldridge and Detective Mike Dansbury of the West Windsor Township Police Department and Detective Brian Potts of the Wayne County Sheriff's Department in Wooster, Ohio, March 1993.

Dedy and Brian grew close in the course of our investigation.

Janice E. Hartman
in 1969, just
graduating from
high school.

John Smith and
Janice Hartman
Smith as they
appeared in
their marriage
announcement
photo in 1970.

The home of Chester and Ethel Chaney, John's maternal grandparents, in Seville, Ohio. John stored Janice's body in the garage to the right of this house for several years.

John's beach house in Milford, Connecticut.

Me reviewing case files in the Justice Center during our visit
to Wooster for the joint task force meeting in March 1993

John Smith and third wife
Diane Bertalan's condo in
Oceanside, California.
John broke down the
steel-framed front door
after Diane filed for a
restraining order and an
annulment.

LaForza/Monster Motors, a specialty car manufacturer in Escondido, California. This was John's final employer before police arrested him and charged him with murder in October 2000.

John Smith sits between his two attorneys, Wayne County Public Defender Beverly Wire and attorney Kirk Migdal, during jury selection.

Photo courtesy of *The Daily Record*, Wooster, Ohio

Wayne County Assistant Prosecutor Jocelyn Stefancin expertly argues Janice's case before the jury.

Diane Bertalan, John's third wife, received an annulment before the trial that allowed her to take the stand.

Photo courtesy of *The Daily Record*, Wooster, Ohio

Wayne County Prosecutor Martin Frantz examines the plywood box in which Janice Hartman's remains were found.

John gets handcuffed after being convicted for Janice's murder. "I can't speak for the parole board," Judge Mark Wiest said, "but I am confident you will spend the rest of your life in an Ohio prison."

My husband, Dave—my compass, my constant—with me in 2004.

Dedy Weiss, my niece and my
partner in investigating crime.

Fran in her element in Houston, 1989.

Noreen explained the importance of phrasing questions appropriately. Psychic energy can be influenced. Therefore, we should be careful not to lead her. A bad question would be, "Does he have black hair?" A better choice would be, "Can you describe this person physically?" But she did want confirmation of factual information she was seeing correctly, what psychics call "hits." Jo would help Noreen channel her psychic energy to enable us to get as much information as possible from our first session. Noreen wanted only basic information. She knew only that Fran was missing, Mike was the detective on the case, Dedy was Fran's daughter, and I was Fran's sister. Noreen had never seen a picture of Fran or anyone else connected to the case. She knew nothing about Janice. Jo asked Mike to repeat the following: "Fran missing since October 1991."

This is one of the ways Jo helps channel Noreen's energy and keeps her focused on the issue at hand. If Noreen's energy began to wander, Jo would softly ask a direct question to bring Noreen back on track. Noreen then began opening the boxes of items we had sent. It's important to know that when holding items, Noreen can see and feel things from both Fran's and John's view as she holds objects belonging to each individual, as well as view them as an outside observer. When holding a particular person's belongings, she's focused on that person alone.

Noreen first wanted to be sure she was "into" Fran. She began to describe her, physically and in terms of personality. It was exact: blond hair, fair complexion, tiny stature. She even told us about the small cleft in Fran's chin and about a small scar from having a mole removed. Noreen commented that Fran's eyes would change color depending on her clothes and surroundings. She identified Fran as a strong-willed and often opinionated woman. Very organized. Someone who wanted everything put away and in its place. After we told Noreen she was indeed into Fran, she proceeded with the reading, while holding items that belonged to both Fran and John. She sensed some breaking up or parting, perhaps a move around Fran. Mike asked Noreen to concentrate on events from September 28, 1991, forward. She felt Fran was expecting someone, that she had plans for later that evening, but that the plans did not material-ize. "A man appeared upstairs. He was not supposed to be there. He was not supposed to have a key. He surprised her. He hit Fran, causing her injury. He then abducted her." As Noreen described this man, she felt head pain. When this happens, Noreen is actually feeling the pain, not just having a sense of pain, and she can become distraught. Jo reminded her to relax, that Fran was fine and that the pain was gone. Noreen also had a sense of premeditation, as in, "I know I am going to kill her. I know where I am going to put her." Fran's relationship with this man was close. He had made threats in the past and caused her to be afraid. Fran's fam-ily knew this man and had reservations about him, she said, but accept-ed him because of Fran. Fran didn't want anyone to worry about her, so she had never told anyone about the threats. Jo reminded us that it was important to confirm correct information for Noreen. Mike confirmed that Fran's residence was indeed upstairs. I confirmed that Fran would not want her family to worry about her.

Noreen continued: After some premeditation, the perpetrator was mad at the victim and went to see her. She knew he would cause her trou-ble because she was asserting herself to get rid of him. Noreen stated that this was the key motive. In the confrontation at the residence, Noreen felt Fran had been hit, specifically struck on the head. Her arms were behind her. Noreen saw her being pushed as they were leaving the residence. Once again, Noreen became preoccupied by the pain, and Jo urged her to move forward.

She went on to relate her psychic impressions of the vehicle and trav-el route. The numbers 8 and 80 were significant; also exit number 14 or 41. Their direction of travel would lead to the residence of a relative who had been visited before. The exit 14 or 41 was definite. Noreen also picked up the presence of hunting dogs. We attribute this to tracking dogs being used outside the condo during the search of the area, when the missing-person report had been filed. These dogs were used to try to find out what direction Fran might have taken in leaving the condo. We again confirmed a hit for Noreen and told her there had been a dog living in the household.

Jo asked Noreen whether Fran was alive. "No" she answered. "No, I feel I am dead. He killed me." Writing this sentence is hard, but to hear it spoken was crushing. Even believing it in our hearts, we seldom had spoken aloud that Fran was dead, and listening to it said from Fran's point of view was overwhelming. We knew we would hear things that would not be pleasant, but we had to know what had happened to Fran. About the perpetrator, Noreen said he had been nervous in the beginning but was more confident now because we had not found anything. No one had been to where Fran was. She said he was in a professional line of work, very smart and health-conscious. Noreen saw a minor move for him but said he was still in the area. (While John was living in Connecticut, he still held his job in New Jersey.) She saw him in running shoes and said that either the man or the woman was very outdoorsy.

Noreen has an unusual system for describing locations. She uses a clock as a reference with the victim's location at the center. She said the condo would be at three o'clock; a small airport between eleven and twelve; an odd-shaped brick building light in color at nine, with a tower of some kind nearby, at nine. Other clues she gave were that there was a small amount of water in the confinement, that it was damp but that the victim was not in water. The bricks or stone seemed to sweat. The smell of the area was sweet, like old lilacs, a burnt smell. The body was wrapped in something soft like a sleeping bag.

Her summary: The victim was hit on the head and abducted from the residence by a man she knew. He took her to another location, where she was somewhat hidden. She was not dead. This part broke my heart. If what Noreen said was accurate, Fran was near death and John just left her. She went on to say that using an aerial map, if one drew a square and divided it into four parts, the number three would be significant to the lower left-hand quadrant. The killer had hiked and played here as a young boy and knew the area well. This place wasn't fun anymore.

As the session wound down, I saw the wisdom in taping it. Noreen's speech came in rushes and spurts, full of half-completed sentences and random visions. There is no pattern to what she feels or sees. She told us that sometimes she sees things backward, as with her uncertainty about the numbers 8 or 80 and 14 or 41. She just knows these numbers are significant. This is one reason she has Jo. Jo can try to refocus her images to concentrate on what the client requires.

Noreen reminded us to study the tapes in preparation for the second session and to let Jo know where we wanted her to guide Noreen. After they hung up, Mike, Dedy, and I remained on the line to discuss the results. We were amazed Noreen could describe Fran so well and felt some of her visions could be of use to us, but at the moment, Mike was more concerned about Dedy and me. He knew that Noreen's accounts had been disturbing. That type of compassion is rare. Cops get exposed to the worst people and deeds our society has to offer and can easily develop a jaded domestic outlook. The average cop marries two to three times in the course of his or her career and is at greater risk of dying from suicide than from falling in the line of duty. We quickly assured Mike we were okay and that we had expected to uncover unsavory details if we went looking for them.

Throughout our search, I had worked to display strength and steadiness, which I felt would help our credibility with the police. It did, but I think I had another, perhaps subconscious, motive. If I were required to remain strong for the case, I wouldn't have time to fall apart with grief over losing Fran. Falling apart would have been easy to do, and I was scared that letting in just a little of that emotion would flood all of my carefully constructed compartments with tears. I couldn't allow myself the luxury of grief until I had the truth.

Yet where does that grief go if it isn't expressed?

I was beginning to find out. In suppressing mourning for Fran, I also found it difficult to grieve for my mother, whom I had promised I would find Fran, and for other deceased family members. Resolving those deaths in my mind was bound up in resolving Fran's, because they required the same emotional vulnerability. Food became a comforting outlet. In the eleven months since Fran had passed, I gained at least seventy pounds, and by October I would be diagnosed with high blood pressure. It got to where every time my elbow bent, my mouth flew open. If I wouldn't let anything out, it seemed, then my body was determined to keep putting more in. As I hung up with Mike and Dedy, I broke my own rule and took time to cry quietly for my lost sister.

We didn't waste any time following Noreen's guidance. Dave and I dug out maps and kept in close touch with Mike and Dedy. Mike studied maps of his local area, Dedy started looking for aerial maps, and Dave and I pulled out the atlas and studied maps of New Jersey, Connecticut, and Ohio. I had a hunch that John had taken Fran to the same area he had gotten rid of Janice's body. He's a creature of habit, and Noreen had said that the body would be located in an area that John was familiar with. If it had worked once and the body hadn't been discovered in almost two decades, it would work again. Dave and I found that Interstate 80, which runs west from New York City, would be the most direct route between New Jersey and Ohio. It cuts through the center of Pennsylvania more or less straight to Youngstown, before sweeping north to Lake Erie. In Ohio, exit 14 is what he would use to go either to his mother's home or to the area he had grown up in. From there, Noreen had supplied the following directions: "We go to that main thing there, not far from a major highway, go to the right, then go left, go down, down, in a lower area, water that changes in depth, a stream, river, running water. I saw a flag." While Noreen was into John and I asked why John was so confident, she said, "Because I can go close to where she is. You haven't been in the area. Where I go a lot is not too far from there. Going up a road, bridges are behind us, to the left, river, stream." As Fran, Noreen said, "If I could fly, after exit 14, I am straight ahead. Oh, what a large rock. What the hell is that thing? I've never seen anything like that before." Jo explained that even with Fran showing her a clue, if Noreen didn't know what she was seeing, Fran could not tell her. The information had to come from Noreen's experience.

Although we know he was with Fran at 10:30 A.M. on Saturday the 28th because of Dedy and Fran's phone conversation, John could have left Princeton, made the trip to Ohio, and arrived at the beach house a little after 4:00 P.M. on the 29th, when Sheila said he came. John had acquired a large number of traffic tickets over the years. He loved speed. Even if we factor in his observing all traffic regulations to avoid detection on the way to Ohio, he could have made up for it on the return trip with the way he drove.

Sheila said that at times John would be awake for days working on a project. When it was finished, he would crash. Dedy and Mike agreed that Ohio was a strong possibility, so Rich and Jan, Dedy's father and step-mother, scoped it out since they live north of Columbus, fairly close to the Hudson area we were looking at. Dedy gave Rich and Jan the clues we had received from Noreen, and they spent the day driving around the area and located an abandoned amusement part called Shady Lake. It fit a lot of the clues, and the directions off exit 14 fit the clues.

Before we called Brian Potts to get search teams and dogs involved, Dave and I felt we ought to reinforce the signs Rich and Jan had found. We left on a bleak, rainy Wednesday morning for yet another trip to northeast Ohio. We had no trouble finding Shady Lake and other land-marks given by Noreen. We took I-80 east and located exit 14. As we left the ramp, the bridges were behind us, and we spotted a huge American flag at a gas station. While the road was somewhat hilly, it was obvious that we were steadily dropping in elevation. Shady Lake seemed to fit the general description. There was a large manufacturing plant. When asked what the local people would do for a living, Noreen had answered, "Some people would work in a large plant, but most make their living from the land." Continuing south from Shady Lake, we found ourselves at Tinkers Creek State Park after a few miles. Some descriptions and landmarks also fit the clues here. It was close to where John had grown up, and as we entered the park, there was a huge rock. An electrical power station prompted us to wonder whether this was in fact the large landmark Noreen had been unable to recognize. I had a feeling that I shouldn't leave. I don't know why. We took many pictures at Tinkers Creek State Park. Overall, Noreen's descriptions, especially the place not being fun anymore, fit Shady Lake better, so we returned there to walk the area in the rain.

Dave went to get permission to explore the park. We lucked out in finding a gentleman who had been the maintenance manager when it was open. He told us the main building was now a commercial popcorn factory. They supplied popped, prepackaged popcorn to local grocery stores. The man gave us the history of the park. In the '50s and '60s, it had been filled with rides and carnie games. The ticket kiosks were still standing, but all the games and rides had been sold. It had gone out of business in the late '60s. We asked ourselves: Was this the place Noreen had described as not being fun anymore? When Dave explained the reason for our visit, he also took us on a guided tour of Shady Lake. Covering the two parks took the bulk of our day, and we were ready to return home after one final task. From Mike's plate check of Sam Malz's car, we now had John's mother's address in Hudson and decided to get photographs of her house as well.

The next morning I called Mike, and we discussed Shady Lake. Mike felt there was enough to go on to organize a search and called Brian to set it up. I spoke to Brian for a long time that day. I warned him of the poison ivy that covered the grounds and told him to be careful. I also told him about Tinkers Creek State Park. It took several weeks to put a search team together because the weather was just too rainy. Brian and officers from many other departments and jurisdictions, deputies from the Medina County Sheriff's Department, and officers from the Magadore City Police, with their K-9 units, conducted the search at Shady Lake. They spent all day there, but they found no sign of either Janice or Fran. We had to consider this one more dead end. It would be a long time before we could put together a team to cover Tinkers Creek State Park.

I couldn't let go of the feeling I experienced at Tinkers Creek State Park, and it haunted me. I really wanted to get back there with a search team. I kept thinking, *What if she's there and I just left her there?* I needed to walk it and get my eyes around it. Mike, Brian, Dedy, and I decided that I would wait until after our second session with Noreen to return to Tinkers Creek.

In the meantime, that left me in the dreaded limbo of not being done with the case but not being able to do anything. The ups and downs were taking their toll on me. Early on, I had battled to hold on to hope of Fran's return, and now I started battling to let go of it. I cautioned myself not to invest too much in each possibility in order to avoid the inevitable heartbreak that would come when the lead resulted in nothing.

I puzzle at how many detectives are men, because so much of investigation resembles shopping at yard sales (with more on the line, of course). To have the best chance of finding what you want, you have to start early when the merchandise is fresh. You can cut down on legwork if you have an eye for selecting the most promising sales, or a talent for haggling with the seller, but some of it is pure chance. Stumbling on the dusty stein at the back of the barn that makes it onto *Antiques Roadshow*. Like shopping yard sales, investigation takes many hours and usually yields few real prospects. It's a job of winnowing the jewels from the junk. But the most satisfying part is watching what you thought was junk turn into a jewel.

CHAPTER 16
The Second Session

The clock read 1:00 P.M., meaning it was once again time to talk to Noreen Renier. The date was October 14, 1992. Our last session, in August, had consisted of our asking questions and her answering as she handled the objects from Fran and John that we had sent her. Noreen still had the personal things we had sent her for our previous session in August, but this one would be a little different. I had mailed the pictures Dave and I took at Tinkers Creek and Shady Lake, Grace's house, and in Hudson itself to see whether Noreen got any feelings from them. The pictures were numbered on the back but otherwise unlabeled. Noreen knew only that Dave and I had taken the pictures. She hadn't used this technique much and wasn't sure whether it would work, but she was willing to try.

As connections were made, we once again identified all people present and said brief hellos. Noreen doesn't go over her previous sessions. Psychic memory is short. She just dives into the new material, so some information tends to get repeated. Mike felt that because I had done the most research on the paranormal, and because I had taken the pictures and had become familiar with the area, that I should be the one to take the lead and ask questions about the pictures.

Noreen again described Fran to our satisfaction, and since we had a suspect, she asked for a name. It caused problems with her psychic flow to continue to call him "suspect." Using the things we had sent of John's, Noreen described the man she was visualizing as having a medium build and being health-conscious and athletic. She said he looked younger than his age. She reiterated that she felt some parting from John around the time of Fran's disappearance. Fran had also been concerned for her mother and a son, she said. "John was not a foolish man," she said, and that there was premeditation. "He knew about smells and other things." Her description of Fran's present location was of small trees close together, wooden benches, and a watery stream-like area. There was a makeshift footbridge over the stream, like logs thrown down. The body was at an old meeting place known to the family. The number three was again significant to a map.

At our request, Noreen responded to her feelings about the pictures. Her strongest reactions were to the pictures of Tinkers Creek and John's mother's house. She said that facing Grace's house, we would need to go left about five miles. When she responded to the picture of the stone and wooden sign that read, "Tinkers Creek State Park," she became very excited and said, "1.6 miles." Noreen also felt very good about a picture of a picnic area in Tinkers Creek State Park that showed a few parked cars. Noreen said, "There, to the left of the cars, over the footbridge." There were only two pictures Noreen felt strongly about that weren't connected with Tinkers Creek: one of a building at Shady Lake that looked much like the ranger station at Tinkers Creek. I hadn't taken a picture of this building. The other photo she felt good about was the one of John's mother's house.

Noreen responded psychically to other questions I asked. She saw Fran as either clutching John to her or attempting to push him away. She was unsure which. Noreen felt embarrassment for Fran, as if Fran didn't want her true feelings to show. She again named 8 or 80 and 14 or 41 as important and used her clock system to give further directions and descriptions of the location of the body.

The significance of the number three, as it relates to a map, is that Highway 3 runs to the southwest of Tinkers Creek State Park and through Seville, directly in front of John's grandparents' home. Noreen went on to say that John was familiar with the area from his childhood. There were small purple flowers around. The body would be located in some position of view; there was stone or a cavelike opening.

As she became more tired, Noreen added, while into John, "My impressions indicate a casual sense that life goes on. He feels little concern about the incident except that the money went fast." We had no idea what "the money went fast" meant. It was just one more mystery. Noreen's most resonant statement for me came at the tail end of the session when I asked whether John was so confident because he had done this before. She said, "If you're looking for another wife, you're looking in the wrong state." We concluded our session with Noreen, and she wished us luck. She said she had a feeling that with what we had, a solving of the case was at hand.

We all spent hours going over the tapes and decided that Tinkers Creek State Park was the best lead we had in trying to find Fran's body. Mike and Brian set about the task of getting a team of dogs and handlers to search Tinkers Creek State Park. It was the middle of October and winter was closing in, so we knew speed was essential. It isn't easy to set up this type of search in this area. Because of county lines (Tinkers Creek straddles Summit and Portage counties), local police departments' jurisdictions, and Tinkers Creek being a state-owned park and a national waterfowl preserve, it would entail the cooperation of many different agencies. Brian worked very hard to make this search happen, and although all the different agencies were more than willing to help, the weather was the biggest factor in holding up the search team. You can't simply say, "Today looks like a good day. Let's go." Many dates were set for the search, but each time it either rained of snowed. By November, our window of opportunity had closed. The park has a lot of marshy areas, and though the officers could dress for the weather, the dogs could not. Frostbite would have been an ever-present risk. The search would have to wait until the spring, and it was going to be a long winter.

CHAPTER 17
Stoking the Media Bonfire

Without some breakthrough leads, Fran's suspected murder was bound for the cold case files. Mike and Brian had other work that required as much dedication as ours, and they stayed very busy. West Windsor is a small department with about five detectives who work everything from domestic cases to major drug cases. Brian's department was just as busy and worked similar cases. These officers could have one or two new cases each day or as many as six. That's why having victims' families contribute is so important. The police must focus on many cases, whereas each victim's family has only one.

Dedy and I refocused our energies on jobs and family. Normal life was calling us, and yet something told me that if I wholly returned to that now and accepted I had done everything I could, life would never quite be normal again.

A search of Tinkers Creek was still on hold until April, and even that wasn't a done deal. Police had now conducted two unproductive searches based on psychic direction: Mike's in New Jersey the previous spring and Brian's search of Shady Lake in the fall. From certain quarters of police departments, there was a belief that we had made a valiant effort to solve the case and that, absent some imminent major progress, it was time to begin devoting resources to fresher cases with better prospects.

I couldn't let it happen. I have to say that Mike and Brian were so dedicated that they used their off hours, comp time, and even vacation time to work the case. And everything we had collected so far pointed to John. If we could just get one piece of physical evidence to connect him, we might really have a case. Again, as a team, Mike, Brian, Dedy, and I decided that press coverage was our best chance for solving the crime. We all realized that if Dedy and I generated good publicity, the bosses would find it difficult to pull Mike and Brian off our case and let the dust settle. With the ear of the media, we could make a department look good or look bad. Dedy and I had been blown away by how compassionate people can be when they know you're in dire need, and we were count- ing on that goodwill one more time. Our advantage this time was that the plot had thickened, and broadcasting it on a news magazine program became a much juicier prospect for producers. Fran missing was an unfortunate family tragedy. Two wives missing was good TV.

I began by circling back to Mark Mueller, who wrote the original arti- cle on Fran's disappearance for the *Trentonian*. It wasn't easy. This would mark the second time in the case that I was humbled by my previous actions when passions ran high. (I counted facing down Hollie Drajin's husband at Canal Pointe, right after I offered her my middle finger, as the first.) I had been livid when I read the *Trentonian* article that implied Fran was erratic and depressed before she had disappeared, and I had ripped Mark hard for it, though I hadn't spoken to him directly. Now it was time to eat a little crow. Mark returned my call on January 12, 1993, the first anniversary of Mama's funeral in Niceville. I was understandably blue that day and apologized for the phone call I had made to his office in October 1991. He was gracious. Competition among papers in that area is intense, and the *Trentonian* uses a tabloid format with sensational headlines to remain competitive. Yet having read a number of editions, I found that the paper is good and that the stories are generally well-writ-

ten and accurate. Mark has proved to be a very talented journalist. I
updated him on the case while leaving out our sessions with Noreen. The
discovery of an earlier wife and John's consistently suspicious behavior
were enough to interest him in some follow-up coverage.

The resulting story, written by Mark, Phyllis Plitch, and Anne Fahy,
made the cover the next day and appeared on page 3 with the headline,
"'He killed them'." The dramatic quote came from Garry Hartman. Within
the article, he had said, "John killed them. He killed them both." I was
surprised after seeing the Hartmans so detached from the case that Garry
would make such a bold statement. The rest of us agreed, but we were
careful not to say it on the record. I did understand he was angry and
frustrated. The article also quoted John, whose comments were, as was
typical, neither here nor there: "The feeling is one of disappointment. I
hoped she would have been home by now." Although there were some
minor inaccuracies, the story summarized well what had happened with
the case in the past fifteen months since the *Trentonian's* original coverage. After a few follow-ups, other papers found us. The team spent many
hours talking to many reporters.

Tami Lange of the *Daily Record* in Wooster, Ohio, was looking into
unsolved local cases at the time, and Brian related our case to her.
Thanks to her frequent stories and the early play in the *Trentonian*, wire
services started picking up on the investigation. Calls from the tabloid TV
shows *Hard Copy* and *A Current Affair* followed. As much as we appreciated the newspaper exposure, TV time was our dream. The audiences
were infinitely larger, and, as celebrities know well, once networks latch
onto a story, the bonfire pretty much feeds itself.

We all agreed we needed a joint task force meeting of the principals.
We'd meet in Wooster to review the case and plot our next steps. With
the discovery of Janice and more digging into John's background, Seville
and the surrounding area had become the epicenter of the investigation.
Hard Copy and *A Current Affair* liked the idea because they could interview
all the key figures at once to save time and cut down on travel costs.

It was almost a family reunion. Dedy had flown into Indianapolis on Friday, February 5, and come over with Dave and me. Brian, whom we would be meeting for the first time, told us to call when we got close to Wooster. He would then park along the road with his lights flashing and escort us to our motel. We spotted an unmarked Mercury Sable as we pulled off the Interstate and got out to finally meet the man in person. Dave and Brian shook hands. Dedy, Brian, and I exchanged hugs like old friends. We had come to rely on and care for Brian just as much as we did Mike Dansbury. At one point I sensed a romance developing between Brian and Dedy. Whenever I talked to either of them, the other's name had a way of entering the conversation. It was not to be—both married other partners—but they remain good friends. I think they were good for each other at that time in their lives.

Brian proved to be a wonderful and thoughtful host. He had arranged for Mike and the captain of the West Windsor Township Police Department, Greg Eldridge, to stay next door to us at the motel. Before going to our room, I knocked on their door. Captain Eldridge was asleep, but Mike immediately answered. Hugs, cheek kisses, and handshakes with Mike lasted a few minutes. It was so good for us to all be together. We spent awhile discussing what we needed to accomplish and how to make the most of our time. We knew we would lose most of Saturday to the media. The interviews and taping times had been set. *A Current Affair* had already interviewed me at my house the night before. We were to again meet producers for *A Current Affair* at the Justice Center in Wooster the next morning and *Hard Copy* at a local hotel in the afternoon.

We also had our first nibble from the latest media blitz. Tami Lange's *Daily Record* coverage had prompted a woman who knew John in the mid-1970s to come forward and asked to speak with Dedy and me somewhat anonymously—we were to know only her first name. She also agreed to give Brian a formal interview. Brian got first crack to avoid the appearance of our influencing anything she had to say on the record. Sandy, an attractive black lady, met John through a mutual friend, Dennis Evans.

She was newly divorced with a young daughter. In other words, her life was a wreck. John moved fast and set her up with an apartment and, within a few weeks, bought her an engagement ring and the first of three Mustangs. Sandy said John was not very sexual, but he did talk frequently of bondage and leather. She felt he might be a closet homosexual.

John told her he needed to establish an image for professional purposes, someone to take to parties and present to the world. She said he was very good to her daughter. He also was not upset that she had another boyfriend who visited her during the week. This wasn't a problem as long as Sandy reserved the weekends for him. He'd arrive on Fridays with gifts and groceries for the week but was never around during the week.

Sandy's mother liked John, but her sister did not because he was white. She also stated that John stayed wired on amphetamines he bought off Dennis Evans. She knew that he had been married before and said that he presented himself as a grieving widower. He told her Janice had been murdered and that he had been taken to see her body. He described it as having semen dripping from her vagina and down her arm. If we were to believe him, this would indicate he had seen her within minutes of her death since the semen would quickly gel with exposure to the air. The story freaked Sandy out, and she became afraid for her life. She felt she was being set up to be murdered.

Sandy moved out of the apartment in the middle of the week and away from the area. She met with John one more time to return the engagement ring and the car she was driving. Sandy was still afraid of John. Hence, her anonymity.

I thought John's story about needing to establish an image was lame. Mixed marriages weren't widely accepted in the 1970s, and in any case John never took her anywhere. Sandy had similar sentiments. She said they never attended any of the parties John had talked about. They were homebodies.

She offered one other piece of information: She had met Mr. and Mrs. Chaney at the time, except John introduced them as his parents. Earlier he said the Chaneys had adopted him.

Although the women in John's life often had similar body types—thin and petite being John's build of choice—most everything else was different. The primary commonality we saw among Fran, Janice, Sheila, and now Sandy is that they were women willing to accompany John for reasons other than love. The only people who have probably ever loved him are his grandparents.

While this trip offered us a lot of opportunities—including getting our message to the public, getting up to speed on others' work in the investigation, and gaining more insight into John's past—its greatest significance was that the case had begun to move beyond our control. Captain Eldridge, Mike's boss, didn't think it was appropriate for us to meet with Sandy. Mike vouched for us, saying, "I trust these women with my life." Captain Eldridge stepped aside, but reluctantly. I don't think he felt sharing information with the team, our primary reason for making the trip, was useful or necessary. I suspect he came mainly to help Mike deal with the media. He was cordial enough; he just didn't think we had any business being involved with a police investigation.

That evening TV producers from both shows met us at the Justice Center. Dave, Dedy, Mike, Brian, Captain Eldridge, and I were all there, as well as Wayne County Prosecutor Martin Frantz. Then Garry Hartman walked into the meeting with his attorney. This really closed the door on a plum opportunity. Once the press was gone, we could have shared a lot about the case, but the police weren't going to talk with his attorney there. I still don't understand why Garry brought him. Over the few days we were there, Garry also revealed John's failed polygraph to the press along with a few other tidbits we weren't ready to discuss publicly. Considered alongside his *Trentonian* quote that John had killed Janice and Fran, I understand why someone like Captain Eldridge would be opposed to allowing families inside access to a case. No officer wants to invite additional barriers into an investigation. We began to question whether we could trust the Hartmans with sensitive case information.

Our standoff with Captain Eldridge made for an awkward dynamic with Mike since he was responsible to his boss but also firmly believed in our participation in the case. That night, I called him over to our room and asked if Captain Eldridge was stifling him. "No, the captain is okay," he said. "Good people." I let it drop. As an Army brat, I'm very familiar with the phrase "keep the brass happy," and I resolved to shut my mouth and avoid causing any trouble for Mike. I also resolved not to let any authority prevent me from making progress with the case.

My dual resolutions came into harsh conflict the next day when the family met Brian, Mike, and Captain Eldridge for lunch. The conversation turned to our sessions with Noreen Renier, and Captain Eldridge said, "I don't know where all this stuff about a psychic comes in." I looked him in the eye and said, "Five hundred and twenty-five dollars of my family's money is where the psychic comes in." Dave put a vise grip on my knee under the table. Dedy left the table with Brian right behind her. We were both mad enough to spit.

During lunch we suggested that while the team was together, we should drive to Tinkers Creek State Park to see whether Noreen's psychic directions meshed with the layout of the park. The captain obviously thought walking Tinkers Creek was a waste of time and told Mike and Brian he wanted a meeting after lunch. The meeting never happened— Mike and Dedy both had bad colds—but in any case none of the police went. Mike returned to the motel and went to bed. Brian returned to the Justice Center alone. Dedy, Dave, and I went to the park to look around.

As we ventured back into the woods from the parking lot, we spotted a log footbridge just as Noreen had described. We found several things that fit Noreen's description of the area, but it was in fact a futile search without dogs and trained people. The park comprises more than eighty acres. On our way out of the woods, Dedy spotted a huge rock that could have been the one Noreen had told us about. We didn't see it going into the woods because weeds and leaves hid it, but it was clearly visible from the other direction. We returned to the motel to report our findings. Mike and Brian have since wished they had gone with us.

Dedy and I set aside a day and a half to review the complete case histories, all the notes from all the interviews—five four-inch binders filled to full capacity—at the Justice Center in Wooster. We were very surprised to find how little there was that we didn't already know. Mike had always said, "No secrets," and we found that to be the case. We made copies of the few files we hadn't seen. The irony is, Captain Eldridge was also against our reviewing the case histories, which essentially confirmed how much we already knew. Although we had permission from Brian to access the files, Dedy and I read exhaustively but almost furtively, half expecting someone to come and kick us out at any moment. We spent the rest of that time guiltily skirting Mike and Captain Eldridge so we wouldn't have to address the case files conflict. We didn't want Mike to be caught in the middle and also didn't want to lose our access.

Reading through the mountains of paper reminded us of just how much work these officers had put into the two cases for the sake of justice. We shouldn't feel too resentful of Captain Eldridge. He is a good man and, though now retired, was a good cop. We also knew he wanted to protect the cases. He deserved better than the spoiled brats we were acting like, and we promised to treat him better.

That night, our *Hard Copy* show aired. No doubt having *A Current Affair* there too pushed them to run their footage so promptly. You can never tell with these shows when something might run, if it ever does. The *Hard Copy* piece felt thrown together and left out a lot of important aspects. There was no mention of all the belongings suspiciously left behind by both wives, and they didn't give a police or sheriff's department number to call with information. We couldn't complain too much though. Most missing people found are located because someone sees their picture and makes a call. We concluded that any show or story that would get pictures of Fran and Janice out there was worth the time to do an interview. *A Current Affair* took more time with their story. Field producer Stephanie Timm caught up with John at the beach house in

Connecticut and got footage of him running from the cameras. You see it all the time on the tabloid and investigative journalism shows, the harassed, frantic subject trying to get away, hand shading the face. Here I can certify that what you see is what you get. Or don't see. Regrettably, the *Current Affair* segment never aired, but I think they did a much better job than *Hard Copy*.

Mike and Captain Eldridge were to leave Tuesday morning, so we made plans to meet them for breakfast and leave things on a good note. Dedy and I felt we did not want to let Mike go, and he felt the same.

"I hate goodbyes," he said. "Now, no tears. Give me a hug." I missed him already, and he hadn't even left yet.

Dedy came back to our house days later after visiting her dad and Jan and before returning to Houston. It occurred to us after talking over the trip together why we disliked Captain Eldridge. Because of him, we felt we had been less than honest with Mike. We had never lied to Mike, but in this instance, by avoiding him and the issue of case file access, we had allowed something to come between us, and we felt we had violated the "no secrets" promise of our team. Later we learned that our promise had not been broken. Brian had told Mike what Dedy and I were doing in the basement of the Justice Center. We appreciated that we were all in this together and would have to set differences aside. Mike vouched for Captain Eldridge, and we trusted Mike implicitly. So, we had to trust Captain Eldridge.

CHAPTER 18

The Feminine Mystique

Not long after the *Hard Copy* show aired, I wrote to John. I had no hopes of gaining any new information; I knew he wouldn't write back or take my calls. It was purely cathartic. I told him he would have been better off if he had just told everyone that Fran was gone and he didn't give a damn. Instead he had chosen to tell lie after lie to unnecessarily complicate a painful situation. I also told him it was regrettable that he had chosen to hurt his family. "It will only get worse from here forward," I wrote. "I am the easiest person in the world to get rid of. Just tell me what you did with my sister after you killed her, and I will vanish from your miserable life."

Many people have asked me whether I'm afraid of John. The answer is no. John, with his superior intellect, is smart enough to realize that the last thing he needs is for anything to happen to me. The caveat for that rationale, however, is he must have something to lose. He was fast approaching a time when that wouldn't be the case. It was only going to get worse for him.

Since the onset of this investigation, many have also asked how I can be so certain John is responsible. "What if you're wrong?" they ask. "What if you have ruined a man's life?" I have to assume those people don't know the case that well. I answer them, "If I am wrong, God have mercy on my soul. But if I am right, I am not a strong enough Christian to ask God to have mercy on John's soul." It's true that spouses and close family members often fall under scrutiny early on, even before there's reason to believe they're guilty of anything. In this case, no one rushed to judgment. Dedy and I simply collected every fact and figure we could about my sister and the circumstances of her disappearance and then did the math. We've done a lot of soul-searching. John has had every opportunity to explain the circumstances, to correct false perceptions, and to exonerate himself. Every time, he has chosen to lie, manipulate, obfuscate, and intimidate. If he were innocent, his actions would be a poor way to prove it.

The media coverage and strategizing in Wooster did yield myriad new leads in the case. Brian had to investigate most of them because of the geography. I think Mike, who had become buddies with Brian, was frustrated that he couldn't be in two places at once to help out. The leads would require a lot of legwork and investigation, not just returning phone calls. Through his interview with Sandy, Brian was able to contact Dennis Evans, the mutual friend who had introduced Sandy to John. Dennis supplied the name of another woman John had lived with. The trick was finding her. Brian, Dedy, and I spent countless hours and many dollars trying to locate this woman. Brian finally succeeded by issuing a bulletin to vital statistics in a county in Indiana. He located a record of marriage, her present last name, and her home address. Brian talked to her at length on the phone and mailed a list of questions to her. She completed and returned the questionnaire. Her name is Maietta.

Maietta was frank and appeared to be honest in her statements. She said she had met John through her sister, who was dating him. Her sister and John had an open relationship, not a real romance. When Maietta expressed an interest, her sister said, "Have at it," faked an illness, and went to bed, leaving Maietta and John to talk late into the night.

Maietta was young and still a virgin, which was a problem for John. She did everything to please him, but he hated having to teach the art of lovemaking. As you can imagine, this hurt Maietta, who felt John was throwing the gift of her virginity back in her face. In her opinion, he might have a sexual fascination with little girls because he insisted that she keep her pubic hair shaved clean. She never felt John was homosexual, but he did like anal sex. John constantly asked her to lose large amounts of weight. At the time, she was five feet, eight inches tall and weighed about ninety-five pounds.

The new couple soon moved to Cleveland, where John put her to work managing a rundown apartment house he owned. City records we found indeed showed that the city had demanded many repairs on the structure. Maietta's mother described the place as a flea trap. Money control doesn't seem to have been an issue in this relationship because he led her to believe there was no money. On a visit to the Chaneys' home, John took money from a drawer, and Maietta questioned him about it. He told her he would leave a note, that the family had an arrangement. She now believes that the money was John's but he didn't want her to know it. She paid her own living expenses and received welfare. John never gave her any money.

He asked Maietta to marry him but always introduced her as his girl-friend. John told her he didn't like the word *fiancée*. He didn't explain why he didn't like the word. Although there was never any money, John drove a new black Corvette, which Maietta totaled on a visit to Connecticut. John later bought a blue Corvette, which he reported stolen. On a later trip to Connecticut, Maietta was surprised to see the blue Corvette in the garage. When she asked about it, he said that only the tires had been stolen. John told her he did not drive the Corvette except during the warmer months because the salt on the roads was hard on the body.

In a question about observing violent tendencies in John, she said she had noticed a scar on John's back that he claimed was from Vietnam. If he should ever become violent in his sleep and strike her, he said, she should wake him immediately. Maietta said that John experienced many bad dreams in which he was being hurt.

He mentioned his marriage to Janice only a few times. He told Maietta that they were married very young and that it was over before it really began. The marriage had been annulled, he said.

At some point during their relationship, John was offered a job through a temporary employment agency at Textron, Lycombing, in Connecticut. Later, Textron hired him full time. John would make frequent trips back to Ohio to do maintenance and repairs on the rundown apartment building, and Maietta made several trips to Connecticut for weekend visits to John. During Maietta's last visit, she discovered women's clothing in the house. When she confronted John, he said that if it bothered her, she should throw it out. That was it for her. Fortunately, she became friends with one of the tenants in the building she managed. As she became ill and continued to lose weight, this man notified her mother, who came to get her. Maietta moved back home with her in the fall of 1984 and resumed her life without John. Maietta says she will never forgive him for the hurt he has caused her and hopes she never sees him again.

By getting a license plate number through a neighbor living across the street from John's Milford beach house, we learned that at least one of his tenants had been a woman. The man who drove the car had picked up a woman at the house on several occasions. Dedy traced this man through the plate number, and it came back to a woman. She had never been to the beach house, but she said her son borrowed her car on occasion. The son supplied the name of his regular passenger, and we reported this information to Mike.

John had told Dedy he kicked the woman out after he realized she used IV drugs and that she had broken every rule of sharing a house. When Dedy asked what he meant, he said she ate food that wasn't hers.

When we traced her in December 1993, we were surprised to find out she was awaiting sentencing and was on her way to prison. She had been convicted of repeated charges of prostitution and drug use. We felt she would talk to family more openly than to the police, especially given her circumstances, and would perhaps volunteer information. That theory didn't hold true; Dedy couldn't get a return phone call. Instead, Mike interviewed her. This woman was also named Janice. We refer to her as "Janice II."

She told Mike her story over the phone while in prison. Janice II said she was five-foot-five and about 110 pounds with blond hair. John picked her up one evening, they had straight sex that night, and thereafter John appeared every night. He started to try to get her to move in with him. She lived with John on a now-and-then basis from August through October 1992. She told Mike he was never physically abusive toward her. "In fact, he treated me pretty good," she said. Janice II had a drug habit, and John would drive her to meet her suppliers and give her the money to purchase the drugs. He'd remain in the car, asking only how much money she needed, which might be anywhere from fifty to three hundred dollars. She said it didn't bother John to go into these bad areas of town.

Although the relationship appears to have been very one-sided, she said John didn't ask for sexual favors. They had sex only two times: the night he picked her up and again two months later. "He said he loved me," Janice II told Mike. John told her of his two marriages. He said Janice had been involved in drugs and was the victim of a hit. He said the FBI had told him Janice was dead but that they couldn't release her body. This was one of only two times he spoke of Janice. John spoke of Fran often. If she and John were together for an entire week, she estimated he brought up Fran maybe five times. John told her they were now divorced.

Janice II thought his behavior was compulsive. She said he stayed busy cleaning the house and washing his car. But it was John's bizarre stories that appear to have driven her away from her easy mark. "He was scaring me," she said. "He was strange. One time, he came home with his wedding band on. When I asked why, he said, 'I was told by my bosses to wear it. They don't want the people at work to know I'm divorced.' When I went after him, he'd change his story." Janice II said John's stories would become more outlandish and he would become frustrated.

John systematically ridded the house of everything Janice II had brought with her, such as clothes and makeup. Soon she had only the things John provided or bought for her. She wore only what he supplied, and he picked out what she would wear. She thought at times she was losing her mind. She'd remember entering the beach house with her things, then either go upstairs or out of the room and return to find the items gone. Everything she owned before meeting John was disappearing.

John picked clothing and lingerie from garbage bags he kept in the attic. Janice II's clothing story makes me think of my visit to the condo in February 1992, when John insisted on discussing his sex life with Fran unsolicited and talked about the lingerie she would wear. "Fran liked to dress up for sex. Half the fun was the effect of undressing," he said at the time. Janice II said John would get defensive about the attic at the beach house. One night he came home and said, "Someone's been in the attic. I can tell by the footprints on the chair." She denied being in the attic but told Mike she'd looked up there. "There were lots of women's clothes up there," she said. "Lots." She said he was sneaky when he went up to the attic. She never knew why. Add the clothing to the wedding band and the missing belongings, and one can certainly understand why she got spooked.

While she lived with John, there were two other tenants at the house. One, a guy named Dave, I knew about because of the conversation I had with John when I needed to get items for Noreen. The other was a man from Detroit named Davis. To her knowledge, John never told him to stay out of the attic. As far as she knew, Davis continued to live at the house after she left.

John was always trying to get her to go away on business with him.

She was uncomfortable with the relationship and refused to accompany him. She did, however, go to Ohio to visit the family. Even though she was not in touch with her family, she faked a call to her mother. She wanted a telephone number where she could be reached while they were away. John gave a long song and dance about not being able to reach his family and no one was answering when, at her insistence, he called to let his family know that she would be coming with him. Imagine her surprise when they reached his parents' house and she found that there were many phones. In fact, everyone had a car phone and beepers. John introduced Janice II to Grace, Sam, Michael, Steve, and even the Chaneys, who were the only people who seemed genuinely happy to see him. She said the nuclear family didn't appear to be close at all. There was no display of affection on their arrival. Grace was businesslike and cold and sent them upstairs. "Get up for breakfast," she added. Janice II said being hospitable was a strain for Grace. Grace wasn't happy that John was involved with another woman and said she couldn't stand John's wife. Grace never mentioned Janice but called Fran a whore. Fran and Grace had never met.

Janice II described John as getting upset when she wanted to return to her own apartment. But he wasn't upset that she had another boyfriend. Janice II doesn't apologize for using John or his money. She says he was aware of her feelings and still wanted her to be with him.

Of Fran, John said she was in constant contact with his attorney and at times called John at his office. He said he spoke to Fran's family often and sent money to her children. The part of speaking to us was of course true, but John didn't send money to Fran's family. The only time he sent money was when he owed Granny for charges to local merchants he had accumulated on her accounts in Florida. My Aunt Betty called to tell him to pay back the money. Only after Aunt Betty got nasty with him did he send Granny the money he owed her.

While he has never sent money to Fran's children, John spent lavishly on Janice II and gave her the impression of great wealth. She was amazed that he would give her anything she wanted and that she didn't have to do anything. This was the only reason she could find that would make her believe John was gay. "He had the money to buy my drugs. Our relationship was based on his ability to provide money. He went to work, and I stayed home and got high." Janice II was sure John was wealthy. He told her about his plans to purchase an island for $1 million. John told her he had had the money at one time, but no longer.

As is the case with all the women in John's past, Janice II doesn't want John to know where she is. These women are all either scared of him or too hurt to desire further contact. The scariest thing about these relationships is that they exemplify not just John's reckless disregard for women but his obsessive quest to somehow mask his own perceived shortcomings—or his dysfunctional relationship with his mother—through tightly scripted dramas in which he controls all the characters. Under this scenario women are less than playthings; they're robots expected to perform for his gratification. Our family and the Hartmans feel we lost our sisters because they didn't get away from John fast enough the way Sandy, Maietta, and Janice II did. We are so grateful that these women escaped with their lives.

Interestingly, John's program of control depended on traditional domestic roles. He enjoyed sex immensely, but that wasn't where he derived his power. Finances and status symbols like cars and houses were how he defined himself, and the women who would be attracted to him because of those spoils were exactly the kind of women he wanted to lure. Janice II, who stayed at home all day (admittedly getting high) while John went to work and earned a paycheck, probably represented the ideal power balance for him. He needed to feel women were completely dependent on him and his generosity.

While he seems to be attracted to women with strong personalities, he becomes frustrated when they assert themselves. When John's parents divorced, Grace made John the man of the family, but nine years later she married Sam Malz. This caused problems between Sam and John. Sam was a strong man, and he was determined to be the head of his household. Perhaps John felt that Grace abandoned him in favor of Sam. Time and again, in assessing John's relationships, we see him asserting control over a mother figure and "conquering" her to reclaim his status as the head of the family.

The case was still up in the air, and we were biding our time on a Tinkers Creek search, but there was some comfort in understanding why John behaved the way he did. More disturbing was our discovery that rarely would John go without a female companion. His self-image required being with a woman and inevitably involved playing out his control-and-conquer scenario. That meant the possibility of many more women than we might have thought who had been at risk while with John, and ongoing risk to any woman who accompanied him now, for as long as he went free. Short of a conviction, protecting other women became our goal. If we couldn't have John, then no one would.

CHAPTER 19
Finally, Tinkers Creek

In April 1993, Mike and Brian made plans to contact the other five police jurisdictions needed to conduct a search of Tinkers Creek State Park as soon as the weather permitted. Waiting was so hard. We knew better than to hang all of our hopes on a successful search, but it was difficult not to. Without something conclusive there, we would have followed even the psychic leads, already a bit of a stretch, to what was most likely a dead end. Doctors equate the psychological toll in a case like this to what soldiers in combat experience, and we had been immersed in it nonstop for eighteen months. I had taken a medical leave from work. My blood pressure was sky-high, and my nerves were taking a beating.

Writing my thoughts about the experience helped. I was able to channel some of my pent-up emotional energy into something useful and lasting, a memoriam to Fran. This has been the ordeal in which I've needed her most, and the one time when I haven't been able to rely on her. You reach a point where you can function, but the empty feeling in your core is always just a memory away. The truth of her death can't bring her back, but I believe it can shrink that hole. In response, on the positive side, I have reached out more to my husband and my daughters. I have come to know Dedy as an eminently capable and intelligent adult in her own right, and as a great friend. I have met Mike and Brian through their sacrifice and tireless work on our family's behalf, and we have become lifelong friends. And I have learned that surmounting small challenges seems effortless after you've faced the life-size ones.

We set a search date of May 29, 1993, the Saturday of Memorial Day weekend, for Tinkers Creek. Dave and I planned to leave home on Friday evening, spend the night in Ohio, and be ready to meet the team early the next morning. Tim Wilmoth, chief of police in Magadore, Ohio, and his wife, Kathy, had agreed to use their dogs Doc and Diane. Brian would also be with us. Friday night, as we were packing to leave, I received news that my father's mother, Nan, had passed away on her eighty-eighth birthday. Dave and I had taken Thursday of that week off to go to New Albany, Indiana, to visit her in the hospital. At the time, Nan seemed to be improving. Getting the news that she was gone was a hard blow for me. I continued to lose treasured family and still felt like I wasn't yet prepared to grieve.

Brian had worked tirelessly to organize this search that I knew we could not call it off. After making sure my grandfather would be taken care of with family, Dave and I left for Ohio. We got in late and went straight to bed, but after the news of losing Nan I couldn't sleep.

We arrived at the park the next morning before anyone else. Tim, Kathy, and Brian arrived not long after. Tim and Kathy put the dogs to work. Doc and Diana worked so hard that day. They scent-searched the entire front half of the park with no strong scent hits. But by mid-afternoon, the weather had gotten warm, and Tim, Kathy, and the dogs were exhausted. In order for a search with dogs to work, they must be rested and cool enough to breathe through their noses. Once they begin to pant, the search is off. Tim and Kathy graciously offered to return the next day to continue the search, and though we appreciated the offer, we decided to leave because of the funeral arrangements for Nan. As a waterfowl preserve, Tinkers Creek tends to be wet anyway, and spring wasn't cooperative in our search plans. It rained there almost daily through spring and summer. We couldn't get to the back of the park to continue our search. Because of the time lapse and decomposition of tissue, we knew that in May, we were already on the outside edge of the window for the dogs to find anything, even if Fran's remains were in the park. By the time the area was searchable, it was too late. A second search was moot.

It was time to reassess. We would continue to run down and check out any lead, but our success now likely depended on someone whom we hadn't found yet coming forward, either through the media, law enforcement, or John's social circle. We were worried, but weren't yet prepared to accept, that he could get away with murder.

CHAPTER 20
The Widower's Third

More than five years later, on July 30, 1998, Mike called to report that the FBI's Cold Case Homicide Division would take a look at our case. Special Agent Bob Hilland had been an officer with the West Windsor Township Police Department early in the investigation, and he hadn't forgotten about Fran when he became an FBI agent. He visited the West Windsor police station while in New Jersey for another case and learned there was nothing new on Fran. Agent Hilland said he might now be able to help, for he was assigned to the Cold Case Homicide Division. He took the files back to the New York office and presented the case to his director, who allowed him to open a federal case file.

One shouldn't be misled by the large gap between our coverage of Tinkers Creek and the opening of Fran's case on the federal level. Rarely did a day go by when someone from the team wasn't working on the case. It might have been a phone call, a letter, or an interview. At times when we had nothing new to pursue, we would review the case files and go over old evidence. All of this didn't translate into any breakthroughs. However, it's important to remember that hitting a dead end in any investigation is not a complete failure. Once you have resolved a particular issue, you can close that door to further examination. At those times, I would accept the physical toll the investigation had taken on me and remind myself it ain't over 'til the fat lady sings.

In October 1996, Dedy purchased a memorial marker for her mother to be placed at the family plot in Valparaiso, Florida. We held a short graveside service and dedicated the marker, anticipating that this could provide the resolution we hadn't received through the justice system or in our own minds. We were wrong. I got no feeling of peace from this empty site—just a stronger determination to find Fran's body and claim the true closure that a proper resting place would bring.

That November, Dedy and I had taken the psychologically difficult step of declaring Fran legally dead. We needed to settle Mama's and other relatives' estates, and we needed to formally face a hard truth. Mike provided testimony, so Dedy and I did not have to appear before the judge to get the declaration of death issued. On January 3, 1997, the judge ordered that it was the court's opinion that Fran should be declared dead as of September 28,1991. Having the court reinforce our own long-held beliefs created a sense of finality. I should have been prepared for the document to arrive, but I remember feeling lost when it came in the mail at work. I read the words in black and white and could not sit still. I went out to walk the parking lot for a long time, just as I had when I heard I wouldn't make it down to Niceville to be with Mama as she died.

So even if the case hadn't progressed discernibly in the intervening five years, we had traveled a difficult spiritual and emotional road. That would continue when the FBI opened its own case. The Bureau doesn't work like the small police and sheriff's departments we were used to. The FBI asks a lot of questions, and while they expect answers, they do not dispense them to family members. From the outset, agents told us that as a family we would have to bow out and let them conduct their own investigation. By this time Dedy and I were both physically and emotionally exhausted. We agreed to the Bureau's demands and prayed they would find something we had missed.

We still called Mike and Brian regularly and spoke with Agent Hilland often, but we were not given any clear vision of where the investigation was headed. The only hints we got about what they might be working on were questions they asked during periodic phone calls. Dedy and I would then call each other and see whether we could get a handle on what the FBI was doing. We were only guessing, but we found our imaginations were similar.

Before the FBI took over the case, we had continued to keep tabs on John and make sure that if he could walk as a free man, he at least wouldn't walk comfortably. During those five years, we traced him from New Jersey to Connecticut to New Hampshire, and then to Ohio. Wherever he went, managers and landlords seemed to discover quickly the storm that was swirling around him, and his tenure at jobs became ever more brief. His earnings and high-rolling lifestyle suffered. But once he left Ohio, we lost him. None of the standard sources could turn him up. I understand it took the FBI nearly three months to find him in California. We didn't know what town; perhaps they did. We took some solace in the fact that he was at least being watched again.

Major news outlets remained interested in the cases, but there wasn't much new to tell, and the fact that John still hadn't been charged with anything left us in limbo at times. *America's Most Wanted* contacted us about doing a segment. The problem with that format was that we knew where John was. They couldn't do anything unless he went on the run. At that point, they could only air a segment on the case stating that John was wanted for questioning. Dedy and I still vowed to do any show and talk to any reporter to help keep the case alive and get Fran's and Janice's pictures out there one more time. The right call with new information would come.

In April 1999 we got one right call. The FBI had briefed John Miller of ABC's *20/20 Downtown* on our case, and he became fascinated by its scope and length and by the dedication of those involved. The show's producers asked whether we would be willing to do an interview with ABC. In May, Dedy flew to Indianapolis for the taping of the show.

John Miller, producer Terri Lichstein, and the entire taping crew were wonderful. I had watched many of John's interviews. I was a little nervous, but I shouldn't have been. They made us feel so at ease. John filled in the pre-taping setup time with humorous stories from the many stories he'd covered. One of the questions the people of *20/20 Downtown* asked me: Did I ever feel like Angela Lansbury playing Jessica Fletcher on the TV series *Murder, She Wrote*? There is a temptation to romanticize an investigation with fantasies of cozily solving a crime by dusting for prints on a museum's painting or pulling chewing gum out of a street-side trash can. My answer for them was that *Murder, She Wrote* is fiction, and this was real life. Real life is messy and much less glamorous. The emotions are real, the outcome is uncertain, and the consequences are permanent. I reminded the interviewers that for most people, guaranteeing the security of family members is a basic need, like food and shelter. Any police officer's spouse will tell you that without that guarantee, it's difficult to focus on higher-order goals. As you go to bed tonight, I said, ask yourselves one question: Can I put my finger on every one of my family members, within a few minutes and a few phone calls, to make sure they are all right? If you can answer *yes*, you and your family enjoy a luxury that my family has not for almost eight years.

We are all, however, equally endowed with this moment, and only this moment, in time to let the ones we love know how important they are to us. No other time is guaranteed.

In the course of taping the *20/20 Downtown* segment, we learned that John had married again, on September 5, 1998. The courtship had been short, and his methods hadn't changed. He didn't meet this woman at work, but he did meet her *through* his work. The company Diane worked for supplied parts to John's company. John Miller asked Dedy and me what message we would send to Diane Bertalan, the new Mrs. Smith. We responded in unison: "Run. Run as fast as you can. Do not look back. Just run."

ABC took their time putting the piece together. John Miller and Terri Lichstein went to California to interview John. He ran, but they did get some footage of him outside LaForza and Monster Motors, a specialty automobile manufacturer he now worked for in Escondido, north of San Diego. ABC also interviewed associates and acquaintances there.

At the same time ABC was putting its show together, on May 5, 1999, the FBI pulled John in for questioning. They set up in a motel room plastered with pictures and evidence from the case. After several hours, he curled up in the fetal position and began to cry. "I want to tell the truth. My life is in shambles, but I am afraid," he said, then faked a heart attack. The agents involved knew it was a fake attack, but they could do little more than call an ambulance to transport John to the hospital.

Agent Hilland called me to say that John was in a delicate state and the agents in on the questioning felt he could commit sucide that night. "I don't believe that for a minute," I told him. "John's too narcissistic to commit suicide. You watch. He'll be back at work tomorrow morning." I called him that next morning just to prove a point and heard John's perky voice on the other end of the line. He hired an attorney again that day, so the interviews with him ended.

The FBI also interviewed Diane. They laid everything out on a table for her and told her exactly what kind of monster she had married. She stuck by John. When we heard Diane's reaction, Dedy issued a challenge to her in the *20/20 Downtown* segment: "You show us your John Smith, and we'll show you ours." We felt she was in grave danger, but there was little we could do. At least she was aware of the danger, an advantage Fran and Janice had not had. We still worried. While ABC was taping our segment, Dedy had a brainstorm. She wrote out a note to Diane telling her how to reach us and offering to answer her questions, and she asked that producer Terri Lichstein deliver it to Diane when they interviewed her (take that, Jessica Fletcher!). Diane refused to talk to them for the show, so Terri overnighted the note to ABC's affiliate in San Diego, and someone there hand-delivered it to Diane's office. We felt she could end up in even more danger than she already was if we were to contact her directly.

———————

The FBI's involvement and corresponding increased media interest had an interesting effect. Suddenly the case moved to the top of some law enforcement agencies' priority lists that were looking for a little taste of the spotlight. From May 26 through May 28, the FBI, West Windsor Township Police, and the Wayne County and Medina County Sheriff's Departments conducted a dig at an apartment complex in Seville that John's stepfather had constructed. They hoped to find Janice's remains. Law enforcement didn't intend for it to be a political sideshow, but when crime-scene tape went up around the dig, it wasn't long before nearly everyone in the small town had converged on the complex. Television crews and newspaper reporters roved the site. We learned of the dig not from the authorities but from the press when they called us for comment.

The big news was this: A confidential source had told the FBI about a wooden box that was supposed to contain Janice's body, and this same source speculated that John might have gotten rid of it here when the apartments were being built. Dave and I high-tailed it to Seville on the 28th, but by the time we arrived, the search team was preparing to leave. They had found nothing. Still, authorities had brought in a body-recovery dog and gotten a good hit. (The publicity hounds were also making good headway. One sheriff's department had brought in a motor home with a large sign identifying which county it belonged to.) For three days, the crew dug up garage floors and sifted through the dirt. The dog had not been wrong; it located a molar that was later determined to be ancient. Another hit supposedly was an old sewer-line break and not the scent of a body.

After the dig failed to produce the expected box, sources say a rift developed between the Medina and Wayne County Sheriff's Departments, perhaps over who had been wrong in choosing to dig there but also over who was now going to pay for repairs to the site. I'll bet if they had recovered a body, those two departments would have been fighting each other over who was going to get to write that check.

I asked about the Hartmans and learned that they hadn't appeared at the site. I couldn't believe they wouldn't show. If it had been Fran they were looking for, we would have had pop, sandwiches, and snacks in coolers for the search team. Dave and I left the site and drove to the Hartmans' home to check on them, but they weren't home—or otherwise were hiding out from the press. Maybe Brian was right. Maybe it was just too hard for them. I left them a note and asked them to call, but I didn't hear back.

I also picked up a little dirt at the site: One of the Medina County Sheriff's detectives told me that Sam Malz had died. The EMTs that came to the house didn't think his symptoms at the time were consistent with his later cause of death. The sheriff's deputy only said that ol' Sam was unconscious when they left with him. He didn't know the cause of death, just that the EMTs thought something funny had gone on at the home. The detective said it was common knowledge Sam had been having health problems, but they weren't life threatening. And it seems John was the only one home with Sam when he became ill.

Our *20/20 Downtown* segment aired the third week of October 1999 and came off very well. The final edit did a great job of fairly covering the main points in the case in limited time and telling an exciting story without overhyping it. On October 7, Diane called me in response to the note Dedy had sent through *20/20 Downtown*. Diane called me first because she said John had talked about me. I guess she wanted to find out whether I was really the person he had told her I was. Or, if her trust in John was wavering, maybe she figured the anti-John would give it to her straight. Right off the bat, Diane said that her marriage to John was one of convenience and that she didn't love him. Their marriage was built on his lies, but they both liked fast cars and doing a lot of the same things. He kept her from being lonely, she said, and being married to him (and its perceived dangers) was no big deal because he was never home anyway. John worked all the time. This established the pattern for many phone conversations and two visits with Diane.

One minute she came off as entirely rational; the next, she seemed off-balance. As time went on, Dedy and I saw that she was very confused and wanted to believe what John told her, but the specter of two missing wives was starting to sink in. She would tell us that he lied to her all time, yet she didn't trust the authorities when they laid out all of their evidence in front of her. I ended our first conversation feeling that this woman was probably living better right now than she had ever lived before. If she accepted what the FBI was telling her, she would be forced to leave. I also intuited that Diane had never been without a man to take care of her emotionally and financially. She would fit into John's control program perfectly, or nearly. I tried to sway her with facts and make her see what a perilous situation she was in. *What is worth more than your life?* I wanted to say. In every conversation, she found reasons to doubt what was before her.

She did tell us immediately that she believed John had killed both Fran and Janice, but for some reason she didn't think she was in danger. "With all this stuff going on around John, he can't afford for anything to happen to me," she said, adopting the same rationale I had used in the past to get to sleep, except that I wasn't the one who had to climb into bed with him. Diane was determined to stay with him but also relieved to have someone besides John to talk to about the conflicting information flying at her from all directions. She said she planned to stay with him but would try to help us as much as she could. We again pleaded with her not to take any chances and to just leave. When Diane refused, we told her we would appreciate any help she might provide.

Diane told us a lot about what her life with John was like. For the first time, it was as if we had real-time insight into John's behavior around romantic partners and could do something about it while it was still happening. (Fran and I shared a lot, but in hindsight I think she screened out much of her troubles with John to avoid embarrassment and spare me worrying about her.) Actually, Diane told us much more than we wanted to know. We heard her suspicions that John was frequenting prostitutes when he was under stress, and that when she could prove this, she intended to leave him. Dedy and I couldn't believe that she was more concerned with his using prostitutes than she was with the fact that two women were dead. She told us that in May, when all this was thrust on her, she had decided to leave John—not because of the two missing wives but because she found out he had continued a relationship with a woman from when he lived in New Hampshire. He bought Diane a Ferrari and begged her to stay. She did.

Diane also said something strange—she said she found no reason to believe John was a pedophile. The only reason we could think of for that statement was that the FBI had told her the story about John trying to get Janice's little sister, Dee, to touch his privates twenty-five years prior. Diane continued, "Besides, that was a long time ago, and people did strange things back then. I would not like anyone to dig too deeply into my past." She also said she had revealed to John at the beginning of their relationship that she really liked sex. When he was upset with her, he would withhold sex and masturbate in the shower instead. Dedy asked her how she knew this. "I don't know if you know it or not," Diane responded, "but John is very well-endowed down there. I can tell by looking at him when he has been masturbating in the shower."

During another phone conversation with Dedy, Diane said that on her first few dates with John, she had asked him whether he had ever been married before. "Yes, I guess I am a widower," he said. On other occasions when she asked about his past, he would just tell her she was nosy. He did finally invent that Fran had died of cancer and that he had nursed her to the end. He told her that I had come and picked up all of Fran's things. When they decided to marry, John told Diane that he wanted to use the wedding band he had worn while he and Fran were married. He carried it around in his pocket. Diane thought this was sweet and agreed but asked that she be allowed to inscribe their wedding date on the inside of the band. John consented. Diane also said John had a very large picture of Fran that he asked to hang in their home and that she agreed to it. John hung the picture directly above the television so that every time Diane turned on the television she was forced to look at Fran. After about six months, she told him it had to go.

John shipped a motorcycle trailer out to California that he kept outside one of the LaForza warehouses, and Diane assumed he had put Fran's picture in that. We asked what else was in the trailer. Diane said that it contained one box of John's personal things and some car parts. His other boxes were in her storage unit. She began to go through the boxes in the storage unit and copy and fax documents to Dedy and me. Most contained only financial information. Dedy and I soon realized that Diane wanted us to help her track money that John had invested. I found it odd that there was any money to track. As far as we knew, John had been unemployed or had very little income before he left Ohio. Diane said that he had worked for his mother and had tried to help her sort out his stepfather's estate after he passed away. She also told us that John and his brother, Michael, spoke often, but that no one spoke to Steve. There was a big fight going on within the family. Steve was supposed to have stolen a lot of money from the estate. Diane also knew that John sent his mother money every month. This seemed odd to Dedy and me because Diane had told us that John was suing his mother for unpaid wages, and in the documents that Diane sent, we found that John had filed a mechanic's lien on the house that Grace had shared with Sam. Diane also told us that John had invested heavily in LaForza. At the time, she was telling us how tight things were financially for them, that she controlled all the money and credit cards. We would ask where she thought John was getting the money for an expensive sports car, large investments, and the frequent use of hookers. Diane would change the subject.

We begged her to talk to the FBI or other authorities as she was talking to us. Diane refused, stating that she could not trust them because they had lied to her. She told of three days in July of 1999 when John disappeared. Someone who identified himself as Special Agent Bob Hilland was supposed to have called a friend and told the friend that the FBI had John, and that he would not be at work for a few days. Diane said she called the FBI and was told that they did not have John. Diane felt the FBI had lied to her because when John called her after three days to pick him up, "He looked like shit, had not showered or shaved. He stank. He had not even brushed his teeth, which he does after every meal." I told Diane I did not believe John, and that I felt certain that if the FBI had taken John, she would have been the one to receive a call, not a friend. I asked whether she was basing her distrust on what she actually knew of the FBI or what John had told her. She had been the one who told us her marriage was all based on John's lies.

After we had exchanged information for about a week and our efforts at persuasion were going nowhere, Diane asked whether we knew about "the box." We did not and asked, "What box?" She changed the subject. Diane would tell us many versions of stories John had told her about the box. She said that Michael had called John in July and told him that the authorities knew about the box and he would not go to jail for John. Diane later called Michael to find out what this was all about, and he told her that the family had found a box in his grandfather's garage in 1979 and that when they saw what was inside it, they called John, and he came and took it away. She then questioned John about Michael's explanation, and John told her that the people he worked with at the time had played a terrible joke on him. The box contained the remains of a goat. When the family called, he borrowed a friend's car, picked up the box, and threw it into a field. Then the elements and coyotes had done whatever. Diane tried to verify this story with Michael.

"Diane, I saw what was in that box, and it was no goat," he said. "It was human. You have to get out of there." With that warning, Michael ended the call.

Diane sounded unconvinced of that in our conversation. Of the box, she said, "I don't think you will ever find anything."

Michael told Diane and John that the grand jury was to meet to obtain an indictment for John's arrest. He gave them the date that the grand jury would convene, and the two of them didn't go to work that day because John didn't want to be arrested at work. Late that day, John's attorney, a Mr. McCabe, called them to check in because he had heard they had made a suicide pact. Diane told him that this was not true, but McCabe wouldn't tell her who had given him this information.

As we heard these stories from Diane, Dedy and I were compiling notes of our talks and faxing them to about six different law enforcement agencies along with the documents Diane was faxing to us. When Dedy and I asked Brian Potts about the box, he said that, in his opinion, Michael wasn't credible and that it was his account of the box that had led to the search of the apartment complex in Seville. I contended that it did not matter whether they believed Michael—John believed Michael. Why else would John have been afraid to go to work and be arrested there? Brian made no comment.

In one of our many phone calls, Diane also told Dedy about a knife that the authorities had. We had heard nothing about a knife. Diane said John seemed to be much more worried about the knife than the box. We called Mike Dansbury for corroboration of this, and he said that when John had sold the house in Connecticut, the new owner had found a knife under the insulation in the attic. They had done forensic tests on the knife but could not at this time use it to further build our case. The knife had been exposed to the elements for too long.

We exchanged all of this information with Diane in just over two weeks. Dedy had a business meeting in Palm Springs toward the end of

October, and she arranged to meet Diane face to face to sort out some of these stories and to try to get more information. We also believed that by meeting her in person, Dedy might gain her trust more and get her to see the wisdom in leaving and being more forthcoming with the secrets she knew about John. Diane felt better about meeting Dedy in Palm Springs than she did about having Dedy show up at their home in Oceanside, and Dedy agreed. After everything that had transpired, Dedy wasn't going to take any chances, even with Diane. Dedy hired a private detective firm to monitor John during the October 23 meeting and also to stay nearby but out of sight while Dedy and Diane were together. This certainly made me feel better about the idea. (Even though Dedy agreed to the meeting in Palm Springs, she drove to Escondido and Oceanside as soon as Diane left so she could get pictures of LaForza and John and Diane's condo. She then copied these and sent them to Mike, Brian, and me.) Diane brought a lot of paperwork with her for Dedy to copy and send to the authorities. Most of this meeting was Diane telling Dedy stories that John had told her and then Dedy correcting her with the true facts.

Diane had first heard from John that both of his wives disappeared while he was at work, that he and Janice were trying to get back together, and that she was living with him. Later, he would tell Diane that *the weekend* Fran disappeared, he had been in Connecticut and that Sheila could confirm his story. He also told her that the first he knew about Janice's disappearance was when the police arrived at his door to ask him where she was. Dedy promptly dispelled many of these myths: that Janice and John were not living together when she disappeared; and that John was the one in both cases who had filed the missing-persons report. For the second or third time, we told her to get copies of both missing-persons reports, compare them, and to pay close attention to who had filed the reports and how similar the reports were in content.

We tried so hard to get this woman to reason out why these facts didn't gibe with what John was telling her, but most of that pleading fell on deaf ears. We can't say for sure what Diane was like before she met

John, but no doubt much of the confusing and conflicted behavior she displayed can be accounted for by living with John. It's probably the same sort of self-doubt Janice II would have developed had she stuck around the beach house for another year after she realized she was losing her mind there.

Also at their meeting, Diane told Dedy that John had paid $38,000 for the Ferrari.

Again Dedy asked, "If money is so tight, and you control all the money, where did John get the money for this car?"

Diane said that when John sued his mother for unpaid wages, he received $113,000. He had used that to buy into LaForza and to buy the car.

Dedy in turn related what I had told her about John being with Sam at home when he became ill, which cast suspicion on John's motives and his actions before the ambulance came. Diane responded with the story John had told her. He said that Sam was on his deathbed, and John was alone with him saying his goodbyes. Sam revealed that his entire estate would go to Grace, and when John left the room, he told Steve what Sam had said. Steve was angry but went into Sam's bedroom to say goodbye. In John's version, Steve was the last to be with Sam in the house before he died.

CHAPTER

Inside the Family

Through the producers at *20/20 Downtown*, I learned that Steve was working for a car dealership right in Indianapolis. The mixed messages I had heard from all corners of the Smith/Malz clan made me determined to separate the spin from the truth, or what passed for it with them. My understanding of the family came from John's invented stories, the interviews with his past lovers and associates, the Hartmans, public records, what the police had collected and shared with us, and limited interviews they had conducted with the family in April 1992. I thought Steve could offer an underrepresented point of view—inside the family but outside the Grace-John-Chaney triangle that we just didn't think we could trust.

I decided to call on Steve. I showed up at the BMW dealership unannounced and asked to see him. I already knew whom I would be talking to because when I walked by the window of one office I noticed a young man visibly pale when he saw me. Steve came out of his office to meet me, and we shook hands. He was very friendly. "I saw you on TV," he said. I asked if he was comfortable talking at his place of business, or if he would like to meet at some other time and place. I wanted him to know that we were going to talk one way or the other, but I would let him choose when and where. Steve said that this was fine and invited me into his office. He said that his coworkers and the management there had no idea about any of this and "thank God I have a different last name." He also recognized me as the lady sitting in front of his house taking pictures in Ohio when the first story broke in the press there. I told him I was just trying to get a feel for what John's life prior to Fran had been like.

No apology needed, he said. I told him I really wasn't offering one. He just smiled.

I told Steve the story John had given of his father's death and what the Medina County detective had told us at the apartment dig in Seville. Steve just shook his head and said, "I'll tell you what actually happened." His eyes brimmed up with tears, and he excused himself briefly but remained seated.

Steve said the day his father got sick at home, he was outside mowing the lawn. John had been playing head games for days about how ill Sam was, so when John came outside and told him that he should go inside and check on his father, Steve didn't pay much attention to him. He continued to work. He then reconsidered and went inside to see how his dad was. Just as he started into the house, the EMTs arrived. Sam was unconscious but alive, and Steve couldn't stand to see his father that way, so he again went outside. Steve said that Grace wasn't home when all this took place and that John had been in the house alone with Sam.

I asked him whether he was satisfied with the cause of death on the death certificate.

Steve said that he was not interested in bringing his father up for an autopsy, which was not done at the time of death. He said that wouldn't get him what he needed—to bring his father back. Around this time Dedy was beginning to investigate ways to have Sam exhumed for an autopsy. After Steve and I talked, Dedy called him to see if he would sign a consent form to have Sam exhumed. It just seemed too convenient that

Sam would die so suddenly. Steve at first agreed but later waffled, even knowing that Dedy would pay for all the expense of having it done. While he seemed to think that John might have done something to the one person he said he loved, he would not help Dedy do it.

Steve said he received nothing from his father's estate and was visibly bitter over this. His father had spent many years building up a business that he thought his son would inherit. Steve had spent his youth and short adulthood learning the business.

He said that he knew there was at least $400,000 that John had stolen from his mother. Grace put on a big show of grief when Sam died; a few weeks later she received approximately $255,000 in insurance, and the grieving stopped. Steve also said there was at least $173,000 in a safe in the basement of the home that was missing.

"Why would there be so much money in the house in cash?" I asked.

Steve looked at me, winked, and said, "My dad was a very good businessman."

I asked why he had not fought for what he felt was rightfully his. He said he had become very depressed. His father had always been his best friend as well as his mentor. Steve felt that when his father passed away, he lost the only person who truly cared about and loved him. Grace had let John take over all the settlement of the estate, and by the time Steve came out of his depression, the entire estate was gone. He said a will had disappeared, and in its place John used one that Sam had made when Steve was just a small child. That old will gave everything to Grace.

He felt his father would be very unhappy with the way things had worked out, that his only biological son who had worked the business ended up with nothing and was forced to work for someone else instead of for himself. He also said that now Grace had nothing—John had stolen it all.

I was surprised because I had thought, from all accounts of Grace's professional life, she had been an astute businesswoman. Steve laughed at this comment. He said image was everything to Grace, and like John she was prone to exaggerate and lie. I was again surprised and said I thought she was a pretty together woman, and very intelligent. He restated that she too was a liar and that she was not all that smart because she could not keep her lies straight. He said he would describe her as a good actress but not a smart one.

I brought up John's passing himself off as an engineer. Steve believes that this is because Sam was an engineer. To obtain Grace's approval, it was important for John to also be an engineer. Steve said that John spent a lot of time studying Sam's engineering books and spent time trying to learn all he could from Sam. Steve felt that John probably had the knowledge to pull off the appearance of being an engineer, if not the degree. We both agreed that John is very intelligent.

Steve didn't spend a lot of time around John growing up—he was much younger, and Sam kept him away from John—but at one point in our interview, he said, "I think I have a pretty good take on John's personality. It's like this," and he pulled out a pen and paper and drew a rough football field shape. Imagine that most people live their lives between the forty- and fifty-yard lines, he said. This represents what we think of as normal behavior. This is the image that John wants the world to see: the perfect husband with the perfect wife and family, status, success, etc. Because John wants to achieve and put this image forward to the public, he continued, this image is built on the lies he tells to sell the package. Between the thirty- and forty-yard lines is just a little left and right of normal behavior. In that zone, it's okay to steal a little and be dishonest in your daily dealings with the public and people you're supposed to love.

When John gets caught, and his lies and perfect life are found to be a fabrication, he is forced to move down between the thirty-yard line and the end zone. At that point, John scraps his perfect life to stamp out unfavorable perceptions of him and starts over again with his core self image. He is then free to move on and rebuild his life between the forty- and fifty-yard lines.

Steve also offered his opinion that he didn't think Grace and John had a normal mother-son relationship. He didn't think it was sexual, but it certainly wasn't normal. John was both more equal and less equal than the average son—the golden boy or the pariah, depending on Grace's frame of mind at any given time.

I would have expected Steve to have had a better home life than John or Michael, since Sam had been his primary parent, but he called the place a "hellhole." I said John had described their family as dysfunctional, and he replied that there weren't enough ways to spell dysfunctional to describe his family.

"You know, if I had a wife and children, I would never want them anywhere around my family," he said. "I would not want them exposed to those people, not even for holidays. The holidays were always the worst. They always ended with a family fight of some kind."

He said that Sam and Grace were total opposites, but both very strong-willed people, and fought all the time. He did feel he was lucky that Sam had been his main caregiver. The rest of the family was nuts. He said that Sam hated John. It was sad: Steve always had his father, and John always had Grace. Poor Michael had only John. Michael, he said, had always done John's dirty work. He felt that Michael was the key to our mystery.

Steve referred to Janice as "Wife No. 1," Fran as "Wife No. 2," and Diane as "Wife No. 3." This was the only way he could deal with what his family is: He had to remove himself emotionally as much as possible. He went on to say that from an early age, he had heard that "Wife No. 1" was buried in Grandpa's garden.

Steve went on to say that because Michael had always done John's dirty work, he would know all the details. He said that Michael would want to do the right thing but would feel the need to still protect John. He said, Michael will make you think he's a total flake but will tell the truth. Because you think he's a flake, you don't give his story much credibility. In this way Michael can be truthful and still protect John.

Steve says he thinks that John did away with Fran's remains in Connecticut. He feels that way because he says he went to New York to buy a car, and when he came back through Connecticut, he was surprised to see that John had just poured a new garage floor and a new driveway. When he asked John about the improvements, John told him a storm had caused all the damage and he had done the repairs. "The next thing you know," he told Steve, "they'll think I put her under the garage floor." Despite what John had said, Steve felt Fran could be buried at sea, because John told him that the police had never considered that he had access to a boat. (John himself never owned a boat, and police couldn't determine whether he might have disposed of Fran's body in the ocean.) Steve said he thought Diane would also be buried at sea. He had little doubt that she would also be killed.

Steve said he almost threw up when he saw the *20/20 Downtown* segment where a reporter said John's grandmother was the only person he cared about. "If John cared so much about her, why didn't he come for her funeral?" Steve asked. He said that when he went to Ohio for the funeral, as they were lowering his grandmother into the ground, his mother had tried to pick a fight with him. When Grace found out she could not get to him, she became "the nice Mommy" and tried to get him to go to lunch with her. Steve told Grace that he had accomplished what he had come to do, that being to show final respects for his grandmother. With that done, he was out of there.

I left my visit with Steve feeling sad for this young man who had been raised with the best of everything and now didn't even have what his father had worked for. It was sad to see someone so young so bitter. But the visit was friendly, and Steve expressed regret that he couldn't help more. He said he didn't want to see John put to death for these murders, but he thought that John should be studied as a multiple killer.

Steve said he was willing to speak with the police again but asked that they not contact him at work. In the dealership's moneyed and image-conscious atmosphere, he didn't want anyone at work to know

what was going on in his family. "I need this job. It's all I have now,"
he said.

A few days later I called Steve to follow up. During this conversation he
said he thought we should look for Wife No.1 somewhere between their
home in Ohio and Chicago. This contradicted his earlier statement about
thinking as a small child that Wife No. 1 was in his grandfather's garden.
I asked him the date of his father's death, and he said it had been
December 29, 1994. I asked why he would have been mowing the lawn in
December. He replied that it had been a mild winter and the yard was
bothering his dad, so he decided to get the yard work done. Besides, he
added, if he were outside working in the yard, he wouldn't have to be
inside with John.

CHAPTER 22
The Missing Piece

Dedy and I flew out to California the first week of December in 1999 to appear on *Leeza*, Gibbons's talk show, another chance to get Fran's and Janice's pictures on the air. With the increased public focus on the case in the past year, we prayed that this time someone would come forward with new information as a result of the show. The producers called and wanted to know whether we could come out a day early and try to get John to talk with us. We agreed but doubted they'd get any footage of John. The off-site crew would pick us up at 4:00 A.M., go to LaForza in Escondido, and try to catch John when he came to work at 7:30, his usual arrival time. After tracking him for eight years through five states, I knew his habits and patterns as well as anybody—maybe even him.

We arrived in good time the next morning and set up near LaForza to surprise John with an interview. He came when expected, but we weren't hidden enough, and he took off. He drove by again a few times, went to a LaForza warehouse to change cars, and entered the complex through a back gate. Not realizing there was another way into the fenced lot, I stood out in front of the business for more than three and a half hours waiting

for him to show up. Finally I called the switchboard and asked the receptionist if I could speak to John Smith. "John, this is Sherrie," I began when
he answered—but before I could say anything else, he hung up. I wanted to tell him I'd send away the off-site crew and that we could talk one
on one. I wanted to let him know we were going to appear on *Leeza* and
that he could also go on to tell his side of the story. I never got the
chance. John has told many people that he hates me and Mike Dansbury
more than any other two people on earth. Mike says we are in good company, but the only reason I know that John would feel that way is that he
is guilty of Fran's murder. I'm intent on finding out what happened to my
sister, and if he had nothing to do with her death, then I pose no threat.

Any chance of getting John on tape for the show was a wash. We left
with the off-site crew and had lunch with them, but Dedy and I had bigger plans for that afternoon, and we needed to lose the film crew in order
to carry them out. We had arranged to meet with Diane to go through
John's things in her storage unit. She had drawn up a document stating
that the storage unit was rented in her name prior to her marriage to
John and that she was giving us permission to inspect items stored there.
Diane couldn't get away from work, so she arranged for her daughter,
Summer, to meet us and go with us. Summer opened the unit and gave
us a small suitcase and a briefcase to inspect and copy documents from.
A quick review of the suitcase and briefcase showed he didn't have much,
at least in Diane's unit. We've never been able to search the motorcycle
trailer, so we still don't know what was in it. Much of what we found was
financial records, bills, etc.—things Diane had faxed to us before the trip.

The suitcase also held a small batch of pictures. At first we thought
they were family pictures, but we found some of two women we didn't
recognize. One was of a woman standing beside an airplane with John.
The other woman seemed to be in a shopping mall. Both were young and
attractive and were not relatives, so far as we could tell. The pictures
were undated, but in investigating John, we learned he had at one time
held a pilot's license. He took his last pilot's physical in 1981. The chill-

ing significance of these photos is that the only other pictures with them in the suitcase were of the two women we already knew to be dead. There were many pictures of Fran and a few of Janice, but no one else—no snapshots, family portraits, or vacation photos. These pictures have haunted us.

The other discovery we made was an address for John in Indiana. Two documents had this address: one from an attorney and one a hospital bill from Hammond, Indiana, with postmarks from 1978 and 1979. We knew he had worked for two different businesses in Indiana through the temp agency Barnes and Reineke in Illinois, but we weren't sure exactly where he had lived. After copying everything, we returned to the storage unit, Summer put it all back in place, and we said our goodbyes. Then we drove to Diane's office to return the key and to thank her. She had really gone out on a limb to help us. John had gotten angry at the beach house when he even suspected that Janice II had been looking in the attic. I wondered what he might do if he ever learned that Diane had allowed anyone—worst of all me—to go through his private papers.

Traffic was terrible. It took us several hours to get back to Los Angeles. We had planned on a casual dinner, a nice bath, and an early bedtime. But the producer from *Leeza* called and said our appearing as guests could present legal problems. The show was about how families had helped police solve the murders of missing wives. In other guests' cases, suspects had been charged or convicted. Because John had never been charged, they were reluctant for us to tell our story on the air.

There was a loophole. If we could get someone to appear on the show to take John's side, we'd have a "balanced" account, and the show would be a go. Dedy and I began making phone calls to everyone we had ever interviewed in connection with the case. We spent fourteen hours on the phone trying to find someone to speak for John. We were calling people on the East Coast in the middle of the night. Surprisingly, not one person got angry we had called at that hour. Everyone we spoke to said that they would be glad to tell what they knew of John, but they didn't think it would help us because they had nothing good to say. Here was a man with forty-eight years invested in life, and no one would even pretend to say anything good about him. He'd been saved for once by his own ignominy.

We spent much of the night talking to the producers as well. Ultimately it would be up to us to persuade the legal department that we should be allowed to appear onstage as part of a panel. Dedy and I were ready for a throwdown. We had set aside the time and prepared to do the show for two weeks only to find out the evening before we were out of luck. When Dedy and I started talking about contacting our attorneys, we all reached a compromise: Leeza would come to us in the audience at the end of the show and briefly talk about our case. She would say only that Fran was missing and that her husband was the sole suspect. Because Garry Hartman wouldn't come to do the show, we couldn't mention that John's first wife was also missing or show a picture of Janice. They did show Fran's picture and ask that anyone with information contact the show. We don't know why the Hartmans declined to participate in even a live phone interview, but Dedy and I felt like we were bearing the weight of two cases single-handedly.

Although not entirely pleasurable, the California trip presented some exciting new possibilities, and a smattering of good news amidst a lot of frustration. *20/20 Downtown* was interested in doing a follow-up segment on the investigation. By doing *Leeza*, we had gotten Fran's picture out there one more time. We had another address to add to John's file, and Dedy and I started trying to get some coverage for our two mystery women as well as Fran and Janice.

Dedy resolved to do everything in her power to have Medina County exhume Sam Malz and perform an autopsy. She found a forensic pathologist that expressed an interest. Months later, after a lot of work on his part, we were disappointed to learn that Medina County would not, at that time, bring Sam up for the autopsy not performed at the time of his death.

Other legal disappointments followed. Dedy made a trip to New Jersey to meet with Agent Hilland, Mike Dansbury, and Mercer County First Deputy Assistant Prosecutor Kathryn Flicker. Ms. Flicker was sympathetic, but she was adamant that there wasn't enough evidence to charge John with Fran's murder. She said she was doubtful what she would do even if she *had* Fran's body. It felt like another dead end. Absent slam-dunk evidence like a confession, they wouldn't move forward. Dedy and I were starting to see how the power of public opinion influenced some authorities' actions more than duty or law did. Elections and political capital were what mattered. Dave reminded us that we shouldn't be too hard on prosecutors. They get one chance at success; if they lose and more evidence comes to light later, it's irrelevant.

Another blow came when the FBI pulled Agent Hilland from the case after almost two years of hard work. The FBI had spent a lot of time and money trying to build a case against John for the murder of both wives, but with Michael as a valuable source, they felt Janice's case was much stronger than Fran's. Wayne County Prosecutor Martin Frantz had Agent Hilland subpoenaed to appear in Wooster and give testimony before the grand jury. When he and Brian arrived, a secretary told them that Mr. Frantz had decided not to convene the grand jury. Since he had come all that way, Agent Hilland asked that he be allowed to submit all the FBI's accumulated evidence but was kept waiting for hours, and Mr. Frantz refused to even see them or to review what they had found. Assistant Prosecutor Jocelyn Stefancin proved to be aggressive in trying to move forward in Janice's case, but she needed support from above to do that. Without it, her hands were tied.

Brian was embarrassed by the way Agent Hilland had been treated at Mr. Frantz's office. After this fiasco, the FBI transferred him out of the Cold Case Division and let it be known through Mike and Brian that Dedy and I would be jeopardizing his career if we were to contact him. Agent

Hilland is young and has a family. We didn't want to do anything to hurt him, and he had worked too hard and had been too good to our family to cause him further grief. But we did want to know why Wayne County was backing off the case. Dedy refused to roll over and let that happen. Brian said he had been ordered not to discuss the case with us, so Dedy began a phone campaign, calling Wayne County Sheriff Tom Maurer every business day for more than a month. He wouldn't take or return her calls. Finally, we decided that I would go to Ohio and at least be ignored in person. We knew the press would enjoy that; let them ask Sheriff Maurer why he wouldn't talk to us. But Dedy suggested a different tack: We'd take our case to the top and call Martin Frantz. It worked, sort of. In a conference call with us, he explained that he hadn't convened a grand jury because he didn't believe the case against John was strong enough. He gave the case a 20 percent chance of conviction if they went to court then.

"How do you know this is a no-win case?" Dedy asked. "You refused to see Special Agent Bob Hilland to review all that the FBI had on the case."

We never got an answer to why he had been treated so badly, or why Mr. Frantz had not withdrawn the subpoena for the grand jury before Agent Hilland had made the trip from New York, especially if Mr. Frantz had no intention of even extending the courtesy of an explanation. In our opinion, this fiasco created anger at the Bureau over spending time and money to produce their agent for no reason. It would have been common courtesy for Mr. Frantz to let the FBI know that the grand jury had been called off. We are also certain this is the reason Agent Hilland was pulled off our case. Why spend the time and money to investigate something or someone when the local authorities have no intention of doing anything with the gathered information?

I should note that Mr. Frantz had not made a good impression on us so far. When we met with Brian, Mike, and Captain Eldridge in Wooster in March 1993, Mr. Frantz had talked freely to Sandy—the woman who had lived with John in the mid- '70s and agreed to answer our questions—during our interview with no regard for her anonymity. He used her last name several times referring to several of her relatives that he knew. We could only promise her that we'd forget we ever heard her name. In our phone call, Dedy and I reminded Mr. Frantz that we had met at that time, but he had no memory of it. Now we couldn't get any straight answers about Agent Hilland's mistreatment in the botched grand jury effort.

I asked how they could just let John walk around, knowing that he had remarried in California and could pose a threat to his new wife or any other woman he came in contact with.

"That's their problem," he said.

Dedy moved to clarify. We couldn't believe what we were hearing. "You mean to say that if this happens again, it's California's problem?"

"Yes."

That comment did nothing good for my blood pressure, I'm sure. I went through the roof. I had felt for a while that many of these elected officials were more concerned with their next photo op than with obtaining justice based on principles and good judgment. I called Mike Dansbury to vent. I needed my friend to listen. Always level-headed, he reminded me that if Ohio lost the case, John could never again be prosecuted for Janice's murder. He could walk out of the courtroom and freely admit to the crime, and there would be nothing anyone could do. John would leave the courthouse laughing at all our efforts to bring him to justice.

The only good news we got from Mr. Frantz was that the case had been turned over to the Ohio Bureau of Criminal Investigation, the equivalent of the FBI Cold Case Division for the state of Ohio. We asked what he thought the OBCI could do that the FBI, with more money and personnel, hadn't accomplished. Mr. Frantz never gave us an answer to this either. Dedy did call these people once, but no one else in the family ever talked to the OBCI.

We were seeing a lot of opportunities slip through our fingers, help-less to do anything about them. While Agent Hilland was in Ohio, he and Brian went to Medina County to persuade the authorities to look more closely at Sam Malz's death. Like Dedy and me, they believed the cir-cumstances of Sam's death were too fantastic and convenient to have occurred innocently. This was based mainly on Janice's and Fran's pre-sumed deaths. John seemed to have people die all around him when they became expendable. Medina County wasn't buying what we were selling. When Brian and Agent Hilland laid out their case for exhuming Sam, the Medina County Sheriff's Department was unconvinced, in my mind because of the political squabble over the dig site in Seville. "You watch too much TV," they said.

Once again, we would form our little team of Dedy, Brian, Mike, Dave, and me. The setbacks in Wayne County and Mercer County with Janice and Fran's cases and Sam Malz's death were disappointments, but the war wasn't lost. We would continue to work to find the answers we knew were out there.

We did receive some overdue good news that Diane was leaving John. She filed for an annulment on December 17, 1999, on the grounds that John had misrepresented himself to her. She requested and was granted a restraining order. Even with all of her denials, she surely couldn't have forgotten that Fran and Janice had lost their lives when they decided they wanted out of John's. His reaction on being served with the papers for the annulment revealed the match-quick temper we think surfaced in the moments he went after Fran and Janice. John went to his and Diane's condo, ran up the stairs, and found the door lock changed and fastened. He knew Diane was home, and she was going to pay. The staircase to the entrance ran up the side of the condo and passed a window near the bot-tom. He attempted to get in through the window, and failing also in this effort, flew into a rage and broke down the steel-framed front door.

Diane's daughter, Summer, was in the condo and described the look on John's face as that of a maniac. Diane was on the phone calling 911. John made for Diane and looked ready to kill her—before he noticed that Summer was there. Then his whole demeanor changed. He began to beg Diane not to do this and to please take him back. The answer was clear enough.

A few days later, the San Diego County Sheriff's Department told Diane she needed to leave the condo to allow John to get his toilet articles and personal belongings. As Diane and Summer were leaving, John pulled up, determined to talk with Diane. She told him he couldn't violate the restraining order and moved to leave.

"You don't understand," John told her. "This is what my last wife tried to do."

Diane and Summer sped away.

Our relief was short-lived. Later that month, the Ferrari's engine blew. Diane dropped the restraining order and her filing for annulment. She did this, she says, to allow John to come back home and get her car fixed. I called to check on her. She didn't want to talk and said contact with us was taking too big of a toll on her health. I wondered whether we were really the problem.

When we first began talking to Diane, she spoke of a bad kidney ailment. She also said that John was very protective of her and made sure she took her medicine exactly as prescribed. She continued to get worse, however, and I asked whether she had any medication-level tests done. She had not.

Dedy also told Diane that one of John's past girlfriends had told authorities that anyone having sexual contact with John should be tested for sexually transmitted diseases. She poked around and found prescriptions for two medications, which I verified were both used to treat herpes. We begged her to go to a doctor. She also had found papers showing that John had gone to a clinic to be tested for HIV. Just as we had offered to pay for her to get an annulment or divorce, we offered to pay for any lab tests and doctor's visits to ensure she hadn't been infected with an STD. She later confronted John with this information. He said the HIV test was for a pre-screen for employment, and that yes, he did have herpes, but that she was never at risk. He said he had not had an occurrence since they had been married. Inexplicably, Diane again believed him, or seemingly so because she never actually told us that she was okay—just that she had been tested. I don't know whether we undermined Diane's health, but Dedy and I felt much better about not having contact with her anymore. We felt we had done everything we could to keep her safe, yet she refused to take the steps to get rid of John or even to protect her health. Having an expensive, fast car was more important than her life.

CHAPTER 23
The Lady in the Box

I'm not kidding when I say that I hadn't gotten a full night's sleep since I learned on October 2, 1991, that Fran was missing. There was always another aspect of the case to contemplate, and some nights I couldn't sleep even when I wanted to simply from being in mental overdrive. I kept replaying one find from Diane's storage unit in my mind: a fax cover sheet attached to a copy of Fran and John's marriage license. This fax was addressed to Sheila Sautter and dated June 5. It didn't include a year. The cover sheet, however, was from Chromalloy, the company John had worked for in Florida. In June 1989, Fran hadn't yet met John, and by June 1991, he was working for Carborundum in New Jersey. It had to be June 1990. Sheila had said previously that she didn't learn of Fran until December 1991, when John abruptly announced at the beach house that he was married and his wife was missing. We can't come up with a reason why she would lie about this except that she wouldn't want her family to know she had continued a relationship with a married man.

Sometimes I managed to get to sleep at night only to sit bolt upright in bed at 3:00 A.M. trying to remember whether I had covered all the possible bases in Fran's case. I couldn't forget that the last promise I had made to Mama was that we'd find Fran and let her know what happened. Eight years later, I still hadn't been able to do that, and I got the distinct impression that it was Mama who was showing up in the middle of the night to nag me about what else I could do for Fran. It always seemed to be at 3:00 A.M.

Many nights I woke up around that time thinking about John's Hammond, Indiana, address from 1979 that we had found in Diane's storage unit. It was on one of those restless nights that something told me we needed to send letters out to coroner's offices in Indiana. Coroners and medical examiners often encounter unidentified bodies, John and Jane Does, that they can't match up with criminal or missing-persons cases in their state or through the NCIC. At the time Janice disappeared, the NCIC didn't carry files for the missing, so unless a case had received national media coverage, a search of the individual state was about all that was done. In cases of unidentified bodies, the remains are usually buried in pauper's graves, most commonly within the county the remains are found in, though this varies from state to state. Any other evidence, such as clothing or jewelry, is logged and held within a case-file box in an evidence locker. This is done in case the John or Jane Doe is ever identified and a criminal case is filed.

I called Brian the next day. He told me he had sent out letters to the Ohio coroner's offices. "Brian, we now know that John lived in Indiana. Let's send letters to Indiana." He agreed but said he was too busy at the time to compile the addresses and compose a letter with all the information we had in the case right away. It would take him a few days. I told him I'd compile the addresses and get them to him. Dave and I had already made a trip to Hammond, in the far northwestern corner of the state near Chicago, and took pictures of the house to send to Brian. We spent a few days online and found that Indiana had a great Web page listing addresses for most county coroner's offices. For those we couldn't find, we used the sheriff's department instead. The night we sent those mailing labels to Brian, in the first week of February, was the first night in weeks I hadn't been thinking of the Hammond address at 3:00 A.M. Mama was going to let me get some sleep.

―――――――――

Brian called me the first week of March. The letters had done their job. Three days after they went out, he got a call from Inspector Gerald Burman with the Newton County Sheriff's Department. "I think I have your girl," he said. Burman remembered when the Jane Doe was recovered because of the unusual circumstances. In April 1980, a Newton County Highway Department worker named Sam Kennedy had been working with a resurfacing crew and spotted a plywood box lying in a drainage ditch off of County Road 400N, near Morocco. He and one of the crew carried it up to the road and, curious about the contents, pried it open with a tire iron. Kennedy used the tire iron to lift up what looked like an old green quilt, and found himself staring at a human skull. He and the crew backed off and called their dispatcher, who made the call to the Newton County Sheriff's Office. The sheriff's dispatcher then requested the Indiana State Police to back up their department's unit. At that time the Indiana State Police were the crime-scene investigative resource for most of the state.

Inspector Burman had been a deputy with the sheriff's department at the time and investigated the case. Morocco is only sixty miles south of Chicago, and it's not uncommon to see bodies dumped in rural Newton County from murders that take place up there. Clues were minimal. They knew only that the body belonged to a young adult female. Burman recalled, however, that it was the only body they had ever found in a box. It was crudely built and about four feet long, too short to hold the body of a full-grown person. Inside, the legs on the skeleton had been cut off below the knee.

The coroner had wanted to create a clay rendering from the skull to reconstruct the face and potentially help identify the body. But the expense was too great, and the remains were buried as a Jane Doe in a pauper's grave near Morocco. He did, however, retain the skull in his office in hopes that funds would become available to do the reconstruction. Early on, some locals thought it might be the body of the Brach Candy heiress who had disappeared not long before. That was soon put to rest when authorities determined that the "lady in the box," as newspapers at the time called her, had been dead long before the heiress had disappeared. So that was the end of it, really, and everyone moved on.

We were incredibly blessed that Inspector Burman had been the one to receive the letter. He was one of the few sheriff's deputies left who would remember the case. Newton County was one of three Indiana counties not on the Web site I had used to compile our addresses. I had to call the county courthouse, and they could get me only the sheriff's department's address. Had the letter gone to anyone but Inspector Burman, it likely would have been tossed. We felt like God was taking care of us in getting that letter to him.

Brian and Ohio authorities needed a few weeks to get their paperwork in order, but once that was complete, they traveled to Morocco to exhume the body. Everything that Michael had reported about the box John built and its contents matched the lady in the box in Newton County. I talked to Brian shortly after he returned from Indiana. "Sherrie," he said, "if this is her, we brought her home on her birthday [March 2]. I think that's nice, don't you?" Brian had begun to think of Janice as a little sister, and he told Dedy and me that on the ride from Indiana back to Ohio, he almost felt as if she should speak to him. I know Brian would have had many questions to ask.

They turned the remains over to the FBI crime lab for DNA testing to see whether they would match Janice's mother. This was supposed to take about six weeks, but six weeks turned into seven months. It seems the FBI had identified the remains as Janice's much earlier but wanted to wait to convene a grand jury and immediately issue a warrant for John's arrest. We had reached the most sensitive portion of the case. In Oceanside, John was just fifty miles from the Mexican border, and the FBI needed to ensure that no press or family leaks could make it easy for him to disappear.

In the meantime, as always, I needed to get my eyes around the place Janice had been found. Dave and I hit the road for Morocco and located the site, about a thirty-minute drive from John's address at the time in Hammond. We took pictures for Mike, again trying to bridge the gap in our worlds, and then just offered up a prayer for the woman who had been cast aside here and forgotten by the world. If this was Janice, she had been left far from home and never given the chance to tell her story. When we got home, I replayed the tapes from our sessions with the psychic Noreen Renier. I took out maps and the drawings we made to interpret her reading. The road John would have taken to get rid of Janice's body would have been I-80—one of two numbers Noreen had given us in speaking of Fran's location—which runs from Ohio directly to Hammond. To get to Morocco, John would have taken Highway 41 south. Noreen's statements about eight or eighty and fourteen or forty-one now made complete sense. The box being in the drainage ditch corresponded to Noreen's sense that she would be found near water, but not in it, and that the water would change depth. There were manufacturing plants in the area, but the land surrounding the ditch was all farmland. When the remains were found, there were many small trees at the top of the ditch. By the time we actually saw the area, the trees had been cut. It was now just overrun with weeds.

Also, at the end of our second session, Noreen had said, "If you're looking for another wife, you're looking in the wrong state."

Since she didn't have anything from Janice to read from, I could only assume that, if this was indeed Janice, John must have been more worried about someone identifying Janice than he was of their finding Fran. When the box was found, there was a lot of press. John was still living in the area, so he had to have known the box had been found. Or maybe Janice was his only true love, and he felt more guilty about her murder. Until we knew for sure that this was Janice, I could only speculate.

We had the press calling us at least twice a week during those seven months. No, we don't know anything yet. Yes, we'll be happy to talk when we do. The longer we waited for results, the more we became convinced this had to be Janice. If it weren't, the authorities would have announced it to the press by now to cut down on all the phone calls. Jane Doe would have been returned to Indiana and her pauper's grave. We talked often of what we should do if this were not Janice. "Continue to march" was our final decision. Even if it were Janice, we'd still have Fran's case to pursue. One found, one to go. Or as Mike and I have said, "Just keep on keeping on." But at the moment, it felt like the entire investigation was on hold. We wanted so much to happen, and we wanted it to all happen soon, sort of like the prayer where you ask God for patience, but you tell Him you need it right now.

PART THREE
The Trial

CHAPTER 24
A Measure of Justice

On October 3, 2000, the phone rang. It was Dedy, and she asked me whether I was sitting down. She asks that whenever she has big news to deliver, so I can never tell whether it's good or bad. My first thought, though, was that Diane was dead. Dedy went on to explain that Brian Potts had just called her on his way to the San Diego County Jail and that they had arrested John at LaForza. He had gone peacefully. The charge was aggravated murder in the death of Janice E. Hartman Smith. Aggravated murder connotes premeditation and normally carries the threat of the death penalty, but this would not be an option in Janice's case. Ohio didn't have the death penalty in 1974, and a sentence can be no more than the accused could expect to receive at the time he committed the crime.

Brian was accompanied by Agent Hilland, FBI agents from the San Diego office, deputies from the San Diego County Sheriff's Department, and Mike, who had paid for his own ticket to California and had taken vacation time in order to be on the scene for John's arrest.

John was being held in the San Diego County Jail pending extradition to Ohio. Wayne County had convened a grand jury and issued an indictment. Relief soon replaced shock as I rejoiced that no one would die at John's hand that night. That was the first full night's sleep I had gotten since Fran disappeared on October 1, 1991—nine years and two days ago. The phones began to ring off the hook again. The press had been hungry for news of the FBI's DNA test for seven months, and now the biggest development in the case was on their doorstep. Reporters wanted our reaction to John's arrest. We could state only that we were relieved that he was behind bars and that, at least if John were convicted, the Hartmans could get their closure. We also emphasized that this was Janice's case. There was still at least one more woman out there to find. I still did not have the answer to the question that had started this investigation nine years ago.

A few days after John's arrest, I called Mike, and he predicted that John would fight extradition. The battle could take months. This appeared to be opening another chapter in our case instead of closing one, but, as I had told the media and reminded Mike, we weren't finished yet. "It ain't over 'til the fat lady sings, and I haven't even warmed up yet," I said. "But Mike, I have made plans to buy a microphone." He laughed, and I joined him.

John's strategy on extradition, as on other fronts in his past, was unexpected. Brian reported to me that John claimed they had the wrong John Smith. He wouldn't even acknowledge at a hearing before the San Diego Superior Court that he was John Smith. The chameleon was out in full force. Mike assured me it was just a scheme that John and his attorney, Mr. McCabe, had cooked up to stall for time. The ruse didn't last long. The arrest team once again boarded a plane for California to bring John back. He wouldn't fight the extradition.

Now that the drama had reached a crescendo, the actions of everyone involved were magnified tenfold and, even if not much different from earlier in the case, said volumes about the people behind them. The Wayne County sheriff and prosecutor were front and center: They put out a press release stating they had worked hard for twenty-five years to solve this case. In actuality, they had worked Janice's case half-heartedly for a few months after her disappearance. Brian had found the micro-filmed files in the basement when he reopened the investigation. At a press conference to discuss the case they'd take to trial, the Sheriff's Department displayed an oversized wanted poster for John. The poster was made specifically for the press conference. There had never been a wanted poster for John. Everyone wanted to step up and take a bow now that the performance was almost over. What really disturbed me about this poster was that the person most responsible for the press confer-ence, Brian Potts, was not pictured. I have always thought that was just as well because Brian is too honorable to ever misrepresent his badge in such a shameless manner.

I credit all the work to bringing this case to pre-trial to Brian Potts, Mike Dansbury, and Agent Hilland. After John's arrest, I placed a call to Inspector Gerald Burman to say thank you for the attention he gave Brian's letter and for making the effort to call. He'd had a long career with the Newton County Sheriff's Department and had enough years in to retire, but he didn't feel ready to give up his badge. He told me about los-ing his son, also a police officer, in the line of duty. He said there have been days he wonders why he goes into work. When Brian and Martin Frantz went out to pick up Janice's remains, they gave Mr. Burman a pic-ture of her. He framed it and has it in his office. On the days when he wonders why he continues, he only has to look at her. "This case both-ered me for too many years," he said.

I talked to a lot of police officers during those nine years, and I always asked them why they stayed on the job. Without exception, they would answer, "Because I want to make a difference." No other reason. I had related that to Brian in expressing my gratitude for his work. I said, "Brian, today you made a difference." I also expressed this to Inspector Burman.

Speaking with him helped turn my attention to more of the good things that had come from our work. He told me that when Janice's remains were buried in Morocco in 1980, a local artist painted a small stone and placed it on Janice's unmarked grave. Thinking about that compassionate gesture made me feel that Janice hadn't been entirely forsaken and unloved even in an anonymous grave far from home. If people who didn't know her could love her in death, then surely the people who had known her and loved her in life were there for her too.

For some time in the later years of the investigation, Dedy had contemplated a civil suit against John for the wrongful death of her mother. Traditionally this is done after the criminal proceedings, a la the O.J. trial, but after a while we couldn't be sure when any criminal court might hear the case. Months earlier, Dedy had contacted the law firm that handled Fran's declaration of death. There at first was some question as to whether the statute of limitations had run out on a civil case, but because law enforcement officials had asked us to wait until they completed their investigation, it could be ruled that the statute would start from the time Fran was declared legally dead—January 3, 1997, rather than September 28, 1991—and we were clear to pursue it. Dedy and her New Jersey attorney had John served with the papers informing him of the wrongful death law suit. I wish I had been a fly on the wall when he got those papers. He was served immediately after he returned to his cell following his extradition hearing. If this was going to be the only way we could give Fran a measure of justice and make John face his crimes, then that's what we'd do.

In many ways, the court proceedings were an extension of the investigative ordeal we had been living since 1991. There would be uncertainty, hope, delays, inconvenience, enlightenment, and lots of red tape. Like when the FBI took over the case, almost everything would be out of our hands, but by now that was an utter relief. All we had to do was summon the strength to accept whatever was decided in the courtroom.

One of the best things about attending the court proceedings was the presence of Ruth Slater and Bette Boldman from the Victim's Advocate Office. Ruth or Bette would be present during all hearings and the trial to offer moral support to us and the Hartmans, explain how the proceedings would work, and run interference with the media if necessary. I was surprised her office would make the effort since we weren't members of Janice's family. Ruth and Bette were even better than you would expect from someone in their positions, caring and genuinely concerned for our welfare. The other personnel within the prosecutor's office proved to be just as considerate.

The first step, on October 11, was the arraignment, where John would have his chance to enter a plea. At that point, his attorney, Kirk Migdal, could either agree to move forward with a bond hearing or ask to delay the bond hearing for the judge who would ultimately hear the case. Mr. Migdal entered John's plea of "not guilty" and chose the latter, which meant waiving John's right to a speedy trial. I don't think John was in any hurry to have his fate decided just yet. The judge scheduled the bond hearing for October 20 and assigned the case to Judge Mark K. Wiest's court. The hearing would be almost a mini-trial where Judge Wiest could weigh evidence from both sides to assess the defendant's flight risk and either deny bond entirely or set a bond that the defendant could then post to remain free during the trial. If there's a reasonable chance a defendant could flee, the judge, rather than deny bond outright, can set it so high the defendant can't come up with the money. Until the hearing, John would remain locked up at the Wayne County Jail.

John's arraignment was one of my first chances to release some of the hatred I felt for him. I had let loose with the occasional tongue-lashing before when he pushed me to the edge, but here he was a fly between the proverbial chopsticks, and he knew it. I wasn't humming "We Shall Overcome" when the sheriffs led John into the courtroom in shackles. I fixed him with a stare of utmost loathing for the entire arraignment from the courtroom gallery, to the right of the defense team's tables and directly behind the prosecutor's table, as you face the bench. I wanted him to stare back and challenge me, to tacitly acknowledge the position I had put him in, but he kept his eyes on the table in front of him. After a while of this, Mr. Migdal must have sensed my eyes on John because he moved his chair back slightly to put himself between us. I just moved further along the bench and continued to glare. I couldn't give him an eye as evil as he deserved, but I could try.

CHAPTER 25
Enraged and Outraged

Dave and I went home to Indiana after the arraignment and returned to Wooster on October 20 for the bond hearing. Neither of us intended to miss a second of John wriggling between the chopsticks if we could help it. Dave had just had knee surgery the day before and was experiencing some pain, but he couldn't be talked into resting. "I have not worked this hard for so many years to not . . . see if the bastard is granted bail," he said. We had a real concern that he could post bond and had no doubt that he'd run if he got the chance.

The proceedings this time were long enough that, like our March 1993 trip to Wooster for the task force meeting, this hearing was a bit like a family reunion. Dedy flew in from Houston. I was pleasantly surprised to see that Rich and Dedy's stepmother, Jan, had come as well. Their being with us shouldn't have surprised me. They have been so supportive of their children and the whole family. Since we arrived for the hearing early, we decided to go to the Justice Center to find Brian before going to the courthouse. He was there briefing an FBI agent, Special Agent Roy Speer, on the relevant facts in the case to prepare to testify. Agent Speer was exactly what you would expect of an FBI agent, pleasant but thoroughly professional. Brian told Dedy that she might be called to testify and handed her some documents to read just to refresh her memory on events that she might have to swear to in court that day.

Afterward, we checked in with Martin Frantz at the courthouse while Brian and Agent Speer met with Jocelyn Stefancin, the assistant prosecutor. Mr. Frantz again surprised us by reacting as if we had never met. Dedy reminded him that we had met in March of 1993 and had spoken to him by phone earlier that year. Mr. Frantz didn't seem to remember. He told Dedy that she might be called upon to give evidence, and she said she was fine and was prepared to testify. We expressed hope that John would be held without bond until the trial. Mr. Frantz's opinion on bond took us aback. He said he almost hoped John would be granted a large bond and then run. That way the bond would be forfeited. "The county could use the money," he said. I nearly came out of my chair. I reminded him that we had a wrongful death action pending against John for Fran's death. Our family had spent enough money trying to keep track of where John was. "Our family cannot afford to find him for you again," I said. Maybe he remembered whom he was talking to at that point. He changed his demeanor and began to say that he thought they had enough evidence to hold John until his trial for aggravated murder. Then he excused himself. We waited there until the hearing was set to begin but had a hard time concentrating on something other than what we had just heard. Dedy and I just looked at each other in disbelief.

When we arrived in the courtroom, I was relieved to see Garry and Isabel Hartman. Isabel and two of her daughters had come for the arraignment the week before, but Garry had been out of town on business. We were all seated in the second row. The first row was reserved for the press and photographers. Our differences in handling the cases for now took a back seat to the common ordeal we'd live through together in court. Isabel and I held hands on my right side while Dedy and I held hands on my left side through most of the hearing. This was not an easy day for any of us, and what we were about to hear was at times difficult.

Ruth Slater, one of our victim's advocates, was right behind us and told us that she could get us out of the courtroom as soon as the proceedings were over if we preferred not to talk to the press. I told her I would speak with anyone at any time about Fran's case.

The FBI's investigative style had left us in the dark about many of the details uncovered in the past two years, and we waited anxiously to hear more about them in the hearing. Both sides would have a chance to call and cross-examine witnesses. John could even testify if he chose. Since it was a pre-trial matter, there would be no jury.

The standard for denying bond is high, and we had no guarantee that the prosecution could meet it, except for Mr. Frantz's dubious statements. In order to deny a defendant the Constitutional right to bail, the prosecution must show that the odds are great that he committed the crime he's charged with; that he poses a substantial risk of serious physical harm to an individual or the community, and that no type of release during the trial can reasonably ensure the safety of that individual or the community; and that the probability of flight is high.

Some of the proceedings were rudimentary but still necessary to enter salient facts into the record for the judge's consideration. Ms. Stefancin called Brian to the stand to establish much of this. He testified at length, talking about how he had come to be involved in the case and reviewing specifics from the missing-persons report John filed on Janice on November 19, 1974. According to the report, at the time of her disappearance, Janice had been wearing a blue top with red stripes, blue jeans, black lace-up shoes, a wedding ring and a diamond engagement ring, and, importantly, a diamond watch. Moving on from the report, Ms. Stefancin began asking Brian about Fran's disappearance. John's attorney, Kirk Migdal, objected, and both parties approached the bench. When they had returned to their places, Judge Wiest agreed the "New Jersey evidence" should not be heard.

In Mr. Migdal's cross-examination, he focused on the inadequate investigation into Janice's disappearance at the time by the Wayne

County Sheriff's Department and the amicable nature of John and Janice's split. They had, in fact, used the same attorney and obtained a dissolution decree, not a divorce (meaning things are less messy; both parties must agree to all terms and secure approval from the court). But what also came out, in questioning about John's assuming other identities, was that he had used the Social Security number of an exotic dancer in Milford, Connecticut, who had later moved to Florida. John had given police the Social after getting stopped for a traffic violation. Only the news of John's using the dancer's identity was new to us.

Agent Speer, whom we had met that morning, gave testimony that would add context to the snitches and snatches of information Diane had provided. He had become involved in the case in June 1999 and knew there had been a massive sweep of interviews conducted by the FBI and other police officers since they had opened their case. A source had stepped forward as a result of this initiative and made contact with Agent Hilland. He flew to New York with his attorney to discuss the Smith case. It would later come out during Mr. Migdal's cross-examination that the source was John's brother Michael, who had directed the FBI to dig at the apartment building in Seville and made phone calls to John for the FBI about fake grand jury indictments to gauge his reaction. But Agent Speer referred to him only as "the source."

Agent Hilland was Michael's contact at the New York FBI office. During those meetings, Michael told of observing John building a box in his grandfather's garage in late November 1974. John told him he was building a box for Janice's things. Michael expected that the box would be more like a hope chest if it were to contain articles from a missing wife and asked him why it was so crude, made only of plywood. John got irate and yelled enough that Michael just let it go and left.

He described the box as being about four feet long, eight inches deep, and sixteen inches wide. Agent Speer testified that Michael had returned to the garage later that day and observed John apparently crying. John had gathered some boxes and bags around him that Michael believed contained clothing and other articles belonging to Janice. He was laying the clothes out, rolling them tightly, and placing them inside the box along the edges. Michael told Agent Hilland that he had later noticed the box in the garage after it was nailed shut. It lay near other bags and boxes that Michael believed to be Janice's.

Michael said he saw the box several times over the course of the next five years. Agent Hilland asked Michael whether anyone had ever noticed any odor. He said yes, there was an unusual odor, but they attributed it to a dead squirrel or a mouse that had crawled inside and died.

Agent Speer testified that Michael had last seen the box in either late May or early June 1979. John's grandfather, Chester Chaney, and Jack Bistor were cleaning out the garage. Mr. Bistor planned to rent the garage to open a small-engine repair shop. In the course of cleaning out the garage, they found and partially pried the box open, but couldn't tell what was inside. Michael was home for lunch, and Mr. Chaney called him to help. Michael carried the box out into the daylight. He also tried to open the box wider but still couldn't tell what was inside. He saw four circles that appeared to be white or gray. He was able to remove one end of the box and took a stick to move the contents around. The contents appeared to be some type of clothing.

As Michael moved to the other end of the box, still using the stick, he discovered what he thought was hair, although it was an unusual color for hair—shades of brown, rust, and orange. Perhaps not quite believing it could be hair he was seeing, Michael continued to shift the hair around until he spotted a face he recognized as Janice Hartman's. He stepped back and returned to the garage to tell his grandfather.

Mr. Chaney decided that they would not call the police. This was a family matter. Instead, he told Michael to call John. John was living in Hammond, Indiana, in June 1979.

Michael asked him for an explanation about the box, and John answered only that he would take care of it. It took him several hours to reach Seville from Hammond. The two discussed what should be done with the box, and John finally loaded it into the fully reclined passenger seat of his 1979 Corvette. Agent Speer stated that the FBI had traced the Corvette to its present owner in Stockholm, New Jersey, and determined that the box would have fit into the car as Michael described. Agents noted some minor scratches on the defroster strips of the rear window, which could have been caused by the box.

The other source the FBI located and interviewed was Kathy McDonald, the daughter of John's manager at two companies around that time, Flexible Steel and Pullman Standard. Agent Speer relayed her statements: She had said she did remember John and a watch that John had given her. Ms. McDonald had said she was looking for a watch with a green face, and John told her he had such a watch and gave it to her. When she asked him about the watch being used, he told her that it had belonged to his first wife and that she was dead. This is the same watch John said in his missing-persons report that Janice was wearing at the time of her disappearance.

All in all, the case for denying bail looked good. Ms. Stefancin had recalled Brian to the stand to testify that John would be a danger to the community because of his temper. Agent Speer related Diane's daughter's story of John's breaking down the door to their Oceanside condo with "the most evil face she had ever seen" and how his demeanor immediately changed when he saw that Summer was present. And of course there was Agent Speer's summary of Michael's statements about the box, Kathy McDonald's testimony about Janice's green diamond watch, and an all-around pattern of conflicting statements and outright lies from John on the record.

Judge Wiest called for a recess, and after closing arguments, issued his ruling: "The Court believes the State has met the three-pronged test" for denying bail to John for this trial. Mr. Migdal had already waived John's right to a speedy trial, which ordinarily would mean within ninety days, so it appeared he would be living in the Wayne County Jail well into the new year.

As a family, we were so relieved that John would be detained while awaiting trial. As we left the courtroom, I had my first opportunity to actually meet Sheriff Tom Maurer (the man Dedy had tried to reach incessantly many months before to find out why they weren't moving on the case). He thanked me for staying on their backs and not letting these cases drop. This meant a lot to me, because I know that at times we were real pains in the butt to these people.

After the bond hearing, Dedy and I went back to Brian's office in the Justice Center. The new owner of John's Connecticut beach house had found a knife in the attic between the ceiling and the insulation and had turned it over to authorities. My nephew Todd makes knives, and I wanted to see whether this knife might have been one that he made for his mother. If so, Dedy and I could contact Todd to verify that the knife had been in Fran and John's household. Also, Dave is an organic chemist and wanted to make sure the knife had been taken apart for testing and not examined only superficially. He knew it was a strong possibility that blood could have been absorbed under the handle, where the blade is attached. Unfortunately, the knife was being held in evidence at the FBI office, and we wouldn't be able to see it. Brian and Agent Speer described it as a regular, serrated household knife and reported that it had been exposed to too many elements to yield anything conclusive. They assured us that it had been completely examined by the FBI lab and that there wasn't anything that could be used for our case.

Brian wondered whether we might be able to get a picture of the knife for Dedy and me to look at. Agent Speer responded that he didn't think the FBI would be willing to spend any more time or money on these cases. I had been told earlier that the FBI had spent about $50,000 on the case at that point. I lost all sense of reason in that moment. The frustration of being closed out by the FBI, Agent Hilland's being taken off the case and transferred out of the Cold Case Division, hearing "no" at every turn as we explored our remaining alternatives—all of that anger came out in my tirade. I told Agent Speer it was a shame the FBI had denied our family access to the one person who knew the most about the two cases combined just because a few egos and feelings had been hurt. I said that I was really angry that while our family did not pay taxes or vote in either Wayne County, Ohio, or Mercer County, New Jersey, these departments had worked their butts off to help us. But, I continued, we do pay a large chunk of our incomes to the federal government. With what our family had spent—now in excess of $100,000—as well as these other police departments, I was not impressed with $50,000 and a few years of their time. Dedy and Brian stared at me wide-eyed. I had never exploded like this before. I have to say Agent Speer was a true gentleman. He just let me rant for a few minutes and then beat a hasty retreat. (After Dave and I got back from the hearing, I called Mike and told him about how I had lashed out at Agent Speer. I told him I felt I owed the man an apology—not for what I had said, because I meant every word—but for attacking him and not his superiors. Agent Speer received a note of apology a few days later.)

That night in Wooster, we taped our second interview with *20/20 Downtown*. As always, the producer and crew were very considerate and kind. I won't say the interview was an ego trip, but it was—and still is— really validating to have people in positions of such power sit down and listen intently and respectfully to what you have to say. Their interest reinforces that victims' families are at the center of the justice equation. It's the families who will have to live day in and day out with the loss of their loved one, whose efforts can influence how crime is investigated and prosecuted, and whose advocacy can make the difference in whether another family endures the same tragedy. We got a plus out of this segment because the producers agreed to air the pictures of the other two women we had found in John's suitcase. Someone recognizing them on TV was probably going to be our only hope for identifying them now. West Windsor, Wayne County, and the FBI hadn't been able to get a clue as to who they were.

CHAPTER 26
The New Jersey Evidence

In January 2001, Brian called to let us know that the Wayne County Sheriff's Department had searched one of John and Grace's storage units. It was a fluke that they even found out about the unit, which Grace had rented in the name of a friend. This friend felt she needed to come forward and told the authorities about their strange arrangement. (I believe that after Sam Malz died, Grace and John were trying to hide assets because of John's inability to manage the Malz businesses. The banks were after anything worth a cash turnaround to cover massive loans against the Malz property.) Wayne County's search rendered four very small pieces of bone, determined to be human and from the head of a female. Other than that, they didn't know anything; they were starting an investigation to determine whom these remains belonged to. The pieces of bone were tiny fragments. Three of them had been burnt. One piece, however, about the size of a thumbnail, still had tissue attached. Interviews with people who had rented the storage unit before or after John revealed they had never stored any cremated remains there.

It took Eagle, one of the best body-scent dogs ever, to locate the fragments. They were in a crevice between the removable walls that divide the storage units. Eagle is the same dog who, on a nursing home visit, was able to determine with remarkable accuracy which nursing homes residents were close to death. Forensic anthropologist Dr. Frank Saul told CBS's *48 Hours*, "If a really good cadaver dog is a ten on a scale of one to ten, Eagle was a twenty." Eagle himself passed away in November 2003. The search results elicited more questions than answers for us. Brian arranged for Dedy to submit a sample of saliva for DNA analysis, and we waited several weeks to learn that the bone fragments didn't match Dedy's DNA and so couldn't be from Fran. We also knew they couldn't belong to Janice because her skull was intact. We had prayed this would give us an answer. Instead, we had one more question: Who is this?

Bette Boldman from the Victim's Advocate's Office informed us in the spring of 2001 that Judge Wiest had scheduled a hearing for May 29 to determine whether the evidence from Fran's disappearance could be entered into the criminal case for Janice's death. We were eager to see this happen both for the sake of Janice's case and because, if we weren't able to get John tried in a criminal case for Fran's murder, this could be our only chance to give Fran a voice and to see prosecutors present to a jury everything we had found in nearly ten years of investigating. Dave and I were growing tired of leaving home at 4:30 in the morning to get to the courthouse in time, so we drove to Wooster the night before the hearing.

The usual gang would be there—Brian would testify, and Mike was coming in from New Jersey—but I also saw a new face. It was Bob Hilland, who had flown in from New York to give testimony. All of my previous contact with him had been over the phone.

As we entered the courtroom, Agent Hilland was sitting next to Mr. Frantz at the prosecutor's table. Ms. Stefancin's daughter was ill, so Mr. Frantz would be representing the state in the hearing. We consoled ourselves that we'd still have Agent Hilland's knowledge from the case to draw on in the hearing.

The defense's table also featured a new face: Public Defender Beverly Wire. That spring the Victim's Advocate Office notified us that Mr. Migdal had asked to be released from the case. John had informed him that he had no funds to pay for his defense. Judge Wiest reviewed John's assets, agreed he was indigent, and appointed Ms. Wire to the case as co-counsel. Mr. Migdal would remain on the case at Wayne County's expense, as would an investigator. In our minds, the wheels of justice too often rolled in one direction only.

To convince Judge Wiest that the evidence in Fran's case also applied to Janice's, Mr. Frantz would seek to establish a "behavioral fingerprint" and highlight the striking similarities between the two cases that, though almost seventeen years apart, demonstrated John's habitual approach to killing. To do that, he called Brian Potts to the stand to outline evidence in Janice's case and followed it with testimony from Mike about his investigation of Fran's case. Under questioning from Mr. Frantz, Brian recited the events of November 9, 1974, that led to Janice's filing a police report for attempted rape and assault. Janice said her assailant threatened her with the statement, "Narcs always have an easy way out." She had been held at shotgun-point while Leonard Bennett was made to get on top of her. He couldn't get an erection, but Janice did say there was digital penetration by the men who were holding her down. She was left with bruises on her face and legs.

Brian testified that the missing-persons report John filed on November 19 of that year had been taken at the home of Kathy Paridon's mother. Ms. Paridon stated she had ridden home with Janice in the early-morning hours of November 17 and left her in the car with a white male with a muscular build, dark hair, a beard, and a bad case of acne. She didn't give a name for the man. Later, upon hearing that description in the trial, I thought, *If I were afraid of John and wanted to describe someone that was his complete opposite, this is the description I'd give.*

Brian said Janice had disappeared without a trace but had left all her belongings and her car. Janice's prized 1974 Mustang was found at the Melrose Trailer Park, John's address. John had reported that Janice might have gone to Florida to visit with relatives. There was a red suitcase missing.

On cross-examination, Mr. Migdal questioned why the rape case was not more strongly investigated. Brian replied that in 1974, even with digital penetration, this wouldn't have been a rape case. It wouldn't even have been an attempted rape case, just an assault, as stated on the report. (A personal note: Thank God the laws have changed and there's a better definition of what constitutes rape and what constitutes assault.) Brian also said he never found any evidence that Janice was an informer for any police department, that he felt Janice had delusions of grandeur, and that being a narc was a story she told her friends and family.

Mr. Frantz then called Mike Dansbury to the stand, and Mike spoke about how we had been a close family and had had no contact with Fran since September 28, 1991. Mike told of all the lies John had told our family and the authorities and explained that Fran was recuperating from a broken hip when she disappeared. She had been in frail condition and, per John's missing-persons report, carrying a yellow suitcase. Fran had also left all her personal belongings and her car behind. Ms. Wire, the public defender, asked Mike if he was sure Fran was dead. "I don't know if Fran Smith is dead, but I believe that she is dead," he said. On follow-up, Mr. Frantz asked Mike what made him believe that Fran was dead. He answered that John had told him Fran was dead in an earlier interview.

So far so good. Judge Weist called a recess for lunch, and as Mr. Frantz left the courtroom, he winked and gave us a thumbs-up. We were optimistic that Brian's and Mike's testimony would be tied together when Agent Hilland was called to testify that afternoon. I went off to call Dedy and let her know how things were going. When she answered, she asked whether I was sitting down. I told her I was, and she broke it to me that Granny had passed away that morning. I was devastated. Granny had moved from Florida to Texas to live with her youngest daughter, my Aunt Betty. I had visited her in January 2001, just after Brian called to tell me about the bones they'd found in John's old storage unit. She was lively at the time and enjoying every minute with my uncle. They liked to pick on each other. This was the second grandmother I had lost while either planning a trip to or being in Ohio. It seemed that every time we were in the thick of Fran's fight for justice, something terrible happened to our family.

I went into a daze and had trouble paying attention when court was reconvened, but I was still shocked to find that Agent Hilland wouldn't be testifying for the prosecution. It didn't make any sense. Even Judge Wiest was caught off guard. His glasses slipped down to the end of his nose as he leaned forward to stare at Mr. Frantz. With no more witnesses, Judge Wiest said he would consider all arguments and make a ruling in a few days. Dave and I walked up to the rail with Brian, Mike, and Agent Hilland. None of us could understand why he hadn't gotten a chance to testify. In several of Mike's and Brian's answers, they had said the questions could be best answered with the FBI case file.

On the way home, it hit us. Agent Hilland had been sitting next to Mr. Frantz for a reason. Mr. Frantz didn't know enough about the two combined cases to do this without his help. If Agent Hilland had taken the stand, who would sit next to Mr. Frantz and tell him what to ask the witnesses? We regretted that Mr. Frantz hadn't asked for a postponement and let Jocelyn Stefancin handle the hearing on another day.

While we waited for Judge Wiest's ruling, Dave and I busied ourselves preparing for the trip to Florida for Granny's funeral. I kept asking myself how our family would be able to let go of this remarkable woman. Our family had gathered just a few years before to celebrate her life and the fact that she had been the church organist for seventy-five years. At the funeral, the hardest part for me was entering the church. I glanced at her empty organ bench and realized she would never again sit there. I would never again hear her play. She was ninety-two when she passed away.

Granny touched so many lives with her love and faith. It was a comfort to listen as her friends told us what her friendship and life had meant to them. I knew then that the quality of her life hadn't gone unrecognized, and that she left this earth a better place for all of us to enjoy.

On May 31, Judge Wiest rendered his decision: "This is a ruling on the admissibility at trial of the 'New Jersey evidence'. A hearing was held on May 29, 2001. The court heard from two witnesses and the arguments of counsel. Evid. R. 404 (B) evidence is admissible only if the state shows by substantial proof that the other acts or circumstances tend to prove one or more of the purposes listed in the rule. Here, the State seeks to introduce the 'New Jersey evidence' to show identity and absence of mistake or accident. In State v. Smith (1990), 49 Ohio St. 3d, 137, the Supreme Court reversed two appeals courts under almost identical circumstances. Here, we don't know the circumstances under which Fran Smith's death occurred. There are certainly some similar circumstances surrounding the disappearance of the defendant's first two wives. But the court finds lacking the substantial proof required before it can admit this evidence."

In a way, it was a ruling in our favor. Based on the previous Ohio Supreme Court rulings, the chance was too great that a conviction could be overturned on appeal. But for this trial, the court would proceed as if Fran's death had never happened, and that was difficult to accept.

CHAPTER 27

This Is Your Life

In opening arguments on July 6, Ms. Stefancin opened with the line, "She will never walk away from him again." She knew the case cold, and she knew that everything in it revolved around John's control of women, from the moment they met him to the moment they tried to leave. She told of the miserable state of their marriage, the fighting, John's physical abuse of Janice, and how they had separated. She told the jury that it would hear evidence from the defendant's brother about the box, how he had discovered what the box contained, and how John had loaded it into his car and driven off.

For the defense, Ms. Wire focused on Janice's immersion in a murky drug-centered underworld and the assault she sustained just a week before she disappeared. She said the defense would show that Janice had left work with a friend, Kathy Paridon, and a stocky, dark-haired man the night she disappeared, and that Janice was not afraid of John and maintained a friendly relationship with him. Ms. Wire argued that the drug dealers Janice was reportedly helping put behind bars were the people that she was afraid of and, in light of the assault report, the people she *should* have been afraid of.

Judge Wiest invited witnesses, and Ms. Stefancin first called Janice's mother, Betty Lippencott, to the stand. The first question Ms. Stefancin asked her was how many children she had given birth to. "Four," Mrs. Lippencott answered. She was then asked how many of her children were not accounted for. "Just one: Janice," Mrs. Lippencott said sadly. She told of being unhappy about the marriage but that the family had come to accept it. Mrs. Lippencott said John often visited their home without Janice. When the defense asked why, since this was such a close family, Mrs. Lippencott replied, "Someone had to work, to pay the bills." She told the court that her daughter didn't stay with her after she and John separated because Mrs. Lippencott had another young daughter. She maintained house rules, and Janice didn't want to follow them. She also told of a late-night visit from the couple. When she offered them something to eat, John pitched a hissy-fit because she had only soup and sandwiches. "Don't you people ever have anything decent to eat?" He yelled, stomped his feet, and banged the cabinets.

Garry Hartman was the prosecution's second witness. Garry related his story of a chess match he and John had played on one of the few occasions John and Janice came to visit. Garry won the game, and John threw the board and chess pieces against the wall. He then yelled to Janice that they were leaving, went outside, and revved up their motorcycle. Janice walked into the room, saw the chess pieces all over the floor, and said to Garry, "I guess you won." Then she went outside, and the two sped off. Garry said the last time he saw his sister was when he went to the Sun Valley Inn to see where Janice worked. "It was a nice place." He said he was surprised and that Janice was a good dancer. Both Garry and Mrs. Lippencott told the jury that John had never contacted them after Janice disappeared to see whether she had been found.

Lieutenant Thomas Gasser and now-retired Detective Sergeant Tim McGuire addressed the 1974 investigation into Janice's disappearance. Neither knew why the missing-persons report hadn't been linked to the police report Janice had filed the week before. The defense ripped them for running a mediocre investigation. The prosecution argued that while both the assault and the missing-persons report were for a Smith, the reports carried different addresses for the person making the report, and the injuries listed were different. The defense noted that the case number for the assault report did appear on a follow-up notation for the missing-persons report, so someone had been able to link them. To me, the important thing about their testimony is that on the missing-persons report, John lists Noda Paridon, Kathy Paridon's mother, as the contact, even though he identified himself as Janice's husband and Janice had family in the area.

Our hearts went out to Mrs. Lippencott. This was the first time she had heard about Janice's being attacked, through two officers on the witness stand. She sat and cried softly. At the close of court that day, Dedy asked Garry why no one had told his mother about the attack on Janice, and he said he assumed she knew. Garry told me they never discussed it because he thought his mother might find it too painful. But Garry didn't go to her after listening to the testimony and comfort her, though she was clearly in pain. Dedy did. She hugged Mrs. Lippencott and whispered what she hoped were words of comfort. We had great empathy for Mrs. Lippencott and the Hartman family, but it seemed there were things about them we could never know, and perhaps wouldn't understand. Garry, Isabel, and their daughters are close, but the rest of the family didn't appear to express much affection for one another.

Mike Dansbury was the last witness called that day and was asked only three questions, all about his interviews with John about Janice's case. I could tell this was a strain for him. He had so much to say and could reveal almost none of it. Any slip-up could cause a mistrial. He clenched the muscles in his jaw and crisply answered only the questions he was asked. If I had been on the jury, however, I would have been asking myself why a detective from New Jersey was involved in the case.

———————

The next morning Agent Hilland and Brian Potts carried the box into the courtroom. I looked to my left to see whether John would have any reaction to this grim spectacle from his past. I was appalled to see him smile and whisper something to his attorneys. From a source sitting near him, I learned later that he told his attorneys he never made that box.

But this was before the box was unpacked. Law enforcement had placed the evidence in a larger, protective wooden box, one actually much more sound and well-made than the one it contained.

The prosecution called its star witness, Michael Smith. He looked very much like his brother: reddish hair, slight build, but maybe a little shorter, and with a beard. Michael began to recount the events concerning John and Janice's relationship. He said that the family wasn't happy that the couple had taken off to Detroit to get married. Their mother was so enraged she forbade John to even come back into the house to get his clothes. Michael told of having a fight with his parents, being kicked out of the house, and going to stay with John and Janice. He said that Janice didn't really want him there because Dennis Evans, John's friend, was already living with them. Michael then told about a time that he had taken the blame when John caught Janice smoking. John didn't want her to smoke and would have thrown a fit if Michael hadn't stood up for her.

Ms. Stefancin asked what Michael knew about the couple's relationship after their divorce. He said Janice had told him they were getting along better now than when they were married. Michael took John to meet Janice on two occasions after the divorce: first he took him to the bar that Michael believed Janice's father either managed or owned; the next night he dropped John off at the Sun Valley Inn to meet Janice.

Ms. Stefancin asked how he found out Janice was missing. Michael responded that John had told him Janice was going into a relocation program because she was a narc. He said John wasn't living with either the Chaneys or Grace in the fall of 1974. After Janice disappeared, John asked him to come to his trailer on Melrose to help him pack up Janice's things. The place was a mess—clothes were strewn everywhere—so he just waited outside while John packed things into boxes and garbage bags. John handed the boxes and bags out to him, and he loaded them into John's van. They then took everything to the garage that had once been a Marathon station next to their grandparents' home.

Through questioning, Michael told of the Saturday after Thanksgiving, when the whole family was gathered at the Chaney home to watch the Ohio State versus University of Michigan game on TV. John wasn't watching, so Michael went to find him. He was in the garage building an odd-shaped box. John told him he was making a box to put Janice's things in. "Why such a shit box?" Michael asked. John became nasty and angry and yelled, so Michael went back into the house to watch the game. Afterward he again went to look for John and saw he was rolling Janice's clothes up and placing them around the edges of the box. He appeared to be crying. The next time Michael saw the box, it was against the east wall in the garage. Later, it was moved to the south wall. The box remained there until the summer of 1979.

Mr. Chaney and a neighbor, Jack Bistor, were cleaning out the garage that summer so Mr. Bistor could rent it. They came upon the box and pried open one end but couldn't tell what was inside. Mr. Chaney recruited Michael to come down and help them. The lighting was bad, and Michael took the box outside. As he got one end open, he found the strangest thing he had ever seen. There were what appeared to be articles of clothing and four white circles. Michael then took the box to his back porch and there opened the other end of the box. He saw multi-colored hair, the second-strangest thing he had ever seen. Mr. Bistor was standing behind him and joked that there was a dead turtle in the box and that it was going to bite him. It wasn't a turtle, or any other animal that Michael saw next. It was his sister-in-law's face. He also realized that the four strange circles he had first seen were the severed bones, the tibias and fibulas, of Janice's legs. They had been cut off just below the knees.

Michael immediately wanted to call the police. Mr. Chaney began to pace the yard and muttered, "It will kill Ethel," referring to Michael's maternal grandmother. Michael has given four reasons for not calling the police: one, that Mr. Chaney told him that this was family business; two, that publicity of the discovery would ruin his grandfather's business; three, fear of going to jail for a crime he didn't commit; and four—what Michael says is the real reason (though the other three he gave, he says, are true to a point)—that he didn't want to be responsible for his grandmother's death. Michael was an immature twenty-five-year-old, and the Chaneys had been more parents than grandparents. The three Smiths had lived with them after Grace's divorce from her first husband, Carl, until Michael was about six. Michael says he knew there was nothing that could be done for Janice but that he did fear causing his grandmother's death. At Mr. Chaney's insistence, he called John instead of the police.

During this entire courtroom exchange, Michael and John never made eye contact. At one recess, Michael turned his chair to face the jury box so he wouldn't have to look at John, and John turned his chair in the opposite direction. John appeared stoic when the box first came out, but he slumped in his chair when Michael identified what it was. I wondered how he felt being confronted by the truth with no way to counter it— unless, of course, he wanted to take the stand himself.

Michael continued with his account. Mr. Chaney said that after they called John, he would never be allowed at their home again. (This was just talk. We know that John spent a lot of time with the Chaneys and even brought girlfriends to visit in the years after 1979.) Michael, always handling the dirty work, was the one who called John and told him they had found the box. John asked whether they had opened it, and when Michael replied that they had, he said only, "I'll be right there."

John was living and working in Hammond, Indiana, at the time, so it took several hours for him to arrive in Seville. When he did, Michael asked for an explanation. John said an FBI agent and a Wayne County Sheriff's Deputy had drugged him. He woke up in a warehouse. Janice was lying beside him dead. The agent and the deputy were laughing at him.

They loaded John and Janice into a vehicle, took them to the trailer on Melrose, and told John they were going to frame him for the murder of his wife. John next woke up in bed again with a dead Janice beside him.

Michael regrets that he told John about some apartments that were being constructed in Seville by their stepfather and mother, and that it might be a good place to put Janice's remains. "No, this is my problem," John said. "I'll take care of it." About nine o'clock that night, Michael moved the box from the porch to a grassy area between the Chaneys' house and the garage. The last time he saw the box, John had loaded it into his Corvette.

It's important to know that when Michael first agreed to talk to the FBI in May 1999 and tell all, he had no guarantee of immunity. His attorneys later obtained one, but then discovered that he could have been charged only with helping to dispose of a body, and the statute of limitations had long expired on that offense. Through hours of intense questioning by the FBI, he stuck to his story, despite having told different versions of events in the past. He agreed to set up a taped phone call between him and John. "All kinds of shit is pouring down on me," he tells John in the call. "I am going to tell them the truth. I am not going to jail for you."

John's reply is meek and low. "I don't expect you to. You have to do what you think is right."

Though not true, Michael tells him he's being called to testify before a grand jury in exactly two weeks. "Holy shit," John says. Michael asks John what he wants him to do, and again John tells him to do what he has to do. The call ends. Michael went on to testify that the next thing he knew, John had disappeared. No one knew where he was. The authorities notified Michael, and he and his family were moved to several motels for protection. Everyone felt John might be unstable enough to come after Michael. He would have been the only witness left that could testify against John about the box. Mr. Chaney and Mr. Bistor had both passed away.

The defense had a tall order trying to control the damage of Michael's testimony. They played up his unreliability and said that the Ohio State-Michigan game had in fact taken place the weekend *before* Thanksgiving. (That discovery only made John look worse. The correct date would have been six days after Janice disappeared, rather than thirteen, as Michael thought.) Michael admitted that he might have the day wrong but that the rest of his testimony was correct. He said he had not seen the written statements he had made to the authorities in more than a year.

"This is something that is like a branding iron, burning into your brain," he said. "You want it to go away, but it just never does." He ended his testimony with a statement directed to the jury. With an unblinking stare he said, "You don't know what it's like to live with this. I've had dreams of Jan chasing me carrying her legs. You don't have the dreams. I do." With that, Michael left the stand. He and John never did look at each other. I remember thinking, as he exited the courtroom, that this was the most wounded spirit I had ever seen. Except for his wife, Tonya, there was no member of his family to praise him for such a brave and redemptive act.

That night, I would write a note to Michael and Tonya. I said that we had no bad feelings toward him and that we were grateful he had done the right thing. I told them how to contact me and gave the note to our victim's advocate to deliver. We met on Sunday, July 15. Tonya revealed that about an hour before they were to leave to meet with Dave and me, Michael had told her he couldn't go through with it. "How can I look this woman in the eye with her knowing that I am responsible for her sister's death?" he said. Shortly thereafter, he changed his mind, and I was able to tell him that now was the time for him and his family to start healing. He made a bad decision at an early age, but he had grown up, and he proved it at the trial.

I also got to hear a little more from Michael and Tonya about the Malz/Smith family. Michael said that Grace and Sam fought often, almost like they planned their arguments. Sam had his own bedroom, Grace had her own, and they kept a third to use when they weren't at odds with each other. Sometimes these rifts could last for months, and then the couple would make up and move back into the shared bedroom. Michael also told us that he was trying to reestablish a relationship with his father, Carl. He had grown up believing that Carl had loved John but not him. His father visited them once when he was a child and bought a bicycle. Michael remembers that the family raised a fuss that Carl had bought a bicycle for John and nothing for Michael. When they reconnected as adults, Carl explained that he didn't have much money at the time, and he had purchased the bike for the two of them to share. It was never intended to be just for John. Michael said this type of deception went on all the time while he was growing up. The family dynamic partially answered Dedy's question about John: "What happened to that cute little red-haired boy?"

When I told Michael what we knew of Sam's illness and death, he again provided a bit more background: Even though Sam and John hadn't been close while the boys were growing up, they had become close shortly before Sam's death. Michael said that Sam was a workaholic and had lived with a lot of stress for many years. He told of the last few evenings they had worked together at the apartments, before Sam became ill. He said that most of the time Sam would work very hard, but the last few nights before he got sick, Sam had simply lain on the floor and slept. When Michael was ready to move to another apartment, he would wake Sam up.

Why, I wondered to myself, had John and Sam suddenly become so close? Is it possible that John could have been giving Sam something that caused the rapid decline in his health?

Michael told us that most of the guidance they got as kids came from their grandparents. They had remained close with the Chaneys throughout their youth. When Grace and the boys left the Chaney home, they moved two houses down the street.

Michael seemed to be shocked when I told him that he and Sam were the only members of the family that Steve spoke well of. He said Steve had always been a very spoiled little boy, and didn't think Steve had particularly liked him. Michael rejected the idea that John had left Ohio with a lot of money after Sam's death, but said that Steve indeed had. I told Michael what Steve had told me: That he left because he couldn't take the manipulation from his family any longer and that he had come to Indiana in an old beat-up car. When John found out Steve was delivering pizzas for a living, he had laughed at him. Michael said Steve had left Ohio in a very nice car, though not the expensive model Sam had leased for him when he completed college.

It's so hard to get a true picture of this family. You're likely to get a different story from each of them on any given subject except one: They all say the others lie about everything. Michael does seem to be the most honest; he has nothing to hide and dosen't seem to care whether he impresses anyone. He's the only person in the family I would trust to tell the truth. For someone who has read about John's crimes in the newspaper and thinks, "Now what kind of parents raise a person like that?" there's your answer. Yes, plenty of talented people have overcome difficult home lives to achieve great things, but a loving family has the capacity—even the obligation—to push that talent in the right direction and ensure that it's wielded by a well-adjusted individual. John has talent, though it's so overmatched by twisted social concepts, the kind you learn in a twisted family, that it will never be put to productive use in society. No one in that family seems to have any true love for the others, except maybe for the Chaneys. Our meeting with Michael and Tonya ended with as many questions as when it started. All I am certain of is that we pray Michael and his family will now begin to heal and find peace.

Agent Hilland would be next on the stand. He explained that he had been assigned to the Cold Case Homicide Unit of the FBI in May of 1997 and had become involved in this case in July of 1998. Shortly after the FBI opened the file on this case, there was a meeting with all the police agencies at FBI Headquarters in Quantico, Virginia. Agent Hilland asked for assistance from the FBI's behavioral scientists. They formed a task force that led to many hours of investigation, and finally to the sweep of interviews that were calibrated for their approach of John on May 5, 1999.

Agent Hilland told how the agents had approached John early that morning as he entered LaForza to begin his workday. They asked him to follow them to a motel, and John agreed. Agent Hilland told how they offered him food and beverages but that he wanted only coffee. Agents read him his Miranda rights, and he still agreed to speak with them. They asked why he had Janice's car after she disappeared, and John denied having the car. As his own statements to the police spanning two decades were presented to him, and proven to be lies, his voice began to shake. He complained of a migraine headache and requested some Advil. An agent went to purchase the medication. John took the Advil and began to cry. They gave him a cold cloth for his head. John asked for a blanket and then asked to lie down on the motel-room couch. There he assumed the fetal position, pulled the blanket over his head, and said, "I am sick of all the lies. My life is a nightmare. I want to just lay on this couch forever." Shortly thereafter he began to complain of chest pain. EMTs were called and transported him to a local hospital for evaluation. (Hospital staff there determined that he was not in fact having a heart attack.)

Some of the most compelling and fascinating testimony during the trial came from bone expert Dr. Frank Saul, who with his wife, Dr. Julie Saul, operates a forensic anthropology laboratory near Toledo. He had examined the bones exhumed from Morocco, Indiana, on March 2, 2000, which were later determined to be those of Janice Hartman. Because of the way the bones were stored, the head and lower jaw previously had been kept in the coroner's office in Newton County Indiana. The leg bones, which had cut marks below the knees, were kept at the Indiana State Police evidence locker, and the rest of the remains had been buried in a pauper's grave in Indiana. The lower leg bones and feet have never been found.

Dr. Saul determined that the three sets of bones were indeed from the same person, a female, approximately twenty to thirty years of age, and at least five feet three inches in height. Using a photograph, he explained to the jury how he had laid out the skeleton to show that the skeleton was intact except for a few small bones and the lower legs and feet. He further explained how the hipbones and the upper thighbones fit together in a way that would suggest that they did indeed belong to one individual. The only other measure taken with the bones was removal of a small section for DNA testing. Dr. Saul really appeared to love his chosen profession. He was able to make the courtroom gallery and, more important, the jury, understand how he had established his findings. The only thing Dr. Saul couldn't determine was a cause of death. He could say only that there were no broken bones, and since the bones were all that remained, he couldn't rule out that there had been trauma to the soft tissue of the body. It was impossible to say how Janice had died. He did know that the legs were mutilated after death.

Dr. Saul said that when he had made these determinations about the skeleton, he recommended that the portion of the legs, just below the knees, be sent to Dr. Steve Symes at the University of Tennessee, the foremost expert on saw marks, what Dr. Saul was sure he was looking at when he examined the portion of the of the legs that had been severed. On redirect, Mr. Frantz asked whether it were possible for death to occur without the skeleton showing trauma. Dr. Saul said that it was possible. For instance, a victim might be shot or stabbed, and if the instrument didn't hit bone, it wouldn't affect the skeleton.

When Sandra Anderson of Canine Solutions International took the stand, I wondered why the jury had to leave the courtroom. We found out that she first had to be established as an expert witness, or more accurately, her nine-and-a-half-year-old cadaver dog, Eagle, did. Ms. Anderson stated that she and Eagle had conducted 277 searches for human remains in the year 2000. She explained that Eagle had been trained to ignore all scents that aren't human. Because these dogs are rewarded regardless of whether they find any remains, they have no reason to react to anything else. For Eagle, this is a game of hide 'n' seek. Ms. Anderson also explained that any type of human decomposition is referred to as human remains. It could be an entire corpse or just odor. Judge Wiest ruled that Ms. Anderson and Eagle were experts in their field, and the jury was led back into the courtroom to hear her testimony.

The prosecution wanted to use Eagle's testimony to show that the box had contained Janice during the years it sat in the Chaneys' garage. Ms. Anderson said she never wanted to know about a case before her search. She wanted to be able to react to what Eagle told her about the scene. The prosecution had a video of Eagle's behavior at the site to show the jury. Many of the spectators, Dedy and I among them, huddled around and craned their necks to watch the video. Ms. Anderson narrated as the tape ran. Eagle went almost immediately to the garage and reacted by barking and then lying down. He was very excited and, as Ms. Anderson said, "showed great will of purpose." She felt that Eagle had picked up a large amount of human remains odor. When she and Eagle entered the garage, Eagle first covered the garage sniffing. When he came to the east wall, he reacted with an excited bark and went down. Ms. Anderson took him away from the area and around the garage again. Eagle would not let the east wall go. He again reacted.

Upon cross-examination, Mr. Migdal questioned Eagle's reliability because the dog hadn't reacted to the south side of the garage, where Michael said the box had been moved. Ms. Anderson held her ground. She said she could only say what Eagle had told her, and that was that there had been decomposition on or near the east wall of that garage. In discussing it later with others, the consensus was that Eagle didn't react to the south side of the garage because decomposition had already occurred and the fabric inside the box had dried before the box was moved to that wall. If there was no moisture to be absorbed into the concrete floor or the wall, there would be nothing for Eagle to hit on. Dedy asked what would happen if Eagle's 100 percent nose ever failed and he reacted to something that was later found to be wrong. "Eagle would be immediately retired," Ms. Anderson answered.

The prosecution had four more witnesses who interacted with John in the summer of 1979 when he had gone to retrieve the box from Seville. Scott Mintier had managed John at Flexible Steel and then at Pullman Standard. Kathy McDonald was Mr. Mintier's stepdaughter and had befriended John. Richard Gromlovits had worked with John at the time. Joseph Dabrowski hired John to work at Copco Manufacturing that June.

Mr. Mintier testified that John had been a good employee. He was shown the diamond- and emerald-green-faced watch and said he remembered it because he had told John to stop wearing it to work. It was clearly a woman's watch, and besides being a hazard on the job, John had to deal with people in the plant making fun of him for it. Mr. Mintier said that John had driven an early 1970s Mustang but that in 1979 he had bought an Indy 500 Pace Car, a Corvette.

Mr. Gromlovits said that he, too, had worked with John during this period of time, and he told about the 1979 Corvette that John drove. He said that John wasn't close to anyone at the plant except for Kathy McDonald: "John followed her around like a puppy dog."

Ms. McDonald said John gave her rides to Ohio to visit her relatives on weekends. She had gone shopping with John and saw a watch with a green face that she wanted. John told her that he had one he'd give her. And he did, a Bulova. She told him it was beautiful and asked where he had gotten it. John answered that it had belonged to his wife and that she had died. Ms. McDonald identified the watch in the courtroom as being the same one John had given her and she had given to Agent Hilland. She also said John had told her he was going to buy a Corvette and asked her what color he should buy. She told him that black was nice. Lo and behold, John got a black Corvette.

I thoroughly related to Mr. Dabrowski's testimony of his experience with John at Copco Manufacturing in June 1979. He said that about a month after he hired John, on a Friday, John had told him he needed to leave early to check on something in Seville. Mr. Dabrowski assumed it had to do with some apartments that John had told him he owned there. The apartments had been a lot of trouble to maintain, and John frequently complained about them. (John did not own any apartments in Seville.) Mr. Dabrowski assumed that John would return to work on the following Monday, but he didn't. On Tuesday, he asked John where he had been and heard a fantastic story about his being cited for driving the Corvette at 170 miles per hour and how the state police had used two semi-truck trailers to block the road. John said that when he appeared in court on Monday, the judge couldn't understand why he had been charged with reckless driving—70 miles per hour was merely speeding. The arresting officer then supposedly explained that the judge had misread the ticket. It said 170 miles per hour, not 70. Mr. Dabrowski said it was such a wild story he had never forgotten it, and that made the time period stick in his mind.

Lodema (Dee) Hartman, Janice's younger sister, came to the stand next. She testified that Janice was living with their father in Doylestown in the fall of 1974 but that she came to their mother's home to visit about once a week. The last time she saw her sister, Janice and John were together at her mother's home. They made plans for Thanksgiving, and for some reason Janice wanted to switch clothes with her. They switched coats and shoes. Then Janice did something strange: She hugged and kissed Dee and told her she would see her at Dee's graduation. Dee was just entering high school, so that would mean that she would not see Janice for four years. Janice also told her that the reason she was working at the Sun Valley Inn was to help agents put drug dealers away. Dee said the family had received nothing that had belonged to Janice after her disappearance except a hope chest they had gotten from the Chaneys. She added that they didn't hear from John one time after Janice disappeared.

After one day of testimony, Dedy and I were already beginning to see how stressful the trial could be. Again, all the uncertainties of the investigation were present but none of the control. (I do confess to having a controlling streak, but don't you dare tell anyone.) We had come so far and wanted so badly to see this all come through.

We recharged our batteries that night and came to court the next day prepared to gut it out. The first witness that day was Dennis Evans, the friend who had introduced John to Sandy and gotten drugs for him. Mr. Evans said that he had known John since kindergarten. They had been close, and in 1971 he moved into John and Janice's home. He said that the couple argued often, mostly about money. By 1974, Mr. Evans had moved back to the Seville area, and was living and working on his uncle's farm. He remembered that John had stopped by to visit and told him that he and Janice were either divorced or were getting a divorce. Mr. Evans said that John was upset that he had co-signed for Janice to purchase the Mustang he was driving. John told him that even though he was making the payments, he couldn't get the bank to give him title to the car. Later during this period, Mr. Evans visited John at the Chaneys' and saw women's clothing all over the back seat and in the trunk of the Mustang. He assumed it was Janice's.

The defense had no questions for Mr. Evans.

With that, the prosecution returned to witnesses related to the discovery of Janice's remains near Hammond. Inspector Gerald Burman of the Newton County Sheriff's Department explained how investigators came to connect Janice's disappearance with Newton County's "Lady in the Box" from 1980. Sam Kennedy, the highway foreman who had discovered the box, told his story. And Larry Bartley, the Newton County coroner who had been a crime-scene technician with the Indiana State Police in 1980, reviewed the items that had been in the box with Janice: a quilt, a cross, rings, and a lot of clothing. At the time the box was found, he had removed these and documented them at the coroner's office, and he now identified them as Ms. Stefancin removed them one at a time from the evidence boxes. There had been about thirty articles of clothing in the box with Janice, and as they removed them for display, the faint smell of death wafted around the courtroom. Brian had kindly warned me about the possible odor, so I was somewhat prepared. One of the jurors was sitting quietly with tears running slowly down her cheeks.

Interestingly, Mr. Bartley had retired from the state police and is now the coroner for Newton County. In Indiana, a coroner, unlike a medical examiner, does not necessarily need a medical degree. As we were sending out letters to sheriff's departments and coroner's offices in Indiana, the coroner before Mr. Bartley had just passed away, and he had been asked to finish out the term of office.

On cross-examination, Mr. Migdal pointed out that the revised death certificate that was issued when Janice's remains were identified did not state a cause of death.

Watching the trial progress firsthand, one gains a new appreciation for the mountain of facts each side must deal with to effectively argue the case. Prosecutors had dug into most every aspect of John's life and found witnesses from all over the country that had interacted with him on a dozen different levels. It was like a broadcast of *This Is Your Life*, except that everyone who came out had something negative to say. Dedy and I tried to see as many of the witnesses as we could after they had testified. We wanted to at least shake their hands and thank them for their help and in many cases for being willing to talk with us. It was nice to finally be able to put some faces with some names. While Fran did not have a voice in these proceedings, we appreciated that these people were present to speak for Janice and the Hartman family.

Dr. Steve Symes, called to testify on July 12, is an expert witness on human bones and specifically on sharp trauma, the study of determining which instruments cause which type of injury to the skeleton. He works at the University of Tennessee Medical School and has a Ph.D. in forensic anthropology. Dr. Symes stated that he became involved with the case when Dr. Saul sent him the left and right tibia and fibula to examine the saw marks. Ms. Stefancin took the bones from among the other pieces of evidence on the prosecution table and walked them over to the defense for examination before giving them to Dr. Symes. John just sat there and looked away from her. Ms. Stefancin remained in front of the table to make John look at the exhibits. He finally did look at the bones and maintained a neutral expression, but I saw that he had begun to rock softly in his chair and his neck was beet red. I knew these as signs that John was extremely uncomfortable. Ms. Stefancin then presented the bones to Dr. Symes.

He began by explaining that the color of the bones was important. The bones were brown, showing that the soft tissue had been intact at the time of decomposition and unexposed to sunlight. Dr. Symes explained that the left tibia was severed about 4 inches below the knee, and because of the position of the normal skeleton, the fibula was cut about 3.5 inches below the knee. The right side tibia was cut 3 inches below the knee, and the right fibula at 1.7 inches below the knee. He said the killer used a back-and-forth motion, which showed that one side of the skeleton was cut, then the body flipped and the other side severed. Ms. Stefancin asked his opinion on the type of instrument used to cut the bone. He answered that the key was to look for "false starts," places where a cut had been started but not completed. These allow an examiner to look at both sides of the bone. From that, he could determine that the instrument used was smooth on one side and rough on the other, consistent with the pattern of a serrated kitchen knife. Dr. Symes told the jury that this wouldn't be an easy thing to accomplish with this type of knife. It would take a lot of force and power, or at least a great amount of determination. I hoped that the jury wouldn't look at John and feel he was too frail to accomplish this. Someone with fear, anger, and adrenaline working for them can move mountains.

Mr. Migdal asked whether the prosecution had the weapon that had been used. Dr. Symes answered that he had no such weapon for comparison. No further questions. Dr. Symes's testimony, like Dr. Saul's and Ms. Anderson's, was powerful because of his deep knowledge of his subject and the ease with which he was able to explain it to others. These people were teachers. Dr. Symes spent much his time in court in front of the jury, explaining clearly how he had reached each conclusion and making eye contact with jurors to make sure they understood. I never detected a trace of condescension. Later we got to have lunch with him, along with Brian and Agent Hilland, and discovered he also has a keen sense of humor, exactly what Dedy and I needed to shrug off the macabre testimony from that day.

As Dr. Symes was leaving the courtroom, I overheard John giggle and say something to his attorney. So far, I had felt as if his attorneys were representing him as best they could, but they didn't appear to have instructed him in the fine art of courtroom behavior. The best thing a defendant in a case this serious could do is remain even-keeled and professional. Anything else could get him into trouble. You'd think John would know all about keeping up appearances. I was relieved to see that a few members of the jury had heard John giggle and were staring at him with astonishment.

Dedy had to fly home the next morning, July 13, to see to her job and family. The day would fall on a Friday, so perhaps it's for the best that there was no court scheduled for that day. She would return on the following Tuesday, the 17th. The good news was that Dave would be back on Saturday. He had left earlier in the week to keep up on the home front. My daughters and their families were also coming to spend the weekend, a most welcome surprise. The trial was supposed to be a time for us to sit back and watch all of our hard work pay off, but it just felt like more hard work. Having the rest of my family there was the antidote. I was going through some serious Grandma withdrawal. This is what truly mattered. I have told so many people that Dave is my anchor, but his role is more like a compass than an anchor. No matter which way you hold a compass, the needle always points north. That's Dave: my constant, my needle that always points north, and I felt confident that he could guide me through one more passage.

CHAPTER 28

Band of Sisters

John had only begun to see the influence he had on the world. On Monday, the women who had come and gone in his life would testify about their relationships with him. The night before, Dave and I had gone out to dinner with Diane and her daughter, Summer. Diane, bless her, brought a box of Fran's things for us that she had hand-carried on the plane from California. It had the set of crystal birds that had been in the beach house and was full of the special little gifts Fran's children had given her. These were the items Sheila had promised to send to Dedy more than nine years earlier, but never had.

The first witness we heard from that morning was Sandy Haynesworth, the lady Dedy and I had the opportunity to talk with while in Wooster for the meetings in 1993. She was even more together and beautiful than I had remembered. Sandy told about meeting John in the summer of 1975 through Dennis Evans. She and John became close very fast and moved to Delaware, Ohio, just north of Columbus. The relationship lasted only about three months. She said she knew that John had been married before and that John referred to Janice as "Tiger." He told her Tiger was dead, that she had been hanging around with a rough crowd and was into drugs. He said she had owed money to drug dealers and that they had killed her. They had taken him to see Tiger's body, which was in a position that made John think of kinky sex. He showed Sandy her engagement ring and wedding band and told her that the drug dealers had let him take the rings from her body and leave. He said he had been afraid to call the police. His relationship with Sandy ended shortly thereafter.

At a recess I had a chance to talk with Sandy for a few minutes. She said she had been so naive as a nineteen-year-old welfare mother. Until she got older, it never dawned on her that the rings John had shown her were probably worth more than the money Janice would have owed the drug dealers. There would have been no reason to kill Janice—they could have just taken the rings and hocked them. She also said she knows there's no way drug dealers would have shown John Janice's body and then let him walk away. I was so happy to see that she was fine and showed no ill effects from her relationship with John.

Janice Miller (whom we had called "Janice II") was sworn in and took her seat in the witness stand. The years looked to have been hard on her. Bleached-blond hair in need of a color touch-up framed a full, squarish face. She would have fit John's preference for petite arm candy when they lived together almost ten years ago, but she had since put on weight. Ms. Miller testified that she met John in Washington Park in Bridgeport, Connecticut. She admitted she had been a prostitute and had been convicted on charges of prostitution. She said that John picked her up in the summer of 1992 and had returned every night thereafter. Ms. Miller said that they sometimes went to the beach house and at other times simply went to the beach and talked. Occasionally they went to dinner. She said that John gave her money to buy drugs. She was addicted to heroin and cocaine. After about a month, she moved into the beach house with him and lived with him until October of 1992.

The night before she was to take a trip to Atlanta with John, he told her about his wife Janice and made a comment about their having the same name. John told her that the FBI had come to him and told him that Janice was dead, that drug dealers had put a hit out on her. John told Ms. Miller that he had never gotten his wife's remains. She became spooked by this and decided not to take the trip with John. She did tell of the trip she took to Ohio with him and how she met the Malz family. She said she began to think that John was really weird when he began talking to her as if she were someone else. He would get upset and say things like, "I've told you about this before," when she knew he had never said any such thing to her. In October, she decided she was going to leave because her personal things kept disappearing. The defense confronted her with the fact that she had used John for drug money. She said that this was true; she had used John to get drugs, not only for herself but also for her boyfriend Robert. Ms. Miller estimated that John had spent between three thousand and ten thousand dollars on drugs for her and Robert. She admitted that the primary reason she left was because the money had run out. Ms. Miller, when asked, freely admitted that she was presently incarcerated in Connecticut on drug-related charges. She spent her out-of-court time in Ohio at the Wayne County Jail.

One of the women we were most curious to see was Sheila Sautter. She didn't look anything like we had expected. Most of the women John had relationships with were blond and had small frames. Sheila was larger and dark-complected. She said they had met at work at Textron Avco and moved in together shortly after the meeting. About five years into the relationship, she found an old resume that said John was divorced with no children. When she confronted him about this, he told her a secretary had made a mistake. "Secretaries don't make those kinds of mistakes," Sheila said. He then admitted that he had been married before and was divorced. John told her that they had married right out of high school and had gone their separate ways after the divorce.

The prosecution then asked her to recall April of 1992, when New Jersey authorities visited the home. Sheila said that by that time, she and John were just friends. Jurors were given a transcript of a taped phone call between her and John. In the call, when Sheila asks John about Janice, he tells her that Janice was his first wife and that he never knew she was missing. He then says, "It's too late," in reference to Janice. Sheila tells him he's "lying, lying, lying." "That's right," he says. The tape ended, and the transcripts were collected from the jury.

Sheila said the relationship ended and that she moved away. The defense had no questions for Sheila, but we weren't surprised. John has always done everything in his power to protect her. We didn't think there was any way he would let his attorneys make it hard for her. Of all his relationships, the one with Sheila appeared to be the most stable, and, though strong-willed, she seemed somehow immune to the dangers John's other women faced. Perhaps because, as a couple, it appears they led their own lives, I don't think she challenged him on any important issues. They were never married; she could take nothing of monetary value from him, as wives could, through community property. Also, until the police knocked on her door, she always allowed John to stay in the home with her.

As Sheila left the courtroom and headed down the stairs, Diane held out her hand to introduce herself. "And who are you?" Sheila asked.

"I'm Diane. You know, the Mrs. Smith that's still alive."

Sheila just shook her hand and walked away.

Trevor Haywood was called and duly sworn. Mr. Haywood had been John's boss at LaForza beginning in October 1997 and had allowed him to live in his guest house until July 1999. When John moved from Ohio to take the job with LaForza, he needed a place to stay. Trevor and his wife, Sue, offered him the use of their guest house. This is one reason tracking him in California had been so difficult. He didn't have his own address and never had utilities turned on in his name. In May 1999, John told them that he had been married and that Fran was dead. After the FBI's first visit to their property, they asked him and his new wife, Diane, to leave. Like other managers, Mr. Haywood told the court that John had been a good employee and had gone to work between 6:00 and 7:00 each morning and usually worked until 9:00 or 10:00 P.M., seven days a week. But on Thursday, July 22, 1999, he didn't report to work, and he didn't return on July 23 either. In fact, John didn't come back until Tuesday, July 27. At that time, Mr. Haywood noticed that he had a cut on his forehead. John told him he had hit his head on the car door. Within a few hours, though, John was circulating a different story—with Mr. Haywood present—that the FBI had done this to him. Two male agents and one female agent had taken him and wouldn't let him leave, even when he asked for his attorney. They had blocked the door, and the female agent had roughed him up. Mr. Haywood said that on the morning of August 5, 1999, John had not come to work but that he did show up that night. This corresponds to the day Michael told him a grand jury would meet to issue an indictment. Again, the defense asked no questions of this witness.

As Summer McCowin took the stand, she appeared determined to tell the truth, but also quite stressed. She explained that her mother, Diane, had been married to John. Upon questioning, she told of the time on July 22, 1999, when she accompanied her mother to the Escondido Police Department to file a missing-persons report on him. Diane was worried because they had no idea where John was. She also told about going with her mother to LaForza on July 24, 1999, to pick him up after he had called them. She described him as being unshaven and dirty and said he looked as if he had not eaten. He was drinking an orange soda when they arrived. They took him home. On that evening Diane asked John to tell Summer about the box. John told her that long ago, coworkers had dumped a box on his grandparents' front porch that contained a goat. He had gotten rid of the box by throwing it into a farmer's field.

About two weeks later, she, Diane, and John had gone to Shelter Island, a tourist destination in San Diego. While there, Summer began to cry. She regained her composure and asked John point-blank whether he had killed Janice. She said that he didn't say yes, but he also never denied it. Summer told of moving into the home with her mother at the time Diane filled for an annulment of the marriage. Diane was afraid of John, she said, and had the locks on the home changed. Our family knew Ms. Stefancin's next question would be about how John had broken down the door to the home, revealing just how strong this man was. The defense objected before she had even finished the question. Judge Wiest sustained the objection. The question would never be asked nor the answer heard inside this courtroom.

Without being able to testify to this story, Diane's appearance on the stand was short. She wouldn't have been able to testify at all if she hadn't been granted an annulment the day before she left California to travel to Ohio. As I understand it, spouses who get divorced cannot generally testify against the other spouse; on the other hand, if a spouse obtains an annulment, the court says the marriage never took place, and testimony against the other is permitted. Because Judge Wiest suppressed any testimony about John's breaking down the door, Diane could state only that she had been married to John. They had dated for about three months and then married. Diane mistakenly gave the date as September 5, 1999. The defense did not ask her any questions. The next morning, however, the prosecution called her back to the stand to clarify that the wedding had taken place on September 5, 1998.

That morning, July 17, the defense did ask her one question when she was recalled to the stand. Was she living with John in October of 2000? Diane said yes, she was living with him at that time. Both times that Diane took the stand, she smiled at John as she walked by. He never smiled back, but he did look at her. Mostly John made it a point not to look at anyone in the courtroom except when trying to make eye contact with one of the nine female members of the jury. I suppose he was hoping to charm them from a distance and soften his image. When he saw that it wasn't going to work, he even stopped looking at them.

The prosecution's case was done. Ms. Stefancin requested the submission of a few pieces of evidence into the record and rested. We weren't sure what might happen next. Some legal wrangling, it turned out. Mr. Migdal asked for an acquittal based on lack of evidence that any crime had been committed and lack of proof that Janice had died in Wayne County. If she hadn't, the prosecution had no business bringing the case to a Wayne County court. Judge Wiest needed to rule on two points: Janice had died of a criminal act, and the criminal act had taken place in Wayne County. Ms. Stefancin countered that Janice had last been seen in Wayne County, that her car was found in Wayne County, and that, despite her being transported to Seville after her death, logic dictated that her death had occurred in Wayne County. A hush settled over the courtroom as Judge Wiest issued his ruling. Based on the evidence, he said, he found that Janice had died of a criminal act and that it had occurred in Wayne County. You could hear the sighs of relief throughout the courtroom.

As Judge Wiest called for a recess, we exchanged hugs with the Hartman family and expressed our relief. I said a silent prayer of thanks. Dave hugged me close as I tried to control my emotions. Theoretically, though, we were only halfway through. The defense team still had to present its case.

Dedy returned to Wooster that same day, the 17th, with her daughter, Nici. We were both excited and relieved that Diane had returned some of Fran's things, but because of the rules of evidence, Brian informed us that the box would have to go from Diane's hands to his. Diane, Dedy, Nici, and I would meet Brian at the Justice Center. Brian would open the box. We were disappointed to learn that Dedy wouldn't be able to take these things home with her. Brian would have to photograph and fingerprint them one item at a time and repack them for submission to the West Windsor Township Police Department, which would photograph them again and return them to Dedy.

Brian, Dedy, and I put on gloves as each item was unwrapped. Nici, Dedy, and I were all softly crying. It was so hard to have these very small pieces of Fran's life and know that we had to turn them back over to someone else. Brian was concerned for us; he had never seen Dedy or me cry. He asked whether we were okay with this, and said that he would do it alone if we wanted him to, but we all understood that this was not an option. We had to verify that all of these things did indeed belong to Fran. One item was a round metal container with a unicorn Fran had painted on it. It had been part of the décor of Nici's bedroom when she lived with Fran and John in Florida. I knew that this child wanted to to keep it with her, but without gloves, she couldn't even touch it.

Diane's gesture in getting these things to us has meant so much to our family. She did her best to make sure the family would receive these few things that had belonged to our loved one. At times we had thought of Diane as unstable because she seemed to change her story or add to the things she had told us in phone conversations. But our family is in total agreement that Diane is a woman with a good and kind heart. She had told us about her kidney illness, and because we were afraid John would try to do something to her or tamper with her medication, we had urged her to see a doctor. After John was arrested and brought back to Ohio, our communication with Diane started again. She seemed much more stable. I commented that she looked so much healthier, physically and emotionally, and Diane explained that she had finally found a doctor who could tell her what was going on with her health. The doctor diagnosed her with lupus, a noninfectious autoimmune disorder that causes the body to attack its own tissues and organs. It can be mild or severe. Now, through better medical attention and the right medication, Diane was feeling like a new person. She said that, as with all lupus patients, she has some bad days but that they are the exception. Most days she feels good.

All things considered, things had turned out well for her, and we were all relieved and grateful for that.

CHAPTER 29
A Graven Image

Judge Wiest didn't waste any time getting on with the trial. The defense began to present its case that same Tuesday, and we were to see a different take on the circumstances surrounding his relationship with Janice in 1974 and an entirely different picture of John, which is to say no picture at all. The defense would not speak of John's character, address his wildly inconsistent statements, counter Michael's testimony of his building and transporting the box, or offer reasons why John might have come to possess Janice's car on the night of her disappearance or her watch later on. As Ms. Wire's opening arguments indicated, their case hinged on Janice's troubling run-in with some local delinquents whose exchanges implied they thought Janice was a narc and might want to silence her.

The defense called Janice's friend Leonard Bennett. We knew little about him, but Mr. Bennet did not appear to be entirely with it. Twice during attorneys' sidebars with Judge Wiest, he fell asleep—while on the stand. He testified that he had gone out with Janice a few times a week after she was done working at the Sun Valley Inn. He said they went dancing at the local bars, although they had never gone to the Sun Valley Inn together. The defense quickly moved him to the night of November 10, 1974, the night Janice was attacked. He said that while he didn't want to go, Janice had wanted to attend a party at Larry Swain's. When they arrived, they just sat and drank and smoked a little pot. He recalled that Janice was asked to dance. After she did, the mood of the party changed. One of the men there grabbed Janice and dragged her into the bedroom. Soon, other men followed. Mr. Bennett said he hadn't been allowed to leave and heard someone shout from across the room, "Watch him. Don't let him go anywhere."

He stated that he was later made to go into the bedroom, where Janice was being held down. Someone threatened, "If you don't get on top of her, we'll get rid of both of you." At that point Mr. Bennett got undressed and got on top of Janice but could not get an erection. After that, he went into the other room, where he saw a blond man holding either a 12- or 16-gauge shotgun. Mr. Bennett said he didn't think he would have been allowed to leave. The attack lasted for about two hours, and Janice actually got out before he did. He saw her afterward walking down the road. He picked her up, and the two of them went to the police station to file the assault report.

Ms. Stefancin asked whether he had felt threatened that night, and Mr. Bennett answered that he had. She then asked what I thought was one of the most important questions of the trial: Had Mr. Bennett ever been bothered by the men at the party since the night of the attack? "No," he replied.

Ms. Stefancin then showed Leonard the cross that was found in the box with Janice's remains. He identified it as the one he had given Janice, but said that the chain was missing. He said she wore it every day.

Ms. Wire asked Leonard whether he had felt threatened by the gun. Mr. Bennett replied that he didn't feel threatened by the gun but by Ronnie, a friend of Larry Swain's.

On re-cross, Ms. Stefancin emphasized that even if he had felt threatened, he and Janice were allowed to leave the party alive, and he had never been bothered again. Mr. Bennett stated that this was correct. As he left the stand and walked by John, Mr. Bennett nodded to John but got no response.

"The defense rests." I looked at Dave, shocked. I did not believe what I had heard. Their entire case rested on one witness, one I didn't think had pushed the scales far enough toward reasonable doubt to help John. The prosecution had no witnesses to recall. Judge Wiest announced that final arguments would be heard the next day, July 18, at 8:30 A.M.

John's demeanor the next morning had totally changed. Whereas before he had limited his focus to the area directly around the defense table, occasionally whispering to his attorneys, he now looked around the courtroom, almost defiantly, and directly at spectators. His gaze settled first on Nici, then his eyes sought out Diane, who, along with Summer, was sitting with our family. Judge Wiest called the court to order and opened the floor to closing arguments.

Ms. Stefancin had nearly two weeks' worth of evidence to distill into a cogent summary. There were so many key points in the prosecution's case for John's guilt that the challenge would be organizing them effectively for the jury. She gathered her breath and began by putting a picture of Janice up on a poster board and comparing the case to a mystery book, with each witness representing a chapter. She displayed an enlarged copy of the dissolution of John and Janice's marriage, which showed a different address for each. Then Jocelyn put up an oversized calendar for November 1974 to outline the events surrounding Janice's disappearance. Then she ticked off the relevant facts in the case that incriminated John and tied them to her visuals. There was the missing-persons report listing the mother of Janice's friend as the contact. There was Janice's green Bolova watch, listed as being with her at the time of her disappearance, that John had later given to another woman as a gift. And there was Michael's damning account of John building the box in the

Chaneys' garage six days after Janice's disappearance. Six days, Ms. Stefancin said, would be too soon to begin packing Janice's things away—unless you knew she was never coming back. Michael said watching John roll up Janice's clothes and place them in the box was the most bizarre thing he had ever seen.

Her presentation was well-thought-out, her arguments clear, and her tone convincing. Then she sprung the prosecution's most memorable moment. Ms. Stefancin picked up a nightgown from the pile of clothes that were found in the box with Janice's remains. She stated that she believed this was what Janice had been wearing at the time of her death, and subsequently in her makeshift coffin. Agent Hilland held up the gown, and Ms. Stefancin picked up the bottom of the garment and lifted it to a position consistent with where Janice's head would have been. Everyone in the courtroom gasped. Held in this way, the gown distinctly revealed the outline of Janice's face. Ms. Stefancin simultaneously held up a picture of Janice's skull, and there could be no mistaking that the jury was seeing exactly what she meant for them to see. I watched as the jury members' eyes made the circuit from the gown to the picture of Janice's skull to the picture of Janice in life. Their eyes continued to take this visual trip, over and over again.

She then held up a pair of plaid pants that had been found in the box. With decomposition in this sealed environment, she explained, the dye from the plaid pants had leached out onto Janice's body and stained her hair in the distinct multi-colored pattern Michael had witnessed when opening the box. Ms. Stefancin took her seat. If this had been a theater, I think the gallery would have applauded.

Mr. Migdal handled closing arguments for the defense. He reminded the jury that they had sworn to be objective and that while he complimented the prosecution on being able to talk to them for an hour without benefit of notes, he didn't think they had proved their case. Mr. Migdal emphasized that Janice had been attacked just days before she disappeared and that Mr. Bennett had feared for his life on that night. Mr.

Bennett testified that the blond man had said, "Narcs always have an easy way out." Mr. Migdal pointed out that Janice had told Dee that she would see her at Dee's graduation and had even switched clothes with Dee. John's defense rested on casting reasonable doubt, that John had not committed something so serious as murder. It could have been the men at the party. Mr. Migdal took his seat.

Ms. Stefancin had a chance for rebuttal. Returning to the calendar for November 1974, she pointed out that Michael had told them that he had taken John to meet Janice twice after the divorce was final. That meant he would have had to meet her on November 15 and November 16. (Their divorce had been finalized on the 14th, and Janice had disappeared by the 17th.) The first night, he and John had left the bar together. But the second night, Michael dropped him off. Ms. Stefancin argued that John didn't need a ride home that night because he knew at the end of the night he would have Janice's car. She again took her seat.

Judge Wiest left the bench to address the jury with final instructions. We were surprised but encouraged to hear that the judge would offer two options for conviction: aggravated murder, the charge John had been arrested on, for premeditation, or a lesser charge of murder, suggesting that the crime had occurred in the passion of the moment. We recognized that the defense had done a solid job of nurturing doubts and were pleased to hear that the jury could also deliberate on the lesser charge. Still, we felt that there was no way to separate John from the box.

Now all we had left was the painful task of waiting. We headed over to the prosecutor's office next door to the courthouse. The staff there had done everything in its power to make us comfortable; some people had even baked treats the night before. Garry and Isabel had brought a fruit tray to munch on. We thought the jury would be back in a very short time, but we were wrong. They began deliberations at 1:30 P.M. and were still working several hours later. After four hours, someone on the jury sent for the transcript of a conversation the prosecution had played during closing arguments. We didn't know why, but it indicated they were taking nothing for granted.

As the clock neared 7:00, someone said we should return to the courtroom; the jury had reached a verdict. We walked next door only to find the jury wanted to leave the deliberation room to stretch their legs. We were then told that when the jury came back with a verdict, we'd have approximately thirty minutes to get back to the courtroom. Dave, Dedy, and I decided to leave for a few minutes to go pick up dinner for anyone who wanted to eat. We paired up people who had cell phones with those who didn't so no one would be left out of the loop when the jury came back. At 8:00 P.M., we got word. Now that they had a verdict, I wasn't sure I could stand to go in and hear it. I do remember telling Dedy that no matter what the outcome was, we would leave that courtroom exactly as we had entered, with dignity, our heads held high.

As the jury members walked in, I scanned their faces to discern what was to come. They were impossible to read. Judge Wiest warned the spectators present not to make any outbursts when the verdict was read. He asked whether the jury had reached a verdict, and the forewoman confirmed that they had. On the count of aggravated murder, the verdict was "not guilty." I squeezed Dave's and Dedy's hands hoping we would gather strength from each other. Judge Weist then asked the foreman of the jury what verdict they had rendered on the lesser charge of murder. The foreman answered, "guilty." Waves of relief and gratitude washed over me. Some of what we had worked so hard for had paid off. After more than twenty-six years, Janice had received the justice she was due. Although Fran had received no measure of justice, it was something.

Judge Wiest scheduled sentencing for 2:00 P.M. the next day, July 19. We exchange teary hugs with Garry and his family. I wished that Mrs. Lippencott could have been there to hear this. Leaving the courtroom, Dedy and I were swarmed by the media and were so tired it was a little overwhelming. We told them that we were understandably disappointed by the not guilty verdict on the aggravated murder charge but relieved by the guilty verdict for murder. Garry ran next door to the prosecutor's office to call his mother. Mrs. Lippencott articulated what we all were feeling when she heard the verdict: "Thank God."

Our family immediately took out our cell phones and began calling the rest of our family with the news. Dedy also called the West Windsor Township Police Department to report the verdict. She relayed the news to Bob Gulden, the detective who originally took John's missing-persons report for Fran, but he told Dedy that they had already heard. The result had been broadcast to the entire department over the police-band radio. This reaffirmed our respect and admiration for the West Windsor police. The whole department continues to take a personal interest in Fran's case.

I learned that evening that both Garry and I would be given the opportunity to address John at sentencing the next day. Mrs. Lippencott had composed a letter to John that would be read into the record. This was one opportunity I didn't want to squander. I sat with Dedy and Nici in our hotel room that night soliciting comments for the statement. I wanted to make sure that, though I was the one speaking, I would be saying the things that they would have said if given the chance. Nici said she wanted to let him know that the year she lived with Fran and John, she felt like a princess. When he killed her Granny, he had ruined even that memory. Dedy wanted me to tell him, in case he wasn't already aware, that this family was a force to be reckoned with. We were not going to go away just because he was convicted of Janice's murder. I had a few choice words of my own to add and spent a couple hours composing a letter of address to John. I had too much to say and couldn't risk forgetting anyone's requested lines, so I opted to read to him what we had to say. I wasn't counting on his making much eye contact anyway.

That evening before the verdict arrived, Diane asked to see John in jail at the Justice Center. Their relationship has always been something of an enigma to me—she appeared to know early on that she was dealing with a dangerous and crazed individual—but I acknowledge that they could have shared something that I don't understand. Maybe Diane has something in her past that has made her more understanding of, or vulnerable to, him. While at the Justice Center, she told John that his past was catching up to him. He replied that he thought she was right. Diane returned to the prosecutor's office in tears. I might have spoken too soon when I once said that the only love John had ever known died with his grandparents.

CHAPTER 30
A Taste of Honey

When we gathered the next afternoon for sentencing, Judge Wiest told the courtroom that he could have pronounced his sentence the night before because he had to revert back to the laws that had been on the books in 1974, when the crime had been committed. He then set sentence: fifteen years to life. Judge Wiest said the court would hear from Garry and me, and then Ms. Stefancin would read a letter from Mrs. Lippencott. Garry approached the podium and stared directly at John. He started by saying that their family had forgiven Michael and that their family prayed that Michael's nightmares would finally go away. Garry said that while his family had forgiven Michael, he, his brother, and his sister would never forgive John. He told John that his past was catching up to him, that he had killed other women, and that this was not the end. Janice's justice was just the beginning. "Sooner or later," Garry said, "you will be tried for the others. Janny is just the first." I think Garry gained strength from glancing at his family, seated just in front of us. He finished by saying he hoped John would never see a free day for the rest of his life. Garry took his seat and his family held hands, giving him what I believed to be an affirmation that he had said exactly what they wanted him to express on their behalf. I prayed I would do as well.

I began by thanking his Honor for allowing me the chance to speak for our family and explained that I had written a letter to John that I would like to read. Judge Wiest nodded his approval.

John, you came into my family's life by way of my sister's love. Because of her love, we trusted you. Trusted you to put her welfare above your own. You have violated that trust. By your hand, Fran's children have lost their mother; her grandchildren have lost their Granny. I have lost my sister, my best friend. As a family, we have proved to be a force to be reckoned with. For the past two and a half weeks, Janice has spoken in this courtroom, and through these proceedings, Janice has found justice for herself and her family. Fran has not spoken yet, but we, as a family, will continue our efforts to give Fran's memory the justice it deserves.

With the help of the authorities, this family has tracked you for nine years, nine months, and eighteen days to get to this day, but this is not over for our family. We are not going away until you tell us what you did with my sister's body after you killed her. I promised my mother on her deathbed I would find my sister. I will work to my last dollar, even my last breath, to fulfill that promise. Then guess what, John? When I am gone, some other member of my family will step forward to continue this investigation. It is our intention to work as hard as possible to see that you are never released to prey on another woman who makes the mistake of loving you. It is my firm belief that if released, you will kill again.

Dedy and I hated you for so long. Then one day Dedy came to

the realization that the hate would eat us up. It was certainly counterproductive to the job we had to do, that being to find Fran. So we have put that hate aside. We only feel sorry that your life, a life that should and could have been so produtive, is a waste, ruined by your lies, your obsession for control, and your temper.

John, for one time, could you just look at me, for I have only one other thing to say to you. I can live with my last memory of my sister. Can you?

For one brief second, as his gaze traveled, he did look at me. His gaze then settled just over my left shoulder, toward the bailiff. Someone looking at him from another angle might have guessed that he was looking at me, which is probably what he intended. Then he just hung his head and looked at the table in front of him. I thanked the court once more for the opportunity to speak.

I felt calm as I spoke those words, but right after I returned to my seat, I began to shake uncontrollably. Dedy took my hand, and Dave wrapped a protective arm around my shoulders and gave me a reassuring squeeze. I realized once more that this is what and who I am, a member of a family that knows the meaning of love and knows how to express that love, even with the smallest of gestures. Dedy said that when I began to shake, it really scared her. She had never seen her Aunt Sherrie go to pieces like that.

Ms. Stefancin then read Mrs. Lippencott's letter. In it she expressed her grief and told John, "You had no right to play God. I hope you feel God's wrath a million times before you die. When you love someone, you give them a decent burial. You do not throw them away like garbage." There was more, but I was shaking too badly to remember what else she said.

I believe that confronting John and finally being able to tell the world exactly who he was, what he did, and how we felt about it was tremendously liberating. In a few short minutes afterward, through that trembling, I allowed myself to release much of the tension that I had been internalizing for years for the sake of the investigation. Emotional comfort, or something like it, was at hand.

Judge Wiest asked John a second time whether there was anything he wanted to say. Very quietly he replied, "No, your Honor."

"I can't speak for the parole board," Judge Wiest said, "but I am confident that you will spend the rest of your life in an Ohio prison." He also said that he hoped that John would find it in his heart to someday do the right thing and tell the authorities what happened to Fran. With that, court was adjourned. I rose to exchange hugs with Dedy and the Hartmans. My heart felt lighter than it had in a long time. I was too busy exchanging congratulations to watch as John was handcuffed while clad in his orange jumpsuit and led out of the courtroom, but Dave says that he looked directly at me with a look of pure hatred in his eyes. It was now his turn to spend sleepless nights thinking of ways to best me—and to torture himself in prison deciding whether to continue stewing in his black thoughts or to choose a new path and offer himself up for forgiveness.

As the Hartmans and our family shared our sentiments, I looked over and noticed that John's half brother Steve was here. I went over to talk, and said I didn't expect to see him here. "I just wanted to see my brother one last time," he told me.

I asked him why.

"I don't know," he said.

As I walked down the stairs of the courthouse, I overheard a man talking to one of the deputies assigned to courthouse security. He was saying something like, What difference would it make if the second family got John charged and convicted? The deputy looked at me and smiled, then said to the man, "See that lady right there? It makes a hell of a lot of difference to her." I smiled at the deputy, and watched as the other man ducked into the men's restroom.

The bathroom-goer had a right to wonder. I had heard Judge Wiest remark at sentencing that he expected John would remain in an Ohio prison for the rest of his life. Once a state has taken on the legal and financial obligations of incarcerating a prisoner, other states aren't so eager to assume that responsibility. In the wake of this successful conviction, persuading New Jersey to bring the case to trial—and possibly take on the cost of caring for someone who's already in prison—would become more difficult. In addition, we faced an uphill battle because of the difference in sentencing between New Jersey and Ohio. At the time of Fran's death, New Jersey had the death penalty; Ohio did not when Janice was killed. If we had found Fran first, the prosecution could have used the threat of the death penalty to prompt a plea bargain, the condition being that John reveal where he put Janice. In getting the Ohio case to trial first, we lost any legal incentive for John to divulge Fran's location.

But that was talk for a later time. We left the courthouse in the sunshine of a beautiful day, thankful that this was at last behind us. John would be in jail for a long time, if not for the remainder of his life. We had been told that if we wrote letters to the parole board, they would become a permanent part of John's prison file. These letters are given heavy weight when an inmate is scheduled for parole, and they follow the inmate for the entire length of his incarceration. We were humbled and grateful to learn that Judge Weist had also sent a letter to the board stating his disapproval for John ever receiving parole. We were also told that when there is dismemberment, either before or after death, the parole board does not smile forgivingly. These inmates are usually incarcerated for the longest possible term of their sentence: In John's case, life.

CHAPTER 31
Civil Peace

When successful court cases like ours take place on TV, the world-weary prosecutors clench jaws and shake hands after the verdict, the victims' families nobly accept justice as their due reward, and the hapless, guilty defendant retires to a cold cell, never to see the light of day. The morning after sentencing, we awoke to harsh reality.

When Judge Wiest had gone to thank the members of the jury for their service, he discovered that evidence pertaining to Fran's case had made it into the jury room. This was evidence that both the prosecution and the defense had reviewed and agreed upon as admissible evidence, a seven-page transcript of Agent Hilland's interview with Michael Smith. The first six pages, except for one question at the bottom of the sixth page, related to Janice Hartman. The last page, however, did contain one question from Agent Hilland about Fran. Upon learning of this, the defense immediately planned to file a motion for a new trial, citing an irregularity in the proceedings. It couldn't claim that inadmissible evidence had been allowed because the defense team had approved it as admissible.

Nevertheless, the mishap prompted a flurry of filings and replies between the state and the defense that kept the possibility of a new trial for John looming for two months. On September 19, 2001, Judge Wiest issued his ruling: The defense's motion would be overruled. He stated that the irregularity in the proceedings did not entitle John to a new trial because the defense team could not be considered ineffective for not objecting to the evidence admitted and the evidence did not deprive the defendant of a fair trial. The transcript page in question only made Fran's existence and disappearance clear; it did not include any of the "New Jersey evidence" that Mr. Frantz had sought to introduce in the trial. Some of the jurors, in fact, had already known about Fran before the trial began. Both the defense and the prosecutor had asked potential jurors before they were accepted into the panel whether this knowledge would influence their ability to render a fair verdict. Each one answered that it would not. With all the media attention these cases had attracted, I felt the jurors would have been living in a vacuum not to know something about the combined investigations. Considering the overwhelming evidence, John's indigent status, and the prosecution's facile presentation, it's amazing that John did as well as he did. The jury's first vote was split 7-5 for conviction, and that was only for murder, not aggravated murder. John had effective counsel, just no defense.

With that settled, we could finally focus on the civil case, Fran's wrongful death hearing. We had been trying to move forward with that for months and kept seeing the date get pushed back to accommodate judges' caseloads and witnesses' schedules. We eventually got a firm date, October 18, 2001, which would come just three days after Dedy and Todd returned from Ireland on a much-needed brother-sister vacation. Dedy would get home on the 15th and fly right back to the East Coast on the 16th. We were gloriously prepared, I felt, psychologically and administratively. We had so much information collected from the investigation that I think the judge in the hearing, Maria Marinari Sypek, moved our scheduled time up from 3:30 P.M. to 1:30 just to fit everything in.

Mike and the officers of West Windsor Township Police Department had made complimentary hotel arrangements for us at the AmeriSuites in Princeton for our stay. Dave, Dedy, and I were all tired by the time we made it in, but it felt good to be together. At about 7:00 P.M., Mike knocked on our door. After hugs and kisses, we spent about two hours getting caught up over dinner. We went to bed after we had done a little family catching up on all the news from Dedy and Todd's Ireland trip. We knew we were going to be busy the next day. We needed to meet with Donald Veix, Dedy's attorney for the hearing (and the same man who had handled Fran's declaration of death for Dedy), to prepare for the next day. And in the afternoon, we had to visit Dr. Richard Rubin so that Dedy could undergo an interview and psychological evaluation for the hearing.

The morning of the hearing, we stopped at the West Windsor police station to review letters that John and Diane had exchanged after his conviction. Diane volunteered to continue to help our investigation by keeping in touch with John and turning over the correspondence to the authorities. After seeing and hugging Bob Gulden, Mike put us in a room and brought out the letters for us to read. There were so many that we knew we couldn't possibly finish reading all of them, so we divided them up. As one of us would find something either sickening or interesting, we would read the passage to the other three sitting around the table. Reviewing the letters, I noticed more inconsistencies in Diane's behavior. In the past, I had been prepared to chalk up many of them to her being caught in John's web, confusion, and overall poor health. Now I wasn't so sure. While we were in Ohio for the trial, Diane told us that John was always asking her for money in his letters. She said she wouldn't send him money because she was having a hard time meeting her expenses as it was. Then I read a letter from John thanking her for sending forty dollars. I realized I still needed to take everything Diane said with a grain of salt. At one point she also told us she had sold the Ferrari, but on the day of sentencing, she was trying to sell it to Steve Malz while Mr. Migdal, the underpaid, court-ordered public defender, sat a few tables away. He had to have heard this exchange and known that this car was still owned by Diane when John had declared himself indigent. Prior to her annulment, Diane continued to tell Steve all the things John had told her to do to hide money.

The hearing that afternoon took place at the Mercer County Courthouse. It felt more like a coming-out party than a legal proceeding. We had overcome so much to make it to that day that we weren't nervous at all. We entered the courtroom and waited for Judge Sypek to arrive and call the court to order.

Mike was called to the stand first. His testimony didn't really break new ground from the criminal trial, but it was a pleasure to see this man at long last have an opportunity to tell the court about a case he had lived and breathed for a decade. This time there was no clenching of jaw muscles; he was relaxed as he told the story. Mike knew our case so well. He didn't even have to refer to the briefcase stuffed with notes he had brought with him.

When Dedy took the stand, most of Mr. Veix's questions centered around what we had uncovered as a family during the investigation and what trauma she had undergone. She also seemed poised and comfortable on the stand, though I could sense a few signs of minor stress as she answered. There were only a couple of times that we were overcome with emotion: when she talked about her last phone conversation with her mother on September 28, 1991, and when she told the judge about finding her mother's clothes in the closet and being overwhelmed by that familiar smell. This was hard for me, and it was also when I'd get the angriest that John had taken Fran away from her. I know that Fran is still with us, but it's not the same as sharing a laugh, a touch, or a hug.

Mr. Veix next called Dr. Rubin to testify to his observations on the trauma that Dedy had undergone. He stated his background and testified that he felt Dedy had been irrevocably injured by the loss of her mother. He said that the only thing that prevented him from diagnosing Dedy as a victim of post-traumatic stress was that her life hadn't been physically threatened. In other words, John had never held a gun to her head and threatened to kill her. He felt that even with psychological help, she would never fully recover from the trauma she had suffered. This was hard for us to hear because Dedy and I always think of ourselves as being strong women, able to face all challenges.

Both of us at times have been overwhelmed by all that's happened to us during the investigation. At different times we have taken leaves of absence from work and sought help with our emotions. At one point, I had become so torn up about being the last of my parents' family left on this earth that I had be placed on medication for a short time. This usually happened to us when the investigation was at a standstill and we found ourselves just going over things we had gone over so many times before, praying to find something that we had missed. We felt there had to be something that we could do but just couldn't find a direction to proceed. I now believe the only reason we maintained our strength is because we have had such great love from our families and for each other.

There was so much to say in our testimony that, as the afternoon wore on, it became clear we weren't going to finish by 4:30, the court's usual stopping time. The court staff told Judge Sypek that they had no problem staying until all the testimony was complete. But because of the time constraints, I was not called to testify. I would have loved to speak my piece, but Mr. Veix asked Dedy and Mike the questions that he would have asked me, so my testimony did in fact get to be heard. Fran didn't need my voice, just the evidence of all the work that our team had done to get to this day.

I should say too that this suit has never been about money for us, although that's the only binding judgment it can offer. John has declared himself indigent and, as we learned from his letters, is taking some money from his only living ex-wife. Dedy pursued this suit at considerable legal expense even when it became apparent that any monetary reward would be negligible. We just needed to hear a judge say that John was responsible for our loss.

Judge Sypek stated that she might have a ruling by the next day, and court was adjourned. That evening, we had plans to meet Mike and his wife, Holly, for dinner. Dedy and I had talked to Holly many times over the phone, but we had never actually met her. We were excited to finally greet this old friend in person. Holly was very much like what I expected: beautiful, sweet, and open to affection. We declared this our retirement dinner for Mike, who left the West Windsor Township Police Department in January 2002. Dedy and I bragged to Holly about Mike's testimony and finally got a chance to tell her how very grateful we were to her for being so patient when Mike canceled family time and vacations to work Fran's case. Holly has never made us feel as if we were an intrusion on her and Mike's life. We were reluctant to end the evening so early, but Dedy had a long drive back to Philadelphia to catch a plane the next morning to Houston. Dave and I would leave to visit his brother for a few days before going home to Indiana.

The one-day wait for Judge Sypek's ruling turned into a week, then a month. She took the unusual step of calling Mr. Veix's office to let him know she would need more time than she had originally thought. Mr. Veix reassured us that the wait wasn't necessarily a bad sign. But coming up on two months, we began to grow concerned. Then on December 17, Dedy called to say that we had a decision. Judge Sypek had ruled that John Smith was 100 percent responsible for Fran's death, and Dedy and her brothers had been awarded a million-dollar judgment, plus the reimbursement of the expenses incurred through this investigation. It was like an early Christmas present, not because we believed that they would ever collect a penny, but because one more judge had said, Yes, Fran is dead, and Yes, John was responsible for your loss. The decision validated not only our loss but also everyone's hard work.

For more than a decade, we have searched first for Fran and then for any remains of Fran's in order to close that hole in our lives. Even if we are one day able to find her, that still won't negate the loss we feel from missing this dear and amazing person. At times, I hear a phrase Fran would have used or news she'd want to know, and I can't wait to call her to share. Then I realize I can never do that again. This is when I feel the loss most intensely. Yet, failing her recovery, we have managed the next greatest success—to piece together her story through continual investigation. Judge Sypek's decision in the civil suit was a culmination of that. Fran had finally spoken on her day in court.

E P I L O G U E

About two months after John's trial, Janice's remains were released to her family, and the Hartmans held a funeral service. As a group we had all the reasons in the world to become close, but Dedy and I remained engaged in a passive conflict with Garry's family over their outward indifference to Janice's case. Once they had agreed on a date for the funeral, Garry contacted us through the Wayne County Victim's Advocate's Office to inform us we were not invited. It was for family and close friends only. During the trial and for weeks afterward, the media bonfire was a full-blown conflagration, and I was in the middle of it, so I recognize that my showing up trailed by a gaggle of television crews would have been inappropriate. I would have expected Garry to contact me himself, however, and I would have liked to send flowers to formally pay my respects to Janice. Only Betty Lippencott acknowledged our role in Janice's homecoming, with a hug and a heartfelt thank-you, and that was enough. Today I have no contact with anyone in their family, except Mrs. Lippencott, with whom I exchange Christmas greetings.

John is incarcerated in Trumbull Correctional Institution in Leavittsburg, about twenty-five miles northwest of Youngstown. The earliest he could be paroled is July 2011. He and Diane exchanged letters for many months after he went to prison (and Diane continued to forward his correspondence to the FBI), but she has since met another man, and I don't believe they're in touch any longer. We know little about his life or state of mind on the inside, although I heard that his responsibilities include scrubbing toilets. Our sole contact has been a letter Dedy received from John in August 2002 that reads like the crazed ramblings of a fallen megalomaniac. In it he claims to have killed at least thirty women and refers to all of us on the investigation team as a "ship of fools." John writes that he has a direct line to Nicolas Cage, the only person who could produce a movie based on a manuscript he's written. This fool has just one response: *John, I go in and out of any door I please without asking anyone's permission. Can you say the same?* I can't be certain he wrote the letter—it was typed—but I did verify his signature as genuine, and the letter is notarized. At minimum, it was sent through John because he had to have supplied Dedy's address.

No law-enforcement agency has been able to link him conclusively to any other crimes. Police believe the small fragments found in his and Grace Malz's storage unit all belonged to the same person, but the identity is unknown. The Wayne County Sheriff's Department continues to hold those remains in case new leads surface. We have no evidence of foul play against the two women we found photos of in Diane's storage unit in Oceanside. The woman pictured next to John in front of a plane died in the late 1990s from breast cancer. The woman in the mall photo could not be located and remains unidentified. Dedy campaigned for well over a year to have Sam Malz exhumed and autopsied to determine a cause of death, but Steve would not agree to that, and the Medina County Sheriff's Department has found no compelling reason to bring him up. We still watch too much TV.

The true nature of John's finances is equally evasive. After hearing the conflicting stories from various family members and assessing the evidence, I've concluded that John is the one who made out like a bandit after Sam's death. Records we obtained from Diane show he was sending Grace eight hundred to a thousand dollars a month after arriving in California, even though his income there wouldn't have allowed for that and he had few earnings in Ohio before he moved. There have been many theories about where the money is but nothing conclusive. We have been unable to trace it to claim the wrongful-death settlement. Michael did say Grace came to him before the trial and attempted to discourage him from testifying against John. Knowing that, I'm guessing that John controlled what was left of Sam's money and that Grace needed him free in order to access it. The last I heard, she had retired from Westfield and was working several retail jobs to make ends meet.

As tragic as this situation has been for our family, we are not a tragic family. Knowing how precious every moment is, we are more loving now than ever but also more skeptical. (The family motto when dealing with strangers now is, "Doubt nothing. Verify everything.") In the midst of uncertainty, family crises, and heartbreak, our family and our detectives' families have also been blessed with wonderful events.

In 1993, Dedy married a wonderful man, Jeffrey, who has been a positive influence on their children. He has been a strong live-in father while understanding that Nici and Jerrad's biological father remains a big part of their lives. Both children are finishing their college careers. Dedy continues to work in the financial planning/investment business.

Fran's oldest son, Todd, has married Fran, a sweet lady who shares not only his mother's name but also her birthday. Together they are raising two daughters from her first marriage. Todd continues his career in banking.

Rodd, Fran's youngest son, married in August 2004. Courtney is just what Rodd needed in his life. Our macho man now claims that the hair on his knuckles has grown back. He no longer drags them along the ground as he walks. His children are all almost grown and are doing well.

Dedy and I joke that if there's one thing we do well, it's produce great babies that grow into great adults. So far so good. Fran bestowed on her children the emotional tools they needed to grow: love, a sense of self-worth, and the embrace of hard work. I know she would be very proud of them.

Mike Dansbury retired from the West Windsor Township Police

Department in January 2002. He and his wife purchased a lakeside home in New York state, where they plan to enjoy their well-earned time together—and do a lot of fishing. Mike and I stay in touch by e-mail and lots of phone calls. As I have said before, Mike is a part of our family, the baby brother I never had.

Brian Potts married a great lady, and they share a beautiful daughter who refers to Dedy and me as "the Ladies." Brian retired from the Wayne County Sheriff's Department in early 2003. He is now a Wayne County court investigator for domestic and juvenile cases. We continue to enjoy a wonderful friendship.

After all these retirements and reassignments, our detectives for Fran's case at the West Windsor Township Police Department are Sergeant Dave Mansue and Detective Bob Gulden. I have to admit I was worried that our case would be left behind when Mike retired, but these two gentlemen have proved to be wonderful and have followed any lead I have presented to them. They both end each conversation with the words, "Sherrie, if there is anything we can do for you or your family, do not hesitate to call us." These are easy words to say, but it is obvious by their voices that they mean them.

Special Agent Bob Hilland is still on active duty with the New York office of the Federal Bureau of Investigation. He remains dedicated to his belief that our case is solvable. Agent Hilland's faith is especially heartening because after all these years, Fran's case is not just considered cold: It's practically frozen. We are still in the damnable situation of "no body, no crime." Yet we have not taken Janice's justice as Fran's own. We continue to search for Fran's remains just as we did before John's conviction.

In June 2004 I contacted Dr. Frank Saul, who examined Janice's remains with his wife, Dr. Julie Saul, and testified on their findings at the trial. Fran suffered from fairly advanced osteoporosis, and I now worried that the unique condition of her skeleton—including multiple fractures in her feet and ribs and the plate and screws in her left leg from her fall in the Poconos—could impede her identification as much as it could help. A medical examiner might interpret the skeleton as that of a much older Jane Doe and dismiss a query about Fran, who was forty-nine at the time of her death. The Drs. Saul agreed and also suggested that with Fran's small stature, inexperienced personnel could identify her as a slightly built male. They thought we should focus our efforts on the route John traveled from New Jersey to Connecticut, because we know that he was with Fran on the morning of September 28 and with Sheila the afternoon of the 29th. On the doctors' advice, I sent out letters to coroners' offices and law-enforcement agencies in New York state with more detailed information about Fran's skeletal anomalies and a request that they re-check their records. She has been gone long enough that obtaining medical records to document her condition for inclusion in the NCIC database has been impossible.

On my more pessimistic days, I wonder how I might have been able to prevent Fran's death. In the spring of 1991, when Mama was in the ICU, Fran came to Mama's house upset with John over something, and I told her to give him a break. He had a mother-in-law in the hospital, a step-son still recovering from surgery, and he was looking for another job. Fran was so hurt. "Don't you ever take his side against me again," she said. "There are things you don't know." What if I had pushed? Would she have told me about John filing for divorce? Would I have had a better chance of getting her home that August when John took off? I might have handled that better, too. Perhaps if I hadn't been so hard on her, she might have taken me up on my offer to come stay. These ruminations won't do Fran any good now. I'm not so sure about me. I suppose if I can replay the scenarios just right, I'll see that I did the best I could and let myself off the hook.

In many ways, I've come to terms with Fran's death (and my health and weight are the better for it), but I still can't bring myself to visit Mama's grave in Valparaiso. She left our family in January 1992 with a promise from me that we'd find Fran. Until I fulfill that ultimate responsibility, I don't think that I can present myself at her final resting place as if all is well between us. I do believe that Fran is at peace with how she passed and the measures we've taken to find out what happened. On my fiftieth birthday, in 1997, I caught a faint whiff of her opium perfume at home. The same thing has happened on a handful of other occasions. I've never known anyone else to wear it, and I think sometimes she just likes to remind me that she's not so far away.

I want others to know that as devastating as this situation would be for any family, it is important that you lead a real life. If you don't, your soul will perish, and you will find yourself forever drowning in a sea of frustration and grief. The worst part is that you will take the ones you love most with you. Everyone must have something outside of the search to sustain him or her. I have managed through unwavering support from my family and a focus on the abundant blessings we witness every day.

In June 2000, Dave accompanied Neva and her husband, Danny, to China to pick up our first granddaughter. I did not go with them because our younger daughter, Mikel, and her husband, Hans, were expecting the delivery of their first child at any moment. Our second granddaughter arrived ten days after Neva, Danny, and Dave got home from China. I think the proudest moments for me are seeing what wonderful mothers my daughters have become. Dave and I have spent a great portion of the last four years enjoying the sight of watching our grandchildren grow into two of the cutest little girls imaginable (no Mamaw bragging rights here, just fact). Our daughters have carried on our family's great child-rearing tradition.

Dave, a chemist, continues to work for a major pharmaceutical firm but is looking forward to retirement and being able to do a little traveling with me. I have retired from Textron and continue to write. My latest project is a little storybook dedicated to safety issues, such as protecting our children from stranger abduction. (A wonderful source for information and education to protect our children is Escape School: www.escapeschool.com.) I have also covered some of the challenges our children are faced with, such as the death of a loved one.

Whenever I'm asked, I speak at rallies for the missing to spread the message that family involvement is essential to missing-persons investigations. My research has shown that in most of the cases that get solved, the family's determination and perseverance in finding answers is what makes the difference. I appear on any show and give any interview that will get this message out there, and during each appearance I show Fran's picture in the hope that someone will come forward with new information.

Helping others cope with the uncertainty and grief I know so well and watching our grandchildren explore a fresh new world gives me the strength to imagine a real resolution for Fran's case. Despite the conventional wisdom that says our odds are slim, we still seek the answers that have eluded us for thirteen years. Consistent and sound investigation worked for Janice's case after twenty-seven years, and we believe it can work for us again, too. Our goal remains to bring Fran home to Florida for a decent burial. After all: IT AIN'T OVER 'TIL THE FAT LADY SINGS.

AUTHOR'S NOTE

This book has been written by my hand. Although I might have made mistakes in the telling of our family's story, I have related the facts as they have presented themselves. I have been as honest as memory and notes allow, and the interpretation of these facts is my own. My objective was to humanize the victims. My hope is that our story might in some way help other families who find themselves in a similar situation.

The best advice I can give to all families is to prepare for a situation like this *before* it happens. Assemble a DNA kit for your loved ones. Look at it as you would life or health insurance. This takes only a few minutes and is easy to do. Baby teeth make excellent samples. Not only do they have the child's blood on them, but they also have gum tissue. Each sample must be placed in a clean, glass, sealable container. (It is very important to use glass containers, because plastic can break down and cause your sample to become contaminated.) All samples must be stored separately. Take a cotton swab and run it around your child's mouth and inside the cheek area. Then store that sample in a second container. The next time he or she gets a cut, swab some of the blood for a third sample and put it in a third bottle. Hair is also a good source of DNA but can be the hardest to get, because each sample must still have the root and follicle attached. I don't know of many little ones who will sit calmly while you pluck out strands of hair, but this is the best way to make sure the sample is usable. Label each sample with the person's name and the date the sample was taken and store it in your freezer. Getting samples is especially important for the families of children who came to them through the heart rather than the womb, as in adoption. DNA might be impossible to obtain from the biological parents.

Be sure to take snapshots often, and make sure you have good pictures of your child's face. Headshots are best, with a label on the back listing name, age, and the date the photo was taken. Children change so much from birth through their preteen years, when facial features mature (Remember how you lost those baby cheeks?) and permanent teeth move into place. *Most missing people are found through the use of photographs.* It's ideal to keep a kit for each member of your family, but it's most important to keep kits for children, who cannot protect themselves.

This book is by no means a how-to, but I do have some advice from my own experience for the families of missing persons and to the police officers working with those families.

I urge family members of missing persons to become a part of the investigation. It is better than sitting at home waiting for the phone to ring. Pick two of the mentally strongest and most intelligent people within your family to act as your representatives. By intelligent, I mean good old-fashioned horse sense. This does not require education. I recommend selecting two people because there will be times when one person cannot drop everything and work the case even though urgent matters require attention. Try to restrict police contact to those two representatives. If everyone in your family is constantly calling the police, they will forever be on the phone and won't have time to work your case. The police will want to question all family members. If anyone is inconvenienced, make sure it is never the police. They are there to help. Although it's almost second nature to protect your family members' reputations, resist doing this, even over something painful or embarrassing. The police, trained professionals that they are, will find out anyway, and in the meantime you've delayed the investigation in its crucial first hours and days.

I recommend getting a good credit card and setting aside money for the investigation. If you need to travel, as we did in our case, you may need to leave on a moment's notice. Also, county and government agencies usually accept credit cards as payment for searches, copies, and mailing of official documents you might need to further the case. Be prepared for large phone bills.

It's up to you to establish your credibility and reputation for perseverance with the police. They will probably be reluctant to discuss the case with you or to use you as manpower. Prove to them that teamwork—with you as part of the team—is efficient and productive. Family representatives should emphasize that they can deal with bad news. Knowing the facts is much better than imagining explanations of what might have happened.

From personal experience, I can say that police officers should not try to sugarcoat bad news. These families are resilient, and should no longer be thought of as just civilians. They just stepped into the world of the investigation. Police officers should not feel threatened by family involvement; after a few days, they'll get to see what the officer's job entails, and believe me, they won't want it. Families of victims know those victims better than the investigators ever will, and the investigators should use that knowledge and listen not only with their trained ears, but also with their hearts. Families can uncover such information as land transfers, marriages, and divorces and turn it over to the police. In our case, we found that some people were more willing to talk to us than to the officers. (A caveat to family members: Civilians presenting themselves as law-enforcement officers of any kind are committing a felony, and a family member who did so would lose all credibility if ever called to testify in court.)

Families have more power than they could ever imagine. It is our right as adults to leave any situation, and we have privacy laws protecting those rights. But family members usually don't have to worry about this. Even if they're sued by the person whose privacy they have violated,

I don't believe a judge would rule against the family. After all, the plaintiff has allegedly put the family through a terrible ordeal because of his or her actions.

Families need to be tutored about how to take clear, concise notes and to document any meetings or interviews: where they took place, the time and date, the people who were present, and exactly what was discussed. Correct spelling of names and addresses is imperative to police follow-up. If it's impossible to take notes during a meeting, family representatives should find a quiet place to reconstruct what was covered as soon as possible afterward. Memories fade, but good notes are timeless. *Document everything*, even if it seems trivial or irrelevant. Those things can become turning points in the case.

If family members get information from the police that is inconsistent with what they know of the victim, the police need to hear it. Families should be prepared to give logical reasons for their feelings. It's possible that the person interviewed either misunderstood or was incorrect. It's also possible that someone lied. The detectives will know how to best use information gathered by the family to further the case.

Families must also realize that detectives are working not only their case but also several others simultaneously. This is where efficient teamwork comes into play. Finding new leads and information is critical. As a case gets colder, the file can sink to the bottom of the stack. Introducing new information forces an officer to pull out that file to make notations and bring it back to the top of the pile. Sad but true: Out of sight often means out of mind. I recommend meeting as a team at least once a week to go over the case, unless something important breaks. Then families should report it immediately.

I have been told that in large police departments, having family involved doesn't work. Both sides should try to make it work. Families that are active in the case are less likely to hamper the investigation. Families should not be afraid to ask questions of the police, but they also need to back off when told that a detective is handling a certain issue. They might not like the answer to their question, but that's the time to prove they can deal with whatever the investigation reveals. Also, families need to know where the law stands with regard to trespassing and harassment. At times, they might approach that line. No family members should ever attempt to use vigilante tactics, even if they believe there was foul play and have a suspect. If they lose control, the family will lose another member—but this time, to the judicial system. For their part, officers should try to obtain legal council for families, either pro bono or at a reasonable expense.

Families who decide to use the press or other media for help should never release any information that law enforcement hasn't cleared. Rather than allow themselves to be threatened or backed into a corner, family representatives should simply refer those types of questions to the authorities. Protecting the case must be the top priority. Families should never use a non-family spokesperson. It is hard for the public to relate to someone who does not have a high stake in the investigation.

The absolute hardest part of family participation is for them to dis-associate themselves from the victim. Families have to GET TOUGH. They must take care of themselves both mentally and physically. There may come a time when they need all their strength and stamina to sur-vive. The mental changes and anguish they go through are normal. Anyone having trouble working through these normal stages need not be proud. They should seek professional help. (Note: Family members should never let themselves be hypnotized. Hypnosis can cast doubt on a witness's testimony in court.)

Family members can relieve some of the burden by sharing their feel-ings with others who are enduring the same situations. We have found very little out there for the families of missing adults, but they can try contacting the victim's advocate office in their county or township. These offices are usually run in conjunction with the local prosecutor's office. A good resource is:

The Nation's Missing Children Organization and Center for
Missing Adults. www.nmco.org; (800) THE-LOST

In addition, the Social Security Administration acts as a mediator for
families of missing people. The local SSA office can guide them through
getting a letter delivered to missing loved ones. Should taxes ever be
filed on their behalf, the SSA will forward their letter to the reported
place of employment. The SSA acts only as a mediator; families will
never know whether the letter has been forwarded unless the missing
person contacts them.

When trying to cope, I've found that gratitude for all the blessings in
my life enables me to continue our search. Prayer helps. Do not give up.
Our timetable is not necessarily God's timetable. There is an answer out
there, though it may be months or, in our case, years before families get
that answer. Even while consumed by the investigation, they must put
family first. That love and support is vital during an intensely stressful
time.

If your family is in this overwhelming situation, I pray you have
obtained some guidance and hope from our story. Dedy, Dave, and I pray
that you reach a happy conclusion in your case. God bless.

A B O U T   T H E   A U T H O R S

Sherrie Gladden-Davis grew up with her sister, Fran, in a military family, living all over the United States and as far away as Panama. She spent many stretches living with her maternal grandparents in Niceville, a small town on the Florida panhandle. Sherrie worked for a while as an ER tech and for twenty-five years as a cost accountant, but she now devotes much of her time to her grandchildren and occasionally speaks to victims' families and others on the importance of family participation in missing-persons investigations. She lives near Indianapolis, Indiana. This is her first book.

Brad Crawford has worked as a magazine editor, book acquisitions editor, agency copywriter, and copy editor. He is the author of *Compass American Guides: Ohio* (Fodor's) and is a freelance writer and editor for books and magazines. He lives in Cincinnati.

BOOKS OF INTEREST

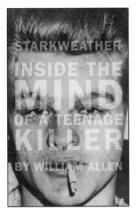

Starkweather
Inside the Mind of a Teenage Killer
By William Allen

"Allen makes the… ambiance of the murders palpably alive…"
– *Publishers Weekly*

"… illuminates Charlie Starkweather from the inside and the outside."
– The *Washington Post*

Nebraska, 1958: Nineteen-year-old Charlie Starkweather massacres eleven people in a grisly murder spree. Emerging into the crime scene spotlight, Starkweather and his fourteen-year-old girlfriend, Caril Fugate, enflame America's growing fears about restless youth and rebellious teens.

A classic of investigative reporting in the tradition of *In Cold Blood*, this revised edition of the *New York Times* bestseller sheds new light on the mind of a young spree killer. Newly released notes from Starkweather's prison journal, plus transcripts of prison interviews between Starkweather and the prison psychologist, take us inside the young murderer's mental state and provide insight into a mind over the edge. Allen also provides further evidence to support his claims that Fugate, often regarded as a kidnap victim, was indeed an accomplice in the murders.

Paperback Price $14.99
ISBN: 1-57860-151-7

To order call: 1(800) 343-4499 www.emmisbooks.com
Emmis Books, 1700 Madison Road, Cincinnati, Ohio 45206

BOOKS OF INTEREST

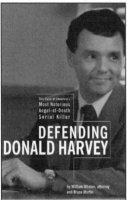

Defending Donald Harvey
The Case of America's Most Notorious Angel-of-Death Serial Killer
By William Whalen and Bruce Martin

Donald Harvey killed at least fifty-nine people while working in Ohio and Kentucky hospitals. In *Defending Donald Harvey*, Harvey's defense attorney finally delivers his perspective on these infamous, terrifying murders.

How could it be that no one noticed that Harvey was mentally ill? Why did he continue to obtain jobs at hospital after hospital despite his odd and suspicious behavior? Harvey performed occult ceremonies to select his victims using a skull stolen from a morgue. He was ironically nicknamed "Angel of Death" by other hospital workers because of his "coincidental" tendency to be nearby when a patient died. And yet he killed with impunity for eighteen years until a chance observation during an autopsy revealed his hand in the death.

With Harvey's cooperation, defense attorney Whalen and coauthor Bruce Martin reveal frightful insights into the mind of a serial killer—facts formerly shrouded by attorney-client privilege. *Defending Donald Harvey* also illuminates the ethical dilemma defense attorneys face when torn between the professional duty to defend a client and the desire to provide closure for victims' families.

Paperback Price $14.99
ISBN: 1-57860-209-2

To order call: 1(800) 343-4499 www.emmisbooks.com
Emmis Books, 1700 Madison Road, Cincinnati, Ohio 45206